An Introduction to Trading in the Financial Markets

Market Basics

R. "Tee" Williams

AMSTERDAM • BOSTON • HEIDELBERG • LONDON
NEW YORK • OXFORD • PARIS • SAN DIEGO
SAN FRANCISCO • SINGAPORE • SYDNEY • TOKYO

Academic Press is an imprint of Elsevier

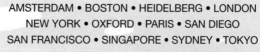

Academic Press is an imprint of Elsevier
30 Corporate Drive, Suite 400, Burlington, MA 01803, USA
525 B Street, Suite 1900, San Diego, California 92101-4495, USA
The Boulevard, Langford Lane, Kidlington, Oxford 0X5 1GB, UK

Library of Congress Cataloging-in-Publication Data
Williams, R. Tee.
    An introduction to trading in the financial markets : market
    basics / R. "Tee" Williams.
        p.   cm.
    Includes bibliographical references and index.
    ISBN 978-0-12-374838-6 (pbk. : alk. paper) 1. Capital markets.
    2. Stock exchanges. 3. Financial instruments.   I. Title.
    HG4523.W555 2011
    332.6—dc22   2010023177
Set ISBN: 978-0-12-384972-4

British Library Cataloguing-in-Publication Data
A catalogue record for this book is available from the British Library.

For information on all Academic Press publications
visit our Web site at *www.elsevierdirect.com*

Printed in China
10   11   12   13   14   10 9 8 7 6 5 4 3 2 1

Contents

The four books in the set are an exercise in reportage. Throughout my career, I have been primarily a consultant blessed with a wide array of projects for many different kinds of entities in Africa, Asia, Europe, and North America. I have not been a practitioner but rather a close observer synthesizing the views of many practitioners. Although these books describe trading and the technology that supports trading, I have never written an order ticket or line of computer code in anger.

The purpose of these books is to describe *what* individuals and entities in the trading markets do. Bob Simon of *60 Minutes* once famously asked two founders of the dot-com consulting firm Razorfish to describe what they did when they got to work each day and took off their coats. That is the purpose of these books: to examine what participants in the trading markets do each day when they take off their coats. These books do not attempt to prescribe what should occur or proscribe what should not.

The nature of the source material for these books is broad observation. In teaching professional development courses over nearly two decades, I have found that both those new to the markets and even those who have been market participants for years become experts in their specific area of activity; however, they lack the context to understand how their tasks fit into the overall industry. The goal of this set of books is to provide that context.

Most consulting projects in which I have participated have required interviews with people working in all phases of the trading markets about what they do and their views on how the markets work. Those views and opinions helped frame my understanding of the structure of the markets and the roles of its participants. I draw on those views, but I cannot begin to document all the exact sources.

I have isolated fun stories I have heard along the way, which I cannot attribute to a specific source, into boxes within the text. These boxes also include asides that are related to the subjects being discussed but that do not specifically fit into the flow.

The structure of the books presents information in a hierarchical form that puts entities, instruments, functions, technology, and processes into a framework. Categorizing information into hierarchies helps us understand the subject matter better and gives us a framework in which to view and understand new information. The frameworks also help us understand how parts relate to the whole. However, my experience as a consultant convinces me that while well-chosen frameworks can be helpful and appealing to those first coming to understand new subject matter, they also carry the risk that their perspective may mask other important information about the subjects being categorized. So for those who read these books and want to believe that the trading markets fit neatly into the frameworks presented here: "Yes," I said. "Isn't it pretty to think so."[1]

---

1   Ernest Hemingway. *The Sun Also Rises*, 1926, New York: Charles Scribner's Sons (Scribner).

FEATURES OF THE BOOKS

Figure FM.1 shows the books in this set with tabs on the side for each of the major sections in the book. The graphic is presented at the end of each major part of the books with enlarged tabs for the section just covered, with arrows pointing to the

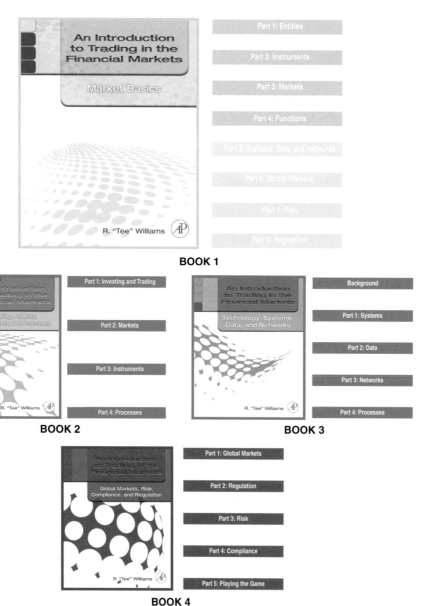

BOOK 1

BOOK 2

BOOK 3

BOOK 4

Figure FM.1   The ***books of this set*** are organized as a whole and concepts are distributed so that they build from book to book.

parts of other books and within the same book where other attributes of the same topic are addressed. I call this the "Moses Approach."[2]

In addition to words and graphics, the four books use color to present information, as shown in Figure FM.2. Throughout, the following color scheme represents the entities as well as functions, processes, systems, data, and networks associated with them.

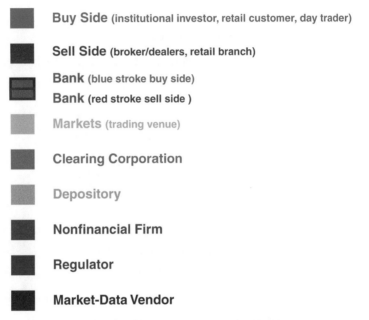

Buy Side (institutional investor, retail customer, day trader)

Sell Side (broker/dealers, retail branch)

Bank (blue stroke buy side)
Bank (red stroke sell side)

Markets (trading venue)

Clearing Corporation

Depository

Nonfinancial Firm

Regulator

Market-Data Vendor

Figure FM.2   ***Color in these books*** identifies entities that are central to the trading markets, and also identifies the functions and processes that are associated with those entities.

A frustration of writing about the trading markets is the wealth of colorful and descriptive terms that permeate the markets. These terms are helpful in describing what happens in markets or where people work, but there is no accepted source that defines terms in everyday usage with precision. Good examples of this problem are the meaning and spellings of the terms "front office," "middle office" and "backoffice."[3] Similarly I use "indices" to mean a collection of individual instances of a single index. (For example closing *indices*—that is, values—of the Dow Jones Industrial Average on January 2, 3, and 4.) I use "indexes" to mean a collection of different copyrighted information products measuring market performance (e.g., the Dow Jones, FTSE, and DAX *indexes*).

I have elected to define the terms, as I understand them, within the books. The first instance of words appear in ***bold italics***, which relate to definitions in the Glossary at the end of each one. The books use more hyphenated adjectives than

---

2   You may remember from the Bible that God took Moses up on the mountain and, in addition to giving him the Ten Commandments, showed Moses the Promised Land. This seems to be a good approach to organizing information. If you expect people to wander in the wilderness of your prose, you at least owe them a glimpse of where they are going.
3   I separate "front" and "middle" from "office" and combine "backoffice." I believe that "backoffice" is a widely used term throughout the economy, whereas "front office" and more particularly "middle office" are nonce terms that may not migrate into common usage beyond the trading markets.

normal usage would require. I believe it is important to remove all doubt that the term "market-data systems" refers to systems for handling market data, not data systems used by a market.

The books in this set contain a large number of graphics. The goal of them is to provide more than decoration. For many people, graphics help them understand the concepts described in the text. Most of them illustrate process flows, relationships, or characteristics of market behavior. There is neither tabular data nor URLs from websites here. Both are likely to be too dated by the time the books are shipped from the publisher to you to provide any real value.

The graphics (and text) build from book to book. For example, in Part 1 of Book 1 the graphic in Figure FM.3 describing institutional investors appears. It shows

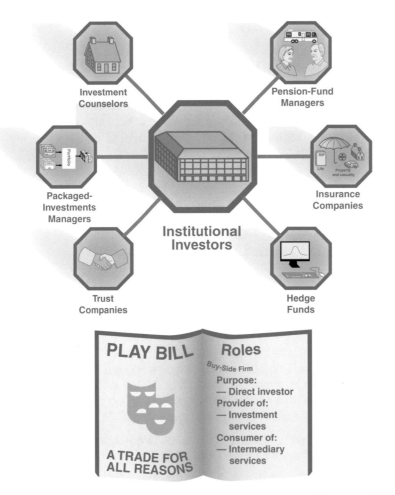

Figure FM.3   ***Institutional investors*** are introduced as important buy-side entities in Figure 1.1.3[4] of Book 1.

---

4   The figure numbers indicate that this is the third figure of the first category (buy side) of the first part (entities.) All figure numbers follow this pattern.

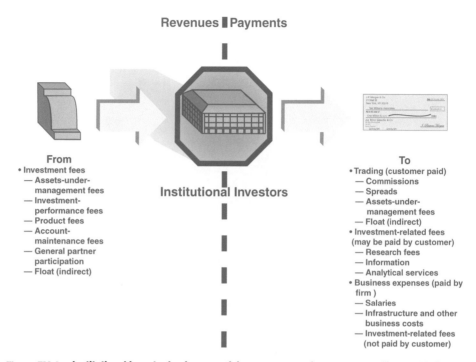

Revenues ▮ Payments

From
- Investment fees
  - Assets-under-
    management fees
  - Investment-
    performance fees
  - Product fees
  - Account-
    maintenance fees
  - General partner
    participation
  - Float (indirect)

Institutional Investors

To
- Trading (customer paid)
  - Commissions
  - Spreads
  - Assets-under-
    management fees
  - Float (indirect)
- Investment-related fees
  (may be paid by customer)
  - Research fees
  - Information
  - Analytical services
- Business expenses (paid by
  firm)
  - Salaries
  - Infrastructure and other
    business costs
  - Investment-related fees
    (not paid by customer)

Figure FM.4   *Institutional investor business models* —revenues and expenses—are illustrated in Book 1, Figure 1.1.3.7.

the customers, the suppliers, and the products and services for institutional investors. (Subsequent sections describe types of institutional investors based on how they are regulated or the service they perform.)

At the end of each entity subsection, the entity's core business model and what services it purchases from vendors and other providers are explained (see Figure FM.4).

Part 4 of Book 1 describes the functions performed by buy-side traders who work in institutional-investor firms (see Figure FM.5). The figure illustrates what tasks the buy-side trader performs (i.e., which other functions), who the buy-side trader serves, which external entities interact with the buy-side trader, and which other functions provide services to the buy-side trader.

Book 2, Part 4, describes the secondary market trading process. The second step in the trading process describes the initial role that the buy-side trader plays in trading.

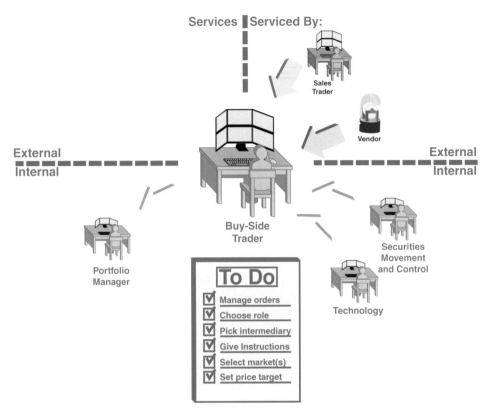

Figure FM.5   ***Buy-side traders*** manage trade execution within institutional investors and their functions are detailed in Figure 4.1.2.1 of Book 1.

Figure FM.6 presents the inputs to and outputs from the buy-side trading process as well as the primary focus of the buy-side trader and the decisions that the person must confront. Subsequent graphics in that section examine some of the decisions and alternatives in more detail.

Book 3 returns to the buy-side trader to understand the role of technology in the process. Part 4 of that book examines the systems, data, and networks that support buy-side trading.

Figure 4.3.2.2 in Book 3 (Figure FM.7, see page xii) shows the systems, data, and networks that support buy-side trading. The text identifies applications supplied by both internal and external sources that support order management. The buy-side trader generates information that is input directly to internal systems and indirectly to external systems. Finally, networks both within the firm and from markets and vendors provide linkages that facilitate the entire process. Subsidiary figures highlight the specific types of systems, data, and networks that are input to and output from buy-side trading.

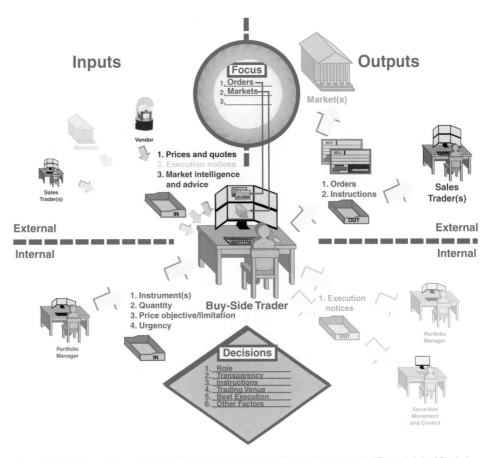

Buy-side trading is defined further as part of the trading process in Figure 4.2.2 of Book 2.

Finally, Book 4, Part 4, presents a hypothetical example that describes how a fictitious British investment management firm with a global presence manages an order across multiple markets with time, customer, and market pressures.

Here, David Anderson,[5] a London-based buy-side trader for Trafalgar Asset Management Ltd., is tasked with coordinating the sale of a very large order (500,000 shares) of In-the-Ether Networks (ticker symbol: ITEN) B.V., a Dutch network company with equities that are actively traded globally on the exchanges, ECNs, and MTFs in Amsterdam, Frankfurt, Hong Kong, London, New York, and Singapore.

---

5   All the names in the "Playing the Game" part are fictitious. However, I do know three different David Andersons, all of whom are Brits and work in some portion of the trading markets. These three gentlemen are the inspiration for the name. However, none of the David Andersons that I know are buy-side traders.

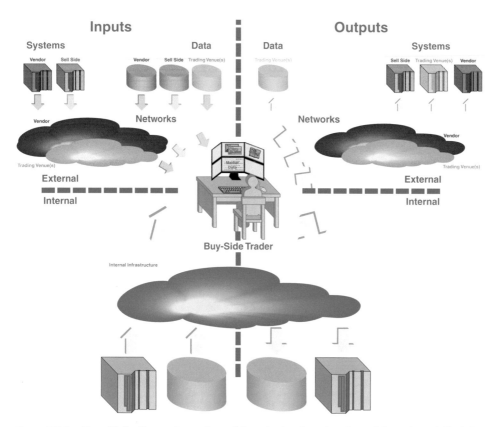

Figure FM.7   ***Buy-side trading*** requires systems, data, and networks and produces data as shown in Book 3, Figure 4.3.2.2.

The graphic in Figure FM.8 shows how the order is received along with instructions for its execution. As the process proceeds, the text describes how the order is then divided among global offices, electronic systems, and intermediaries to be executed through a continuing global process over two elapsed London days. The text also describes the settlement process following the trade. A large trade in multiple markets strains systems data and communications that were created when national markets were insular and did not interact. Subsequent graphics show how the process described in the narrative unfolds.

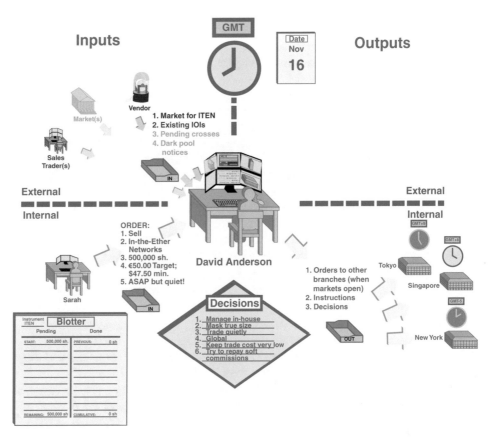

Figure FM.8 ***Buy-side trading*** is finally illustrated through a hypothetical example bringing together the decision process, technology, and interactions in Figure 4.2 of Book 4.

Similar linkages among the graphics in this set of books occur in describing instruments and markets.

As noted previously, a Glossary is included at the end of each book. For convenience, there is a Visual Glossary of the graphical metaphors and elements used in the images for the book. The visual glossary follows this preface to the set.

ACKNOWLEDGMENTS

This project began as an attempt to write a history of the markets beginning in the 1060s. There are a number of individuals who held important positions in the trading markets during and after the "backoffice crisis" in the late 1960s who helped me understand the markets early in my career. I thought that a book about them and the work they did to hold the markets together and then reshape those markets would be interesting.

There are several good books describing how Felix Rohatyn, Sandy Weill, and many others worked to bail out firms that were in trouble, but they do not describe the activities that occurred in the backoffice in the midst of the crisis. That book on history did not happen, but these books are my attempt to "pay forward" all the help I received from many different people. The descriptions of the markets in these books are built on the foundation of the knowledge that these people unselfishly imparted. I hope these books will in turn help those entering the markets.

In a real sense, these people and many more than I can list are the true footnotes and references for these books. My earliest teachers included

- Junius "Jay" Peake, University of Northern Colorado, R. Shriver Associates, Pershing and Company, and Shields and Company. (Jay was my first and is still my most influential teacher.)

- Morris Mendelson, The Wharton School of the University of Pennsylvania. (Morris offered Jay and me entre into the academic community, and Jay chose to stay. He and Jay wrote many papers together on market structure and automation, and they allowed me to help with some. Jay and I miss Morris very much.)

- Ray Holland, Triad Securities, A.G. Becker. (For more than 30 years, Ray has been a continuing source of information and advice about the mechanics of the backoffice processes required by the markets.)

- Dick Shriver, R. Shriver Associates. (Dick, my first boss, introduced me to consulting and many in the financial community including Jay. Dick remains a lifelong friend and mentor.)

- Don and Jack Weeden, Weeden & Company, and Fred Siesel, Weeden & Company and the NYSE. (Jay introduced me to Don, Jack, and Fred in the mid-1970s, and for a time we tried to foment a revolution in trading mechanics. Over the period since, they have been a source of information and insight that has helped me understand the way the markets operate.)

More recently, a number of others have provided important views on the workings of the trading process and supporting technology. Most of these people worked with me, or I worked for them on projects that form the basis for the books. These people include the following:

- Mike Atkin, Electronic Data Management (EDM) Council and Financial Information Services Division (FISD). (I have worked with Mike over the past 20 years first at the FISD and later at the EDM Council. Together, we have come to understand the processes required to manage data.)

- Dick Cowles, Telerate and CBOE. (I met Dick at the CBOE, interviewed him at Telerate, and worked with him for USAID as we tried to establish an over-the-counter market in Poland. Along the way, we became friends.)

- Andrew Delaney, A-Team Group. (Andrew taught classes with Craig Shumate and me. Parts of these books related to infrastructure technology, news, and research rely on Andrew's insights.)

- Tom Demchak, Brian Faughnan, SIAC and NYSE Euronext. (Tom, Brian, and their staffs were liaisons on a project to establish a capacity planning methodology for the equity and options markets in the United States and then to understand the impact of the conversion from fractional units of trading to decimals. They explained the issues of managing huge volumes of data message traffic, functions of the technologies that underpin trading markets, and methods for mitigating message volumes in excess of economically manageable capacity.)

- Deb Greenberger, Skyler Technologies and Dow Jones Markets. (In an attempt to resuscitate the Dow Jones Telerate subsidiary, Deb and I visited and interviewed customers in Asia, Europe, and North America to understand how they use data to manage their trading and related businesses.)

- Thomas Haley, NYSE (Tom was a coauthor of *The Creation and Distribution of Securities-Related Information in North America*, a description of the market-data industry that we worked on in 1984. That book presented an explanation of the processes in the market-data industry and was written by Tom with several other industry experts at the time on behalf of the FISD of the Information Industry Association [now known as the Software and Information Industry Association]. I met Tom and the others in the FISD when I served as editor for the book. Tom has been a friend and a constant source of information and advice on the market-data industry ever since.)

- Dan Gray, U.S. Securities and Exchange Commission; Lee Greenhouse, Greenhouse Associates and Citibank; Frank Hathaway, Nasdaq; Ron Jordan, NYSE; and George McCord, McCord Associates. (Dan, Lee, Frank, Ron, George, and I worked with their associates and people from SIAC to define and then specify a methodology for allocating market-data revenues for the different markets that trade NYSE- and Nasdaq-listed securities in the United States. The project caused us to examine the quoting behavior in the markets in great detail and to wrestle with issues such as locked and crossed markets.)

- Sarah Hayes and Kirsti Suutari, Thomson Reuters. (Sarah and Kirsti managed a project in which we visited many major financial centers globally to understand how people trade and the impact of those trading practices on information needs.)

- Alan Kay and Charlie Pyne, On Line Markets. (Alan and Charlie invited me to join them in a project to evaluate the meaning of the information business and how to use information as an entre to create trading venues.)

- Tom Knorring, Chicago Board Options Exchange; Joe Corrigan, Options Price Reporting Authority; and Tom Bendixen, Mark Grinbaum, and Jeff Soule, The International Securities Exchange. (Projects with and for these gentlemen formed the basis of my understanding of the mechanics and economics of the options markets.)

- Don Kittell, SIFMA, NYSE. (Don was the Securities Industry Association [now SIFMA] manager of a series of projects to forecast the impact of the conversion to decimal trading on message volumes. I was fortunate enough to work as a consultant with Don on those projects, where I learned much.)

- Brian McElligott, Kendall Vroman, and Brian's staff, CME Group. (The people at the CME took me to interview important constituencies in the futures markets to understand how they trade and use information.)
- Peter Moss, Thomson Reuters, and John White, State Street Global Advisors. (Peter and John were forceful advocates for these books. They have also been sources of understanding about the issues facing vendors and market-data users.)
- Leonard Mayer, Mayer & Schweitzer. (Lenny attended one of the classes Craig Shumate and I taught on new trading systems. [He should have been teaching me.] He cofounded one of the premier Nasdaq wholesale firms and was gracious enough to me help understand the business of being a dealer.)
- Lance Riley, SRI Consulting. (Lance was my first boss at SRI Consulting, and together we worked on many projects and interviewed countless people over 20 years. I miss Lance greatly.)
- Richard Rosenblatt and Joe Gawronski, Rosenblatt Securities. (Dick and Joe have been kind enough to take me along as they were trading on the floor of the NYSE. They have also shared their insights on the workings of the markets that they write in an ongoing series of white papers for their customers.)
- Craig Shumate, The Morris Group. (I met and worked with Craig at my first job at R. Shriver Associates, and we have worked together constantly since. He brought me into the business of professional training. It is Craig who pioneered the concept of the eight steps in the trading process and "Playing the Game" as a way to draw together all the aspects of trading in a single process description.)
- Herbie Skeete, Mondovisione and Thomson Reuters. (I met Herbie in London at least 20 years ago, and I try to see him every time I am in London or when he comes to the States. He is a wealth of information on market data and knows a huge number of people. Herbie introduced me to Elsevier and is responsible for my writing these books.)
- Al Thomson, Instinet; Lynch, Jones and Ryan; and AutEx. (Al and I have been collaborators and friends from my earliest work in the trading markets. He set up a great many of the interviews and provided insights that underlie the knowledge presented in these books.)
- Wayne Wagner, The Plexus Group (JPMorgan). (Wayne invited me into a project for the Department of Labor on the meaning of "best execution" in the early 1990s. He patiently explained how many different buy-side motivations resulted in very different expectations from trades.)

I am not able to remember and therefore thank all those that I have interviewed and the many others who worked at the firms for which I consulted for more than 35 years. (By my best estimate, I have averaged several hundred interviews each year since 1974. Therefore, the total number of interviews and thus people to whom I am indebted numbers in the thousands.) Rather than name a few and forget many, I would simply like to thank them all. This book is dedicated to them and most particularly to Jay Peake and Morris Mendelson.

This book is the introductory unit in a set of four books intended to provide the reader with a basic understanding of the structure, instruments, business functions, technology, regulation, and issues for the trading markets. Each of the additional three books provides an overview of a single aspect of the trading markets. This book is an introduction for the set that will serve as a foundation for the other three books.

We use the term *trading markets* as shorthand for trading in the financial markets. The books are focused on trading and not about financial markets as a whole. Therefore, we describe not only the act of trading but also the decisions that lead up to the execution and all the processes that follow the trade until money is exchanged for ownership, and even the accounting for positions acquired in the trading process. We do not cover many important financial products and services such as insurance and commercial banking except to the extent that those firms become involved in trading.

We use the metaphor of *the Street* to represent the market and those who participate in the market (see Figure FM.9). *The Street* was probably first used to refer to Wall Street, although every major financial center has its own "street." It is an area where the majority of trading and ancillary activities that support the trading environment take place. Harbor View Street in Hong Kong, Lombard Street in London, Diagonal Street in Johannesburg, Bay Street in Toronto, and Bahnhofstrasse in Zürich were all centers of local trading markets for their respective nations.

As the markets have become more electronic in nature, the notion of a physical place—a street—has become more symbolic than necessary. A street, an exchange, or a coffee house where traders meet to exchange information and trade is less important, but being physically near the locus of trading is now important to reduce trading ***latency***,[1] which is the time required to transmit orders to the place of execution. We return to this metaphor throughout the set of books when we are viewing an aspect of the markets from the perspective of the entities that operate in the markets.[2]

---

1 Throughout this book, when we use a term for the first time, we put it into ***bold italics***. This means that the term is an important concept in the industry and is defined in the Glossary at the end of the book. We also invite you to look at the term on the website that accompanies this set of books, where you will find not only interactive definitions but also links to other related terms and concepts.

2 Ongoing updates and changes to this book and those in the set will be collected at *http://teewilliamsassoc.com/*.

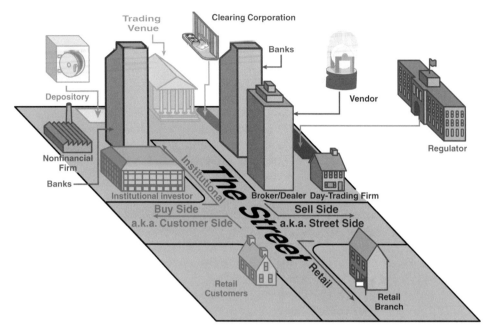

Figure FM.9   **The Street** introduces a recurring metaphor representing the individuals and entities that participate in the trading markets.

Our focus in this book is to describe the industry in general, but along the way we will try to point out unique country-specific features of the markets, entities, and processes. Therefore, we hope to describe the trading markets in a very generic sense and not any particular market. We use the term "instruments" rather than securities because we explore instruments that are not, strictly speaking, "securities" such as currencies, **derivatives**, and those physical commodities for which there is an active trading market.

This book intends to provide you, the reader, with a fundamental understanding of the business of the trading markets. The intent is not to teach you to be an expert **broker** or **portfolio manager**, but rather to help you understand what these individuals and others do as they perform their roles in the markets. We begin with an overview that describes the trading process, which gives you enough information to understand the balance of the book.

Following the overview is a brief historical background that provides context for our exploration of the trading markets. The main substance begins with Part 1. If you are generally familiar with the trading markets and how they evolved, you might want to skip the overview and history.

Throughout the book, we follow the path of orders moving from investors to ***intermediaries*** to markets themselves for execution and then to the utilities supporting the markets. We use this sequence to introduce the entities that participate in the markets and the functions performed within each entity.

The trading markets are complex, and the complexity is growing. Therefore, we present a very high-level view. There are many specialty firms and job functions that are beyond the scope of this book. Some of these functions are described in subsequent books in this set, but others can be found in the books that we reference and many other books on the industry as well.

Finally, we try to explain some of the jargon widely used in the industry as such terms arise. We attempt to define these terms, but we warn you that definitions implied by common usage are often imprecise. People in the markets use terms loosely, and you may run across people who use a term we have defined in a certain way to mean something different. Welcome to the trading markets!

This book describes the trading markets from several different perspectives. We begin by describing all the entities that participate in the markets and the variety of instruments traded. Next, we categorize the different types of markets, explaining how they operate. Returning to the entities, we explore the functions that are performed within each to facilitate trading. We then briefly discuss technology, global markets, risk management, and regulation. The structure of this book corresponds roughly to the flow of topics through the books in the set as shown earlier in Figure FM.1.

For those of you new to the trading markets, this overview provides a foundation for understanding the discussion throughout the remainder of this book and the ones that follow. Because these books are about the trading markets, it is essential to understand the trading process to make sense of the discussion.

If you encounter terms that may not be familiar, you might wish to refer to the Glossary at the back of this book. We have tried to highlight all terms with special meanings in this book and provide explanations in the Glossary. We note the correspondence between concepts in each section with topics covered in the other books through maps at the end of each section. There is also a brief description of the other books at the conclusion of this book.

THE TRADING PROCESS

To provide context for the discussions that follow, we describe here the typical steps in the trading process, which can be applied to most traded instruments.[1] By understanding these steps, you have a basis for understanding the entities and functions that are a part of the market.

Figure OV.1 illustrates the process for an order from an **institutional investor** through **execution** and **settlement**. We chose an institutional order because such orders require all the steps in the order process. (A retail trade from an **individual investor** is simpler, but most of the steps described for an institutional order can be found in a retail trade, albeit on a smaller scale.)

We return to the trading process in Part 4 of Book 2, *An Introduction to Trading in the Financial Markets: Trading, Markets, Instruments, and Processes,* to examine factors such as the focus of the process, necessary inputs and outputs, decisions required, and tools employed at each step.

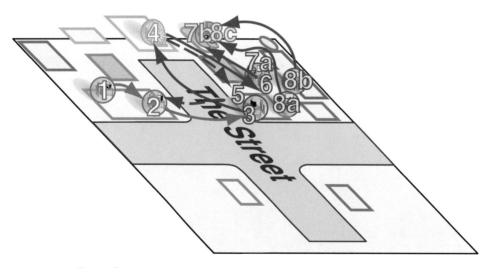

Figure OV.1   The **trading process** involves eight steps from idea to settlement.

---

1   Although the trading steps have similarities across instruments, the details of the trading process for various instrument markets differ considerably. In the instrument part of Book 2, *An Introduction to Trading in the Financial Markets: Trading, Markets, Instruments, and Processes*, we describe the different characteristics of the market's several different instruments.

Step 1: Pre-Trade Decisions

Trades are initiated when a portfolio manager at an institutional investor or a professional trader decides to buy or sell a security (see Figure OV.1.a). The reasons for the decision vary. A buyer may have information that a security is attractive; a security already owned by the buyer may be so attractive that it justifies buying more; often the buyer may have funds that need to be invested; or a **market maker** may need to provide **liquidity** to the market.[2] The seller may need cash; may have become convinced that a security owned is no longer attractive, or that another security is more attractive; or the market maker may need to satisfy the demands of a buyer who cannot find a willing public seller. Whatever the nature of and reason for the decision to trade, the portfolio manager decides what to trade and the urgency of the execution.

Step 2: Buy-Side Order Management

An investing institution is likely to have a dedicated **buy-side trader** charged with managing the execution of a portfolio manager's orders in accordance with the general directives of the portfolio manager. (See Figure OV.1.b.)

Once given the request to trade and the urgency required to complete the trade, the buy-side trader is responsible for deciding where to place the order (perhaps more than one place), the price to request or demand, and other contingent instructions such as whether to place all the order at once or to divide it into portions to be executed over time. For simple orders, all this can happen quickly. For difficult orders, trading can involve complex processes that can take hours or even days to complete.

Figure OV.1.a   **Step 1: Pre-trade decisions**—portfolio managers decide which instruments and what quantities to buy or sell for their customers and firms.

Figure OV.1.b   **Step 2: Buy-side order management**—buy-side traders determine when, where, and how to execute orders from portfolio managers.

---

2   We describe these functions in more detail in this overview and then motivations and detailed processes in Book 2, *An Introduction to Trading in the Financial Markets: Trading, Markets, Instruments, and Processes.*

Step 3: Order Routing

The routing of orders may involve use of automated algorithms through electronic connections to a network and then onward to a market center (see Figure OV.1.c). Alternatively, an order may be placed over the phone with a trading room that then routes the order to a market. Whatever the exact mechanism for moving the order to a market, a firm acting as a **broker/dealer** is expected to take responsibility for the order-routing process and to provide the financial guarantee for the trades.

Step 4: Execution

The execution of orders—matching a buy order with a sell order—was traditionally done in two different ways (see Figure OV.1.d). In **agency markets**, orders from two **principals** are matched according to the rules of the **marketplace**. In a **dealer market**, all orders are matched against the **dealer**. In effect, the dealer buys orders from the seller into the **inventory** of the dealer. The position in inventory is subsequently sold to the buyer.

Step 5: Trade Confirmation

When a trade is completed, the buyer and the seller must be notified, and the price (paid and received, respectively) must be confirmed (see Figure OV.1.e). Prior to settling a trade, the parties may also need to be notified of their responsibilities. The buyer or his or her agent must move money or provide a check in **acceptable funds** to the intermediary, and the seller must provide instructions for transfer of the security, or even produce a **security certificate** if so required.

This confirmation process may involve a phone call, email, or a letter by post, and the market may specify the exact form of the notification. In any event, it makes

Figure OV.1.c   **Step 3: Order routing**—intermediaries route orders from their customers to a trading venue.

Figure OV.1.d   **Step 4: Order execution**—trading venues match buy orders with sell orders to execute trades for market participants.

Step 5

Figure OV.1.e   **Step 5: Trade confirmation**—the sell side notifies buy-side customers of prices and quantities for each execution.

Step 6

Figure OV.1.f   **Step 6: Trade allocation**—the sell side computes an average price for a total order for all executions required to complete the order for every participating account.

good business sense for an agent to notify a principal when a trade is consummated even when **regulations** do not require it.

Step 6: Trade Allocation

Orders from institutions are often quite large, sometimes even involving many instruments in a single order. Tens or even hundreds of executions may be required to fully satisfy the total order. This means that many of the executions may be at different prices. Moreover, an institution may also be trading for many different accounts or customers. **Trade allocation** involves a broker/dealer computing an average price and allocating that price and specific numbers of instruments to each of the accounts for the institution (see Figure OV.1.f). No matter how many trades are required to satisfy an order or how many accounts participate in the order, the trade allocation process resolves the number of **shares** (or any other **unit of trading**) to each of the participating accounts at the computed **average price**.

Step 7: Clearing

In the period between an execution and the settlement of the transaction, a number of tasks are required that are generally referred to as **clearing** a trade (see Figure OV.1.g.a). When there is a physical market, there is always the possibility that the details recorded for the trade from the buyer's broker/dealer will differ from the seller's broker/dealer, and these differences must be resolved.[3]

---

3   In automated markets, the buyer or seller may make an error entering orders, but after they are in the system, the details are fixed and no errors are permitted. A broker/dealer entering incorrect information must accept the results of the trade.

Step 7a

Figure OV.1.g.a   ***Step 7a: Clearing***—the sell side receives reports, fixes problems, and prepares for settlement for each execution.

Step 7b

Figure OV.1.g.b   ***Step 7b: Clearing***—the clearing corporation (trading venue) compares trades and guarantees settlement for each execution.

The broker/dealers representing the buyers and sellers must ensure that they jointly have the money and securities' delivery instructions (or certificates) required for settlement. In markets where there are **clearing corporations**, the clearing corporation may step into a completed trade and guarantee the successful settlement of the trade to the buyer and to the seller (see Figure OV.1.g.b).

Although specifics of clearing differ from market to market and regulatory environment to regulatory environment, the clearing process encompasses all the necessary steps after a completed trade to ensure successful settlement.

Step 8: Settlement

Settlement is the process of exchanging the buyer's money for the seller's proof of ownership, and the subsequent registration of the change in ownership to the buyer (see Figure OV.1.h.a). The details of settlement depend on both the requirements of the market and relevant commercial laws and regulations.

The buyer, often through a department within the chosen intermediary known as the **cashier**, must deliver **good funds** to the seller. Most often this is accomplished by presenting the acceptable form of payment at the clearing corporation at an agreed time on the **settlement date**.

The seller must present **proof of ownership** in a form that can be transferred to the buyer for settlement. Often a department of the seller's intermediary known as the cage does this (see Figure OV.1.h.b). This process is known as making **good delivery**. This also occurs at the clearing corporation at the appointed time on the settlement date.

Step 8a

(for buyer)

Figure OV.1.h.a   ***Step 8a: Settlement*** —the sell-side cashier (buyer) delivers good funds to the clearing corporation on the settlement date at the specified time for each execution.

Step 8b

(for seller)

Figure OV.1.h.b   ***Step 8b: Settlement***—the sell-side cage (seller) makes good delivery of *transferable ownership* to the clearing corporation on the settlement date at the specified time for each execution.

The clearing corporation facilitates settlement by providing a location (physical or electronic) where settlement can occur, by establishing standard times for settlement, and by establishing rules for the process (see Figure OV.1.h.c). The rules may include the standards for good funds and good delivery.

Further in this book, we examine certain of the instruments involved in trading and take a closer look at the participants and functions performed. We begin in Book 2 by exploring the details of the trading process in much more detail. First, however, we look at the history of the financial markets to help put the current markets in context.

Step 8c

Figure OV.1.h.c   ***Step 8c: Settlement***—the clearing corporation receives good delivery from the seller and good funds from the buyer and delivers good funds to the seller and transferable proof of ownership to the buyer for each execution.

Although not a history *per se*, this book offers a basic knowledge of how the securities markets evolved in order to help the reader understand market structure today.

Trading in commodities and, later, finished goods dates from earliest recorded history. On the other hand, trading in financial instruments is a more recent phenomenon. The first recorded trading market for financial instruments began in the city of Bruges in what is now Belgium. The trading took place in a tavern owned by a family named Van der Bourse. Interestingly, in much of the developed world, the words "beurs" (Dutch), "bourse" (French), "börse" (German), and "bolsa" (Spanish) are used instead of "exchange" to signify financial markets. A physical place was necessary so that traders could meet to "discover" the current value or **market price** for the financial instruments they were buying and selling.

The Dutch East India Company created the first active exchange, independent from a pub, by establishing its Beurs in Amsterdam in 1602. The company initially invited investors to help underwrite the costs of sending ships on trading expeditions to the East Indies. If the expedition were successful, the investors would be paid off with a share of the profits proportionate to their investment. If the ship were lost or cargo was damaged, stolen, or sold for less than the cost of the trip, investors lost most or all of their investment. Therefore, by the early 1600s, the Dutch East India Company began to solicit investment in the company itself rather than in riskier individual expeditions.

This marked a seminal change because an ownership investment became a perpetual ownership interest—a **common share** or **ordinary share**—or stock. An investor wanting to liquidate an ownership interest needed to find someone willing to buy the stock for the original investor to be freed of ownership. The "Amsterdamse Effectenbeurs" (Amsterdam Stock Exchange) became the first dedicated "place" for sellers of shares in a company to find buyers and, consequently, establish prices.[1]

London quickly copied both the Dutch company structure (with the creation of the English East India Company) and the Dutch practice of stock trading. Trading in London initially took place in coffee houses such as Jonathan's on Change Alley. Subsequently, informal trading in the alleys and coffee houses evolved into a formal exchange, The London Stock Exchange.[2] Rapidly, other major commercial cities in Europe copied these remarkable innovations. In the United States, Philadelphia created the first exchange with New York following a year later, but trading had existed in taverns for some time before formal exchanges were established. Other cities in Europe had exchanges, but Asia, initially hobbled by colonialism, did not follow suit until later.

1 William N. Goetzman and Rouwenhorst K. Geert. *The Origins of Value: The Financial Innovations That Created Modern Capital Markets.* (New York: Oxford University Press, Inc., 2005).
2 England and the Netherlands were officially tied together during a critical period in the growth of both countries' economic development through the marriage of William of Orange and Mary Stewart, daughter of Charles I.

In addition to standardized **equity** (ownership) shares, trading markets served as the venue for buying and selling standardized **debt instruments** or **bonds** as well. Bonds continue to be listed on many exchanges, but during the world wars most actual trading moved from the exchanges to an over-the-counter system of trading among large banks. This happened because the explosion of governmental debt to fund the war efforts overwhelmed the capabilities of exchange market makers, typically small partnerships, which lacked the capital to handle much larger fixed income or fixed interest trades.

Exchange trading continued, largely unchanged, into the mid-1800s. One of the first milestone changes to the industry occurred in 1867 when several different inventors[3] created the **ticker** for reporting prices for equities and gold. Based on telegraph technology, the ticker's unique attribute was the capability to print stock prices on a paper tape on devices remote from an exchange. Exchanges sold trading firms access to the pricing information on ticker machines, thus creating the market data business.

The next major financial innovation was a centralized settlement facility; the first such institution known as Kassenverein was created in Germany during the reign of Otto von Bismarck. Early stock trading involved bespoke transactions between buyer and seller, with each party depending on the good faith and creditworthiness of the other to settle the transaction. Moreover, there was no guarantee that either trader would record the details of the transaction identically, which made settlement problematic. Common clearing and settlement facilities provided a means for members of the trading community to ensure mutual agreement as to the terms of trades and to facilitate the corresponding exchange of money for the financial instrument.

In the late 1950s, the growing use of computers created opportunities for automating securities processing. However, securities processing was considerably more complex than the banking and other financial processing functions that had begun to be automated in the 1950s. Moreover, because securities firms were typically small partnerships, investing in automation required partners to forgo short-term personal gain with little apparent benefit. So long as there was no crisis, partners had no incentive to invest in automation.

At the same time, two other developments began to impact the markets. First, a small band of computer specialists developed technology that permitted security prices to be transmitted on demand. Stock tickers, like those offered by exchanges, printed prices on paper tapes sequentially as the trades occurred, and the continuous paper tape often came out of the machine into a trashcan. A trader wishing to find the most recent price for a security would look along the tape in the trashcan to find the most recent (**last sale**) price. Because the ticker machines were provided by exchanges, there was a separate machine for each exchange.

---

3 Thomas Edison greatly improved on the price ticker, and his design continued to be used into the late 1950s.

With the new computer technology a trader could enter the ***ticker symbol*** for a security and retrieve the latest price without searching along the paper tape. Moreover, independent market-data vendors could provide prices from multiple exchanges on the same machine. As a consequence, dissemination of securities prices began to occur in "real time."

The second development was the social transformation that occurred as prosperity spread to larger segments of the world's population. First in the United States, next in Western Europe, and then on to larger portions of the rapidly developing world, individual wealth and retirement accounts generated increasing demand for professional ***investment management***. This, in turn, led to significant structural changes in the markets as institutions inevitably traded in larger quantities and much more actively than most individuals.

As trading volumes grew rapidly because of institutions, broker/dealers were slow to adopt automation and were unable to handle the volume of trading. This brought on the near collapse of the securities markets in the United States in the late 1960s as transaction volumes overwhelmed the capacity of manual trading systems that were based on the transfer of paper ***certificates***. Ironically, this situation occurred in the midst of what seemed to be a ***bull market*** with firms scrambling to do more and more trades. A number of firms were bankrupted, and others were forced into hasty mergers with stronger firms.[4]

The aftermath of what became called the "Backoffice Crisis" was a series of new governmental regulations enacted as the *1975 Amendments to the Securities Act* (the '75 Amendments). This Act required the end of fixed ***commissions*** on most securities transactions, the creation of a National Market System, and a National System for Clearing and Settlement. Many in the industry claimed that these changes would spell the end of the securities industry. The law went into effect on May 1, 1975, which came to be known as "May Day," a play on the name for a distress signal.

Far from causing the end of the U.S. securities markets, the markets rapidly became much larger and stronger. By the late 1970s, Great Britain instituted a review of its markets under former Prime Minister Harold Wilson ("The Wilson Report") that recommended similar changes to the London markets. These changes were implemented on October 27, 1986, in what came to be called the "Big Bang." Over time, most other major markets adopted similar changes in one form or another.

The period since the major market changes of the 1970s and 1980s has seen the demise of the Soviet Union and rapid development of economies in Asia. Both events resulted in the explosive growth of trading markets in all these economies, with all the strongest economies now having markets of global importance.

---

4 These details are based primarily on discussions and personal communications with Jay Peake, Ray Holland, Don and Jack Weeden, and Fred Siesel.

This section explains some of the visual cues found in figures throughout this book in particular, but many can be found in the other books of this set as well.

The entities on the Street all have different colors to differentiate them (see Figure VG.1). These colors are used throughout the set to distinguish functions, processes, and attributes related to specific groups of entities. Note that banks, although green, have either a blue or red stroke to denote that they perform different functions for the buy side and sell side. Note that the icons representing many attributes are color-coded to reflect the entity they represent.

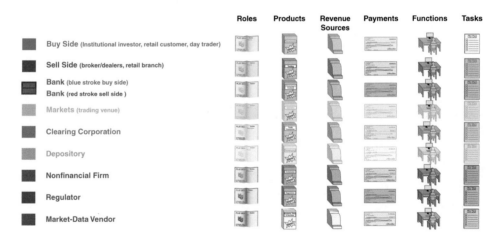

Figure VG.1   The color meanings are shown in this graphic.

PREFACE

We use the metaphor of the Street to define and categorize entities. The Street runs north/south and is bisected by an east/west street. The left side of the Street is the buy side, and the right side is the sell side (see Figure VG.2). Beyond the buy side and sell side, there are supporting entities. Entities north of the cross street are institutional entities, and those south of the cross street are retail.

Each figure (except book maps) has a Caption (1). The purpose of the caption is to distill into a simple declarative sentence the meaning or purpose of the concept illustrated in the figure.

Each type of entity has a unique icon (see Figure VG.3). The icons are used repeatedly throughout the books in this set.

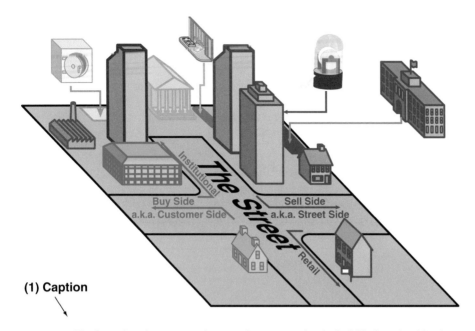

(1) Caption

Figure VG.2   *The Street* introduces a recurring metaphor representing the individuals and entities that participate in trading markets.

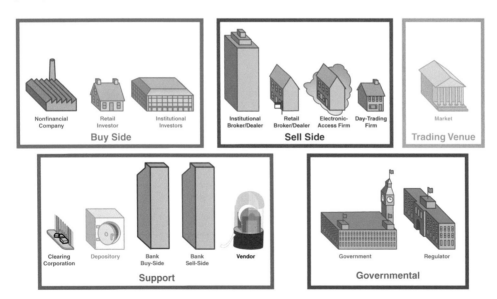

Figure VG.3   This graphic shows the *entities'* icons.

The book images with boxes indicating the major areas of content appear throughout the set of books to suggest areas of interest and to map sections with related content (refer to Figure FM.1). The content boxes do not include incidental sections such as the Preface or Overview.

OVERVIEW

Sections at the end of Book 1, *An Introduction to Trading in the Financial Markets: Market Basics,* present a brief view of the contents of Books 3 and 4. Figure VG.4 shows how content in Book 1 relates to content in Books 2, 3, and 4.

The trading process is laid out on the background of the Street (see Figure VG.5). Each step was described briefly earlier in the main Overview section (p. xxi). A complete examination of the process is carried out in Book 2, *An Introduction to Trading in the Financial Markets:Trading, Markets, Instruments, and Processes*.

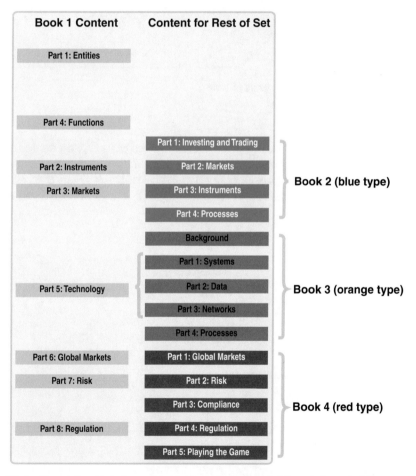

Figure VG.4   The relationship between this book's content and that of those in the rest of the set.

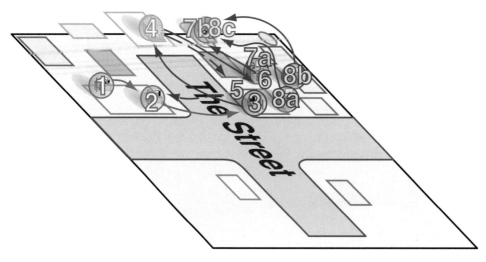

Figure VG.5   This is a graphic of the ***trading process***.

Throughout the books in the set, steps in a process are presented on circular backgrounds that are color-coded to indicate which entity group is involved (see Figure VG.6). Function icons (described in Part 4 of Book 1) are placed on the background. Each step is numbered sequentially with letters added when events happen in parallel.

Figure VG.6   This is a graphic for the ***process steps***.

PART 1: ENTITIES (THE PLAYERS)

Some entities are part of groups that share common characteristics even though members of the group also have unique characteristics (see Figure VG.7). Every entity group figure includes a "Play bill" (2) that describes the "roles" the entity plays: its purpose, what it provides, and what it consumes. Every entity in Part 1 is placed on a color-coded Icon background (3).

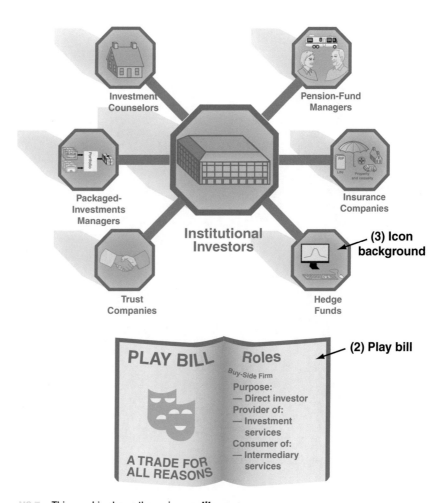

Figure VG.7   This graphic shows the various *entity groups*.

Every entity figure shows its subject surrounded by the other entities that support it and the entities it serves. The left side of each entity figure shows the Customers (4) of the entity. The right side shows the Suppliers (5) that supply services to the entity in question. Each entity figure also includes a product icon that describes the Products (6) or services the entity provides to its customers (see Figure VG.8).

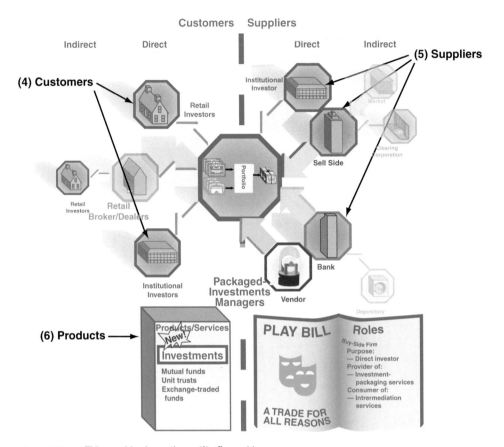

(4) Customers

(5) Suppliers

Customers   Suppliers

Indirect   Direct   Direct   Indirect

Institutional Investor

Retail Investors

Market

Sell Side

Clearing Corporation

Portfolio

Retail Investors

Retail Broker/Dealers

Bank

Institutional Investors

Packaged-Investments Managers

Vendor

Depository

(6) Products

Products/Services

New!

Investments

Mutual funds
Unit trusts
Exchange-traded funds

PLAY BILL

Roles

Buy-Side Firm
Purpose:
— Direct investor
Provider of:
— Investment-packaging services
Consumer of:
— Intermediation services

A TRADE FOR ALL REASONS

Figure VG.8   This graphic shows the *entity figures'* icons.

Every entity business-model figure shows the entity with its revenues and expenses (see Figure VG.9). Each one shows

- Revenue sources (7) represented by a stylized cash register
- Expenses or payments (8) categories represented by a stylized check (cheque)

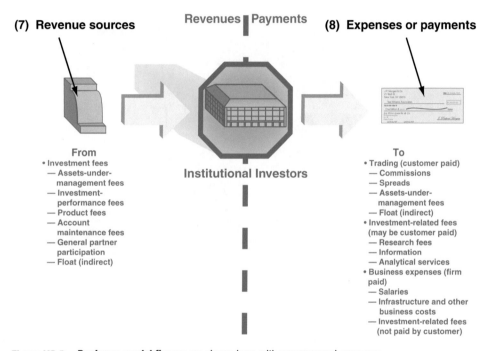

(7) Revenue sources

Revenues **Payments**

(8) Expenses or payments

From
- Investment fees
  — Assets-under-management fees
  — Investment-performance fees
  — Product fees
  — Account maintenance fees
  — General partner participation
  — Float (indirect)

Institutional Investors

To
- Trading (customer paid)
  — Commissions
  — Spreads
  — Assets-under-management fees
  — Float (indirect)
- Investment-related fees (may be customer paid)
  — Research fees
  — Information
  — Analytical services
- Business expenses (firm paid)
  — Salaries
  — Infrastructure and other business costs
  — Investment-related fees (not paid by customer)

Figure VG.9   ***Business-model figures*** are shown here with revenues and expenses.

PART 2: INSTRUMENTS

We categorize instruments in three major groups (see Figure VG.10). Although there are different types of packaged instruments, we use one icon to represent them all. Each type has its own Instrument icon (9).

(9) Instrument icons

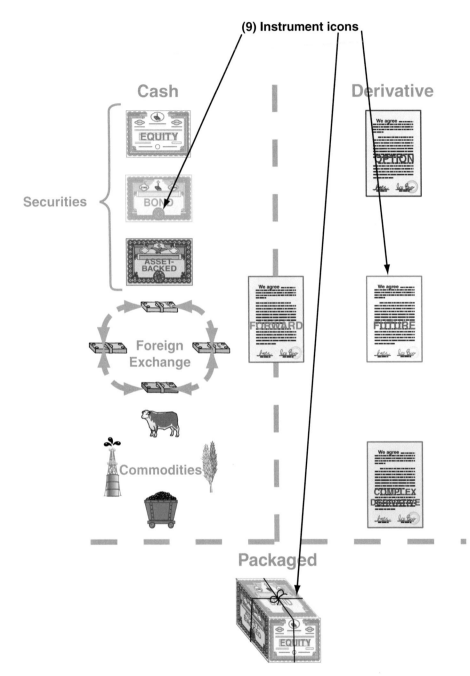

Figure VG.10   *Instrument summary*

For each major instrument type, we summarize the cash flows that are generated when the instrument is issued, cash flows that occur over the life of the issue, and any flows that occur (for those instruments that have a finite life) when the instrument terminates (see Figure VG.11). We examine secondary market transactions. We also summarize the cash-flow economics for a holder of the instrument.

The left side of the figure shows the Cash flow (10) that occurs when an instrument is created. For instruments that pay income, the chart shows Interim payments (11) over the instrument's life. Cash-flow figures show the Holder's economics (12) for each of the instruments. If the holder at instrument creation has a different economic situation than subsequent holders, two economic summaries are shown. For instruments with a finite life, the right side shows the Cash (13) flow that occurs when the instrument matures or expires.

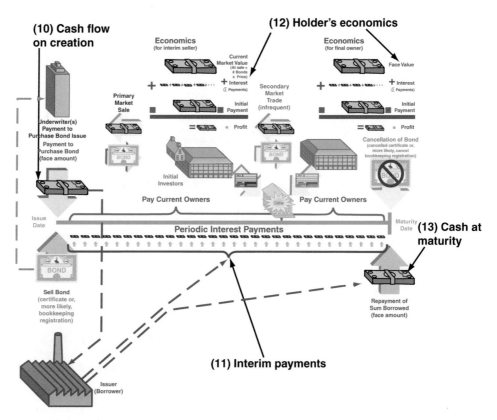

Figure VG.11   *Instrument cash-flow figures*

Throughout the books (at the end of each major part), there is a book map (see Figure VG.12). Beside the cover art for each book are boxes listing the major parts of the book. The book part in which the map is located is enlarged, and an arrow or arrows point to parts of other books or other parts within the same book where you can find more information on different aspects of the concepts covered in the part just completed. We attempt to differentiate sections with comparable levels of detail from parts with lesser or greater detail.

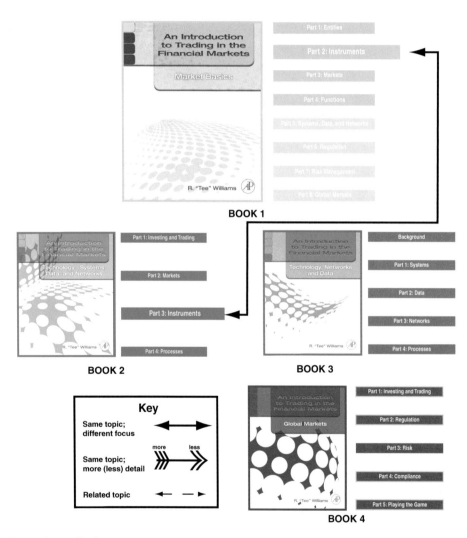

Figure VG.12   *Book maps*

PART 3: MARKETS AND MARKETPLACES

The market charts show the participants and contributions to the market (see Figure VG.13).

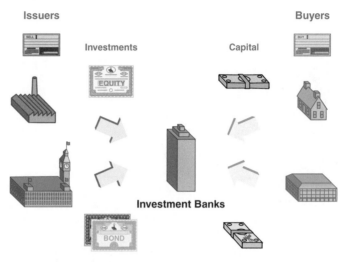

Figure VG.13   *Market types* (e.g., primary)

PART 4: FUNCTIONS (ACTIVITIES)

Every function for each entity type has an icon (see Figure VG.14). For each icon type, there are displays with one or multiple screens. The number of screens indicates both the number of different areas of focus for the function and the willingness of the entity to spend resources from the technology budget for the function. In subsequent books, we use the screens to differentiate focus and technology used.

Figure VG.14   *Function icons*

For the buy side and sell side, there are groups related to primary focus (see Figure VG.15). There are three groups of Buy-side categories (14). There are also three primary Sell-side categories (15), but the front office also has three major subareas.

For every function category Figure VG.16 shows the functions belonging to that category. An icon represents every function within the category.

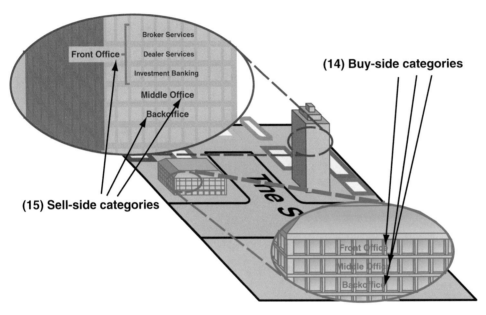

Figure VG.15   *Function categories*

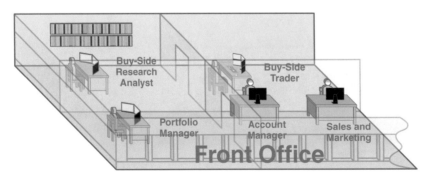

Figure VG.16   *Function-category members*

Every Function (16) covered has a figure that lists its primary tasks and describes which functions it services and what functions service it (see Figure VG.17). The related functions are broken down into internal and external categories. Every function has a "to do" list indicating its primary Tasks (17).

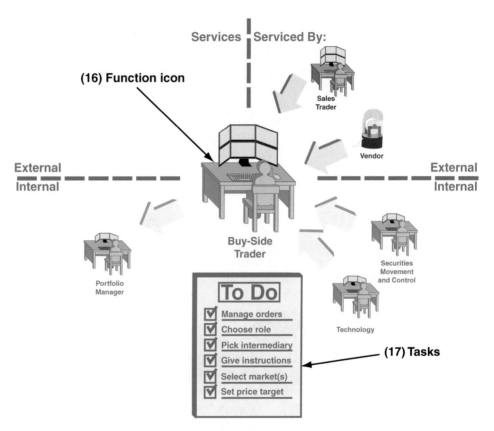

Figure VG.17   *Function figures*

The functions at some supporting entities are not broken out. We describe only entity-level functions (see Figure VG.18).

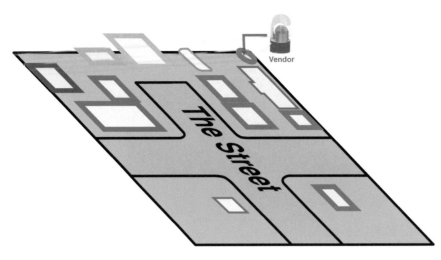

Figure VG.18   *Support functions*

PART 5: TECHNOLOGY: SYSTEMS, DATA, AND NETWORKS

Systems, data, and network icons are distributed among entities on the Street (see Figure VG.19). A red cloud represents Networks (18). A stylized mainframe represents Systems (19). A disk represents Data (20) stores.

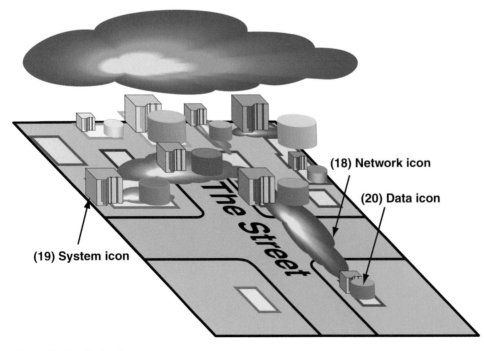

Figure VG.19   *Technology*

PART 6: GLOBAL MARKETS

Market icons of different sizes indicate global, regional, and some important local markets (see Figure VG.20).

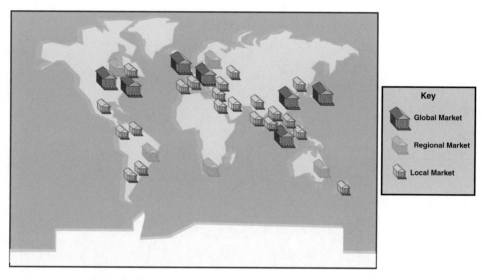

Figure VG.20   *Global markets*

Entities (The Players)

In most countries, the entities that operate in the traded-instrument markets are highly regulated commercial organizations with some activities required and others prohibited. In the past 20 years, however, the unique characteristics of individual firms in many countries have blurred as entities such as banks and broker/dealers have been allowed to merge with one another. National characteristics and differences have also been diluted as large numbers of firms have merged across national borders, or as firms have won the right to register in other countries. Moreover, countries have actively copied policies from one another, which has increased the similarities among entities in different regions.

Therefore, the types of entities we describe exist in many countries, albeit with some differences that reflect the characteristics of the culture, national regulations, and local legal systems of their respective nations. For example, most countries have some form of private or company-sponsored pension or retirement plans even if there are established national retirement programs. Similarly, although differences in regulation exist from country to country, most countries have independent entities referred to as "exchanges."

Figure 1 returns to the metaphor of the Street to examine some terms and distinctions for the different entities involved in the trading markets. We have already used the idea of "the Street" as the basis for the trading process in Figure OV.1 in the "Overview" at the front of this book.

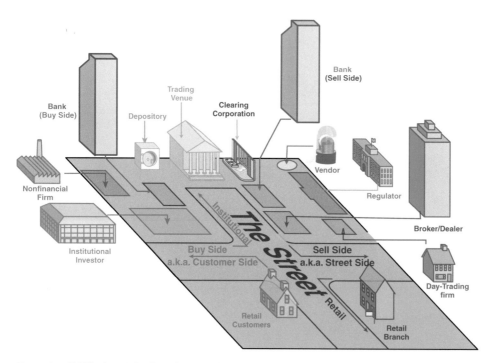

Figure 1   **Entities** invest, **trade**, and support the trading process to implement investment ideas and profit from trades for themselves and their customers.

An important way to categorize the trading markets is to distinguish between *retail* services and *institutional* services. The term "retail" refers to individuals participating in the markets directly. By contrast, the term "institution" refers to an organization that operates in the markets professionally. (An institution may manage the money for a group of individuals, as in the case of a mutual fund or unit trust, but a professional is making investment and trading decisions on behalf of the individuals that have entrusted their money to the institution.) Similarly, broker/dealers often split their operations into retail and institutional departments, each supporting the corresponding investor groups.

The entities reflect the distinct regulatory environments under which they operate, although many may coexist as divisions or departments within a single, larger company. For example, large commercial and investment banks have departments and divisions that operate as broker/dealers, investment managers, and processing facilities. Although they are all part of larger organizations, each separate division operates under differing sets of regulations that reflect the division's specialized financial purpose.

Holding companies often have subsidiaries or departments that are registered as the types of entities described in this part. Part 4 focuses on functions performed by individuals and departments within different entities. These divisions are usually more similar to independent companies with the same operational purpose than they are to other divisions within their own parent organization with different operational purposes.

In the remainder of this part, we describe the entities in the trading markets focusing primarily on regulatory distinctions. In most countries, regulatory categories do not necessarily correspond to distinct companies.

The Buy Side 1

We begin our discussion of participants in the markets by exploring the **buy side.** These are firms and individuals that use the services of intermediaries (the **sell side**) to raise capital and to trade instruments both for investment and to profit from trading. Figure 1.1 shows buy-side entities.

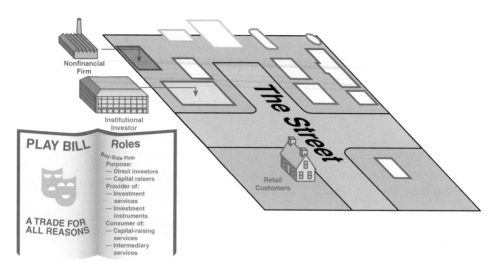

Figure 1.1 *Buy-side entities* raise capital and invest disposable funds directly and use intermediaries in the trading markets.

NONFINANCIAL COMPANIES

Nonfinancial companies have two primary roles within the trading markets (see Figure 1.1.1). First, nonfinancial companies, together with many financial companies,[1] are customers of the *investment banking* activities that comprise the *primary market* described in Parts 3 and 4. In addition, some nonfinancial companies are active participants in trading either by actively purchasing *commodities* (Part 2) in the cash market, hedging their financial transactions with derivatives (also Part 2), or in some cases actively managing their excess cash by investing in securities and other instruments.

---

1   We use the simplifying assumption throughout this set of books that the customers of investment banks for services in the primary market are nonfinancial companies. In fact, banks and broker/dealers need to raise capital like any other organization. When financial firms need to raise capital, they generally use another investment bank instead of managing the process themselves. Thus, they function as any other nonfinancial company when they need to raise capital.

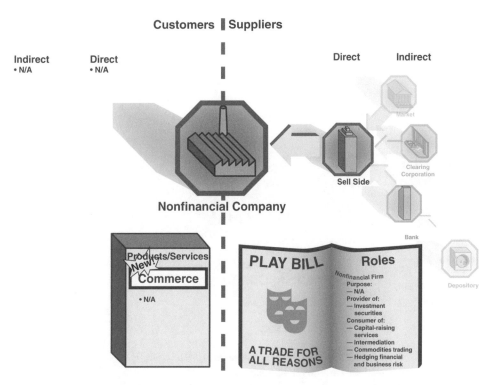

Figure 1.1.1 ***Nonfinancial companies*** raise capital primarily but also invest surplus funds and trade for raw materials in the trading markets.

Business Models

Nonfinancial companies do not typically profit directly from the financial markets (see Figure 1.1.1.1). Some nonfinancial companies do invest cash balances and trade in commodities markets to fulfill needs for raw materials, but such companies are just traders and investors in the context of the markets. Nonfinancial companies are major contributors to the revenues of the sell side when they buy investment banking and ***securitized financing*** services. (See Book 2, *An Introduction to Trading in the Financial Markets: Trading, Markets, Instruments, and Processes,* for an explanation of **securitization**.)

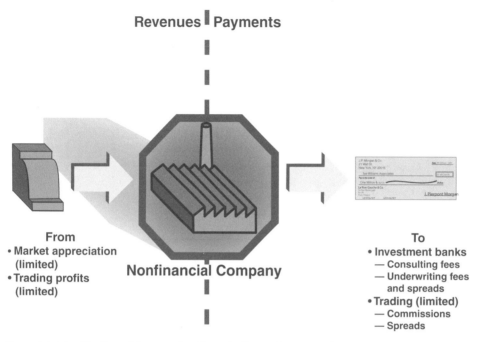

Revenues ┃ Payments

Nonfinancial Company

From
- Market appreciation (limited)
- Trading profits (limited)

To
- Investment banks
  — Consulting fees
  — Underwriting fees and spreads
- Trading (limited)
  — Commissions
  — Spreads

Figure 1.1.1.1   *Nonfinancial companies* offer no trading products or services; however, they pay to raise capital and provide intermediary services in the trading markets.

RETAIL INVESTORS

Individuals investing for their own accounts are small players by themselves in the over-all markets. Collectively, however, **Retail investors** represent a significant portion of the total invested funds. Although the investments of individuals are significant in most markets, they typically represent a smaller portion of aggregate assets than institutional investors (see Figure 1.1.2). Individual investors perform most of the tasks described in the trading process (see the discussion around Figure OV.1 in the "Overview"), although they typically do not have a say in where their **orders** are routed.

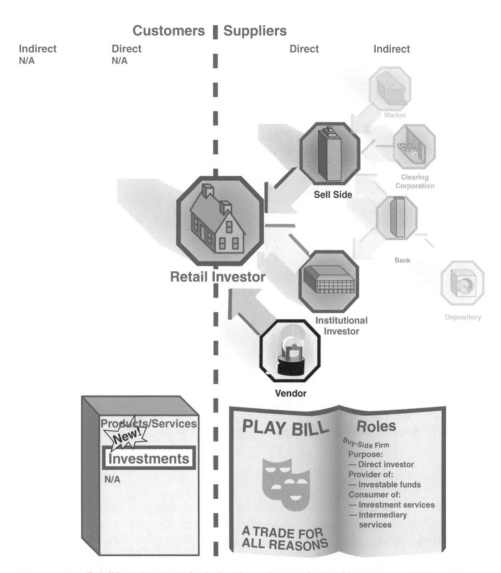

Figure 1.1.2 **Retail investors** invest funds directly or rely on professional investors to profit from their disposable funds in the trading markets.

Business Models

Retail investors profit from income paid by traded instruments and from appreciation in the market value of their instruments (see Figure 1.1.2.1). Individuals provide revenues to the institutional buy side through the fees they pay, both directly and indirectly, for investment management services. They pay commissions and spreads to the sell side for direct securities purchases and sales and fees for assets held for their benefit by sell-side firms. They are indirectly responsible for institutional commissions and spreads for the funds managed on their own behalf.

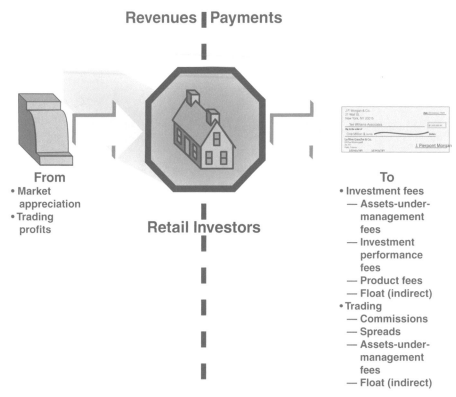

Revenues | Payments

From
- Market
  appreciation
- Trading
  profits

Retail Investors

To
- Investment fees
  — Assets-under-
    management
    fees
  — Investment
    performance
    fees
  — Product fees
  — Float (indirect)
- Trading
  — Commissions
  — Spreads
  — Assets-under-
    management
    fees
  — Float (indirect)

Figure 1.1.2.1   ***Retail investors*** earn income on investments and profit (or sustain losses) from changes in asset prices while paying for intermediary services in the trading markets.

INSTITUTIONAL INVESTORS

Firms that have as their business purpose the management of money for others are collectively referred to as investment managers, institutional investors, or ***money managers***. These generic terms refer to a wide array of entities operating under differing financial regulations. The financial regulations generally circumscribe the activities of entities within each regulatory category, define the way the regulated firms must conduct their business, demand a level of professional conduct, and require explicit reporting on activities. Most regulation is intended to protect the interests of the customers of these institutional investors. Typical regulatory distinctions for investment managers include the categories shown in Figure 1.1.3.

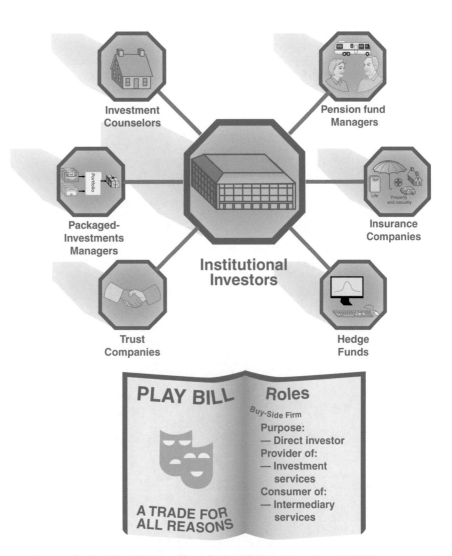

Figure 1.1.3 *Institutional investors* provide professional investment services to individuals, corporations, governments, and other entities through six different organizational structures.

Investment Counselors

Investment counselors typically manage investments for individuals as separate accounts owned by the individual (see Figure 1.1.3.1). Each account in turn may be invested either in part or completely in pooled investments, but the counselor has a direct relationship with the investor.

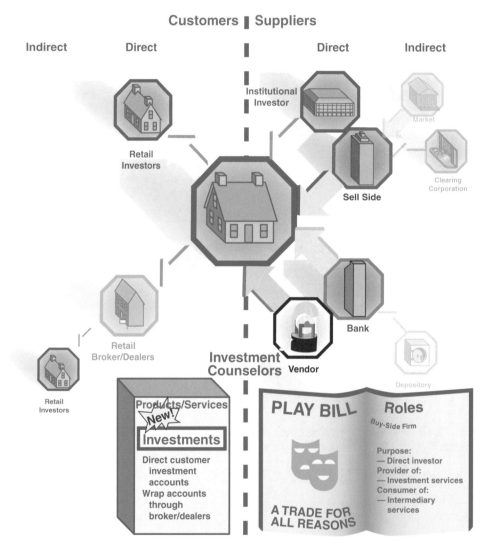

Figure 1.1.3.1   **Investment counsel firms** manage money for individuals directly in accordance with the individual's specific goals and objectives in the trading markets.

Providing individualized services to retail customers involves significant administrative burdens for the investment counsel firm. As a result, these services have typically been reserved for very wealthy individuals. However, broker/dealers have created products known as **wrap accounts** in which a broker/dealer offers individualized investing to the broker/dealer's customers. An investment firm actually manages the investment activities, and the broker/dealer handles the direct customer relationship. This makes individualized investment services possible for less wealthy retail customers.

Packaged-Investments Managers

Mutual funds and **unit trusts** permit an investor with limited funds the opportunity to purchase a share in a pool of investments that contains the combined funds of a large group of smaller investors. These investment pools offer the benefit of a professional manager and **portfolio diversification** that would otherwise be unavailable to an investor with modest funds.

Unlike an investment counselor, a mutual fund or unit trust manager does not have a direct or personal relationship with the individual investor. Instead, the investor purchases shares or units of the investment pool, and must rely on the stated purpose of the investment's funds or units defined in marketing materials to assess the suitability of the investments for his or her purposes (see Figure 1.1.3.2).

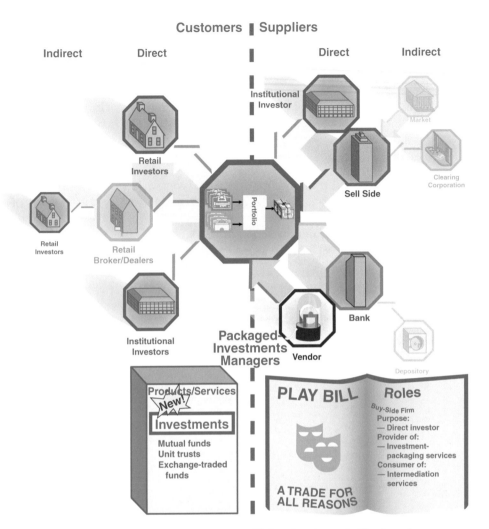

Figure 1.1.3.2 **Packaged-investments managers** provide investment opportunities through participation in shares or units of comingled funds to make professional management affordable to investors with limited funds.

Trustees

Some investment organizations such as **trustees** assume special responsibilities beyond managing invested funds for a profit (see Figure 1.1.3.3). One typical case occurs when funds are placed in a trust for an individual, and the manager is given responsibility not only to invest the funds, but also to control how and when money from the fund is paid to the individual and how it can be used. This is referred to as a **personal trust**. A second case involves a situation in which the money left by an individual at the time of his or her death is managed while the funds are being paid out as instructed by the individual's will, or managed over longer periods of time for specific purposes established by the will.

A fund managed on behalf of a person who is deceased is called an **estate**. A third type of trust is created when money is donated with specific instructions concerning how the donated funds are to be managed for an organization or special purpose. There can be a wide variety of trusts or estates with differing characteristics.

The authority for managing funds in these manners may require a trustee, who is an individual or organization granted the authority to manage trusts and estates by regulators. Banks and lawyers often have **trust powers**. Trust accounts may have the standing of an "individual" under the law. Therefore, trustees are able to bring lawsuits on behalf of the trust, and trust accounts may have special tax obligations that the trustee must file and pay.

In addition to other special trust powers, trust and estate managers have special responsibilities known as **fiduciary obligations**. A **fiduciary** is required by law to act with respect to the funds in his or her care as a "prudent man would manage his own money." This is known as the **prudent man rule**.

Eleemosynary funds refer to money set aside to be invested to benefit charitable purposes and educational institutions. Eleemosynary funds may require unique management skills and responsibilities as well. Managers of these funds are treated as fiduciaries, and some are trustees.

Pension Fund Managers

Pensions and other types of retirement funds often have special tax treatment or implications for the individuals who benefit from the pensions. Retirement funds also require

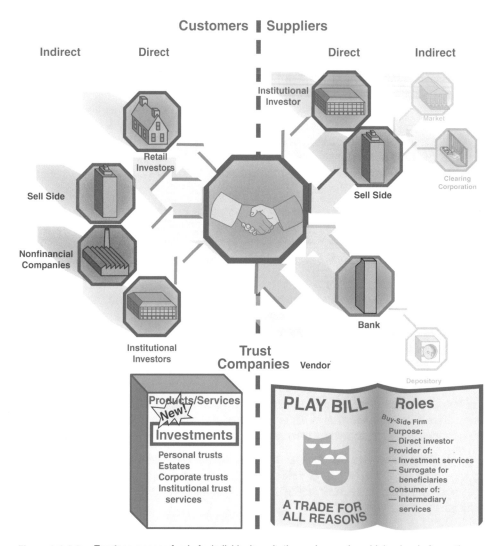

Customers | Suppliers

Indirect   Direct   Direct   Indirect

Institutional
Investor

Market

Retail
Investors

Clearing
Corporation

Sell Side   Sell Side

Nonfinancial
Companies

Bank

Institutional   Trust
Investors   Companies   Vendor

Depository

Products/Services   PLAY BILL   Roles
New!   Buy-Side Firm
Investments   Purpose:
                                          — Direct investor
Personal trusts   Provider of:
Estates   — Investment services
Corporate trusts   — Surrogate for
Institutional trust   beneficiaries
  services   Consumer of:
                         A TRADE FOR   — Intermediary
                         ALL REASONS   services

Figure 1.1.3.3   **_Trustees_** manage funds for individuals and others who require a higher level of care than just professional management and who surrender significant authority to the trustee.

that managers of the funds act as fiduciaries on behalf of the individuals covered by the plan. In particular, pension managers must take special care to ensure that the funds under their control are managed in a reasonable manner without excessive risks, and that all aspects of management are conducted in a professional manner. Pensions were among the first funds for which managers were charged with **_best execution_**[2] requirements, which demand that all trades for the fund be effected with the lowest possible net transaction costs (see Figure 1.1.3.4).

---

2   Best execution is described in more detail in Book 2, _An Introduction to Trading in the Financial Markets: Trading, Markets, Instruments, and Processes._

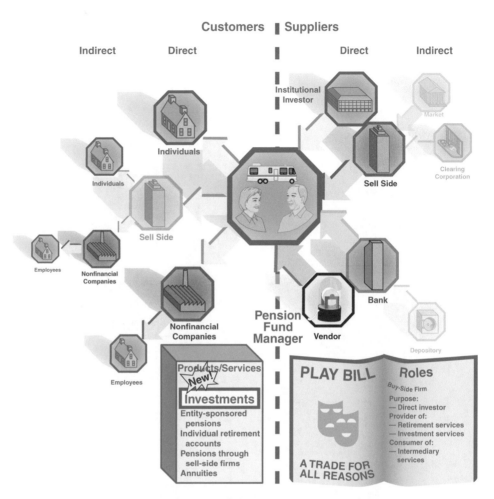

Figure 1.1.3.4 **_Pension fund managers_** manage retirement funds for individuals and corporate employees to ensure the availability of promised levels of funds when the beneficiary retires.

Insurance Companies

There are two primary types of insurance in most markets. **_Life insurance_** provides a component of protection against death and, in the case of **_whole-life insurance,_** also provides investment returns as well. Whole-life insurance is one of the first forms of private investment in most markets, and the **_premiums_** paid are invested on behalf of the insured (see Figure 1.1.3.5). Premiums for whole-life insurance have two components. The first component pays the cost of the insurance against the death of the insured. The second component is an investment that belongs to the policy owner. **_Term-life insurance_** provides protection against death only and does not include an investment asset.

The second type of insurance is known as **_property and casualty_** insurance. "Property and casualty" is a collective term for insurance against specific types of risk

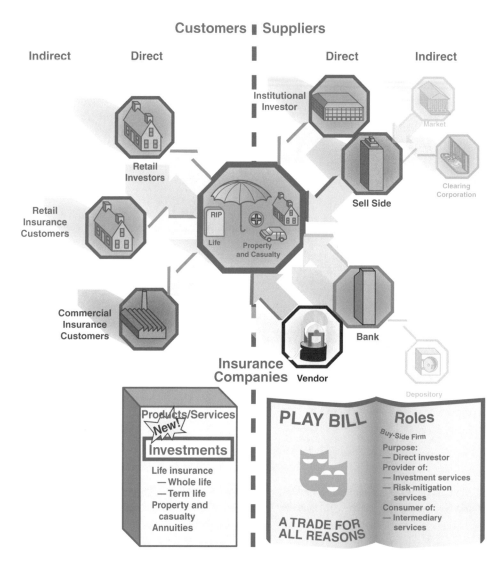

Customers ▌ Suppliers

Indirect   Direct   Direct   Indirect

Institutional Investor

Market

Retail Investors

Clearing Corporation

Sell Side

Retail Insurance Customers

Life   Property and Casualty   RIP

Commercial Insurance Customers

Bank

Insurance Companies Vendor

Depository

Products/Services
New!
Investments
Life insurance
— Whole life
— Term life
Property and casualty
Annuities

PLAY BILL

Roles

*Buy-*Side Firm
Purpose:
— Direct investor
Provider of:
— Investment services
— Risk-mitigation services
Consumer of:
— Intermediary services

A TRADE FOR ALL REASONS

Figure 1.1.3.5   ***Insurance companies*** manage money from premiums to permit promised levels of funds to be paid in the event of defined but uncertain future events to provide protection for individuals or entities.

such as property loss through fire, flood, or theft as well as medical costs and business losses. Premiums for property and casualty insurance are paid to the insurance company, which has the obligation to protect against the insured type of loss but is free to invest the premiums as it sees fit. However, insurance investments are often constrained by regulations.

For the purposes of this set of books, insurance is of interest primarily because it generates huge quantities of investable funds. We leave the description of the risk mitigation part of the insurance business to others.

Hedge Funds

Finally, the most aggressively managed fund groups are collectively known as **hedge funds** (see Figure 1.1.3.6). Hedge funds originally got their name from investing in a variety of different strategies in order to "insure" or **hedge** portfolios. These hedging strategies often included aggressive techniques. Regulators do not believe risky strategies are appropriate for less sophisticated investors who may not understand the risks involved or investors who are not able to absorb a significant loss. Therefore, hedge funds are not permitted to seek investors who are not able to demonstrate a level of sophistication and a relatively high net worth. (Actual requirements differ from country to country and over time.) Also, hedge funds are often regulated as **partnerships**, and the total number of investors may be limited.

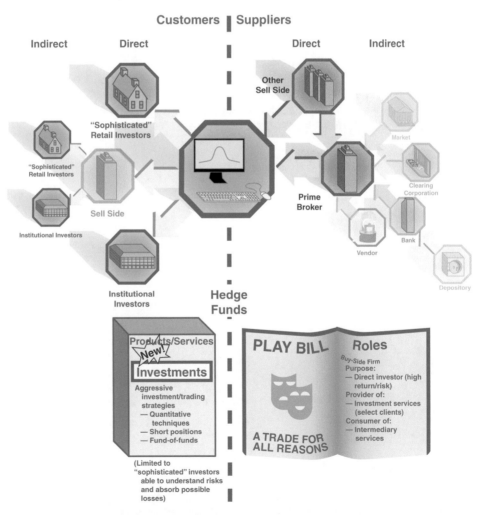

Figure 1.1.3.6   **Hedge funds** engage in high-risk investment strategies to achieve higher than normal investment returns for sophisticated investors.

Buy-Side Business Models

Generally buy-side firms charge fees for managing funds that are a percentage of the funds being managed (see Figure 1.1.3.7). These fees vary but are usually only a few percentage points of the ***funds-under-management*** except for hedge funds that often charge substantial fees for presumed better returns. The advantage of a fee based on a percentage of funds-under-management is that there is an implicit incentive for the manager to make money for the client because the fees rise as the value of the fund increases. For some kinds of funds and in some regulatory environments, fees may be regulated or capped. In most markets, competitive forces limit fees.

An important factor in the economics of fund management is that any costs directly attributable to the management of the fund are charged against the fund. This means that the customers pay ***direct costs*** while the investment manager pays ***indirect costs*** from the manager's revenues. Regulators may define the distinction between direct and indirect costs, but a working definition is that a direct cost is any cost necessary to provide the investment service.

As an example, the commission paid for a trade is a direct cost, whereas rent on the building where an investment manager works is an indirect cost. Because direct costs are paid by the fund, there is a strong incentive for the manager to convert as many costs as possible to direct costs. We explore this topic in more detail in Book 2, where we discuss ***soft dollars*** or ***soft commissions.***

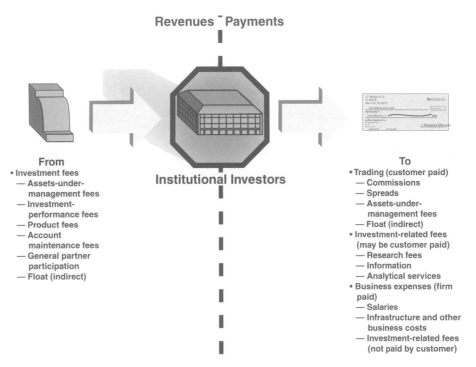

Revenues ⁻ Payments

Institutional Investors

From
- Investment fees
  — Assets-under-management fees
  — Investment-performance fees
  — Product fees
  — Account maintenance fees
  — General partner participation
  — Float (indirect)

To
- Trading (customer paid)
  — Commissions
  — Spreads
  — Assets-under-management fees
  — Float (indirect)
- Investment-related fees (may be customer paid)
  — Research fees
  — Information
  — Analytical services
- Business expenses (firm paid)
  — Salaries
  — Infrastructure and other business costs
  — Investment-related fees (not paid by customer)

Figure 1.1.3.7   *Institutional investors* receive a percentage fee based on the size of the assets they manage or a percentage of the returns they earn less the cost of their operations to provide an incentive for the manager to increase the value of the funds they invest.

The Sell Side 2

Next, we look at the organizations that provide intermediary services, that is, the sell side. Sell-side firms provide both capital-raising and trading services to the buy side (see Figure 1.2).

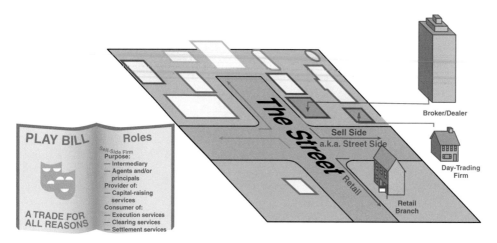

Figure 1.2 ***Sell-side*** firms act as intermediaries and financial guarantors for the trades of their customers.

BROKERS, DEALERS, AND BROKER/DEALERS

The sell side is composed of firms performing the functions of brokers and dealers. These functions are described in detail in Part 4, but briefly a broker (or agent) operates on behalf of investors or other brokers. Dealers act for their own benefit buying and selling as principals. Firms that act as both brokers and dealers are referred to as "broker/dealers." Broker/dealers are also commonly referred to as "brokerage firms" or "investment banks" although we use the term "investment bank" more narrowly.

Broker/dealers perform a variety of tasks, but they have two major roles. The first role is to help companies and governments raise money to fund their operations by issuing new securities. The second role is to help customers buy and sell securities that are already issued. We describe the many tasks of broker/dealers in Part 4 on functions.

It is important to understand what we mean by the terms "broker," "dealer," and "broker/dealers." Categories of sell-side firms are grouped by these three categories in Figure 1.2.0 and are also differentiated by whether they service retail or institutional customers.

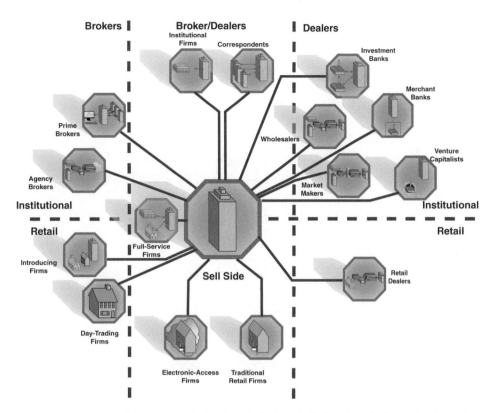

Figure 1.2.0 The *sell side* may act as broker (agent), dealer (principal), or both (broker/dealer) depending on need and the situation for their customers.

BROKERS OR AGENTS

A broker is an individual or organization that is permitted to buy or sell securities or other instruments on behalf of others. Another term for a broker is "agent." An agent or broker is paid a commission for the transaction by the individual or organization for which the service is performed. A broker is expected to look out for the best interest of his or her customer, and the broker should not profit from knowledge of a customer's intentions at the customer's expense. This is shown in Figure 1.2.1.

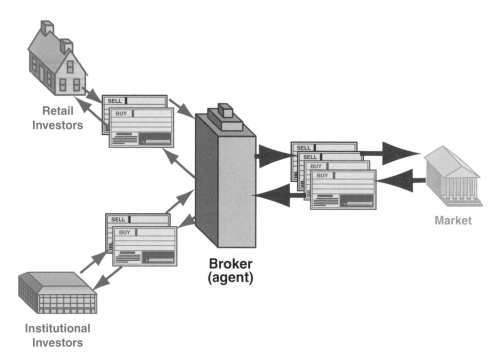

Figure 1.2.1 ***Brokers (agents)*** take orders from their customers and represent those customers' orders in the markets.

Several types of firms specialize in doing agency-only business. These firms often promote their business by emphasizing that in trading they are always acting in the best interest of their customers. Also, the amount of **capital** required for trading as an agent is substantially less than is required for a dealer.

Retail

A number of firms specialize in offering agent-only services to retail customers. The **retail brokers** we place in this category tend to have branch offices in shopping malls, on high streets,[3] and in other public places. **Retail sales** agents operate from these branches dealing with customers in person or by phone. Figure 1.2.1.1 includes two different types of firms that in most cases provide only agency services for retail customers.

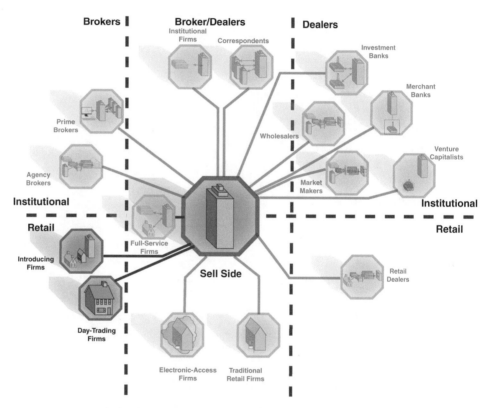

Figure 1.2.1.1   **Retail brokers** provide intermediary services through several alternative delivery channels to individual investors.

---

3   American readers may not be familiar with the term "high street," which is a British term that most closely corresponds to "main street." The primary street in many English towns and villages is known as "High Street" (e.g., Kensington High Street).

INTRODUCING FIRMS

Some retail brokers do not perform their own processing for customers, securities, or both. They use the services of a **correspondent broker/dealer** described later. Firms that perform only the selling function of the brokerage process are known as **introducing firms** because they "introduce" their customers to the markets (see Figure 1.2.1.1.1).

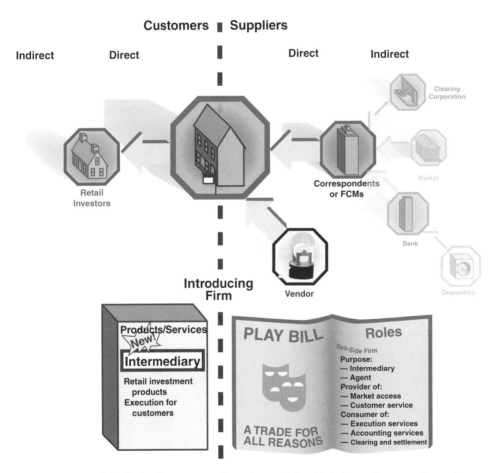

Figure 1.2.1.1.1   **Introducing firms** manage the customer relationship but leave the accounting and even trade execution to correspondents and Futures Commission Merchants (FCMs) to keep costs low, to minimize their need for capital, and/or to focus on servicing retail customers.

DAY-TRADING FIRMS

Some firms offer very sophisticated trading tools to retail individuals known as **_day traders_** who want to trade substantially full time. Day traders historically operated from trading rooms within the office of a day-trading firm. The key difference between day traders and institutional traders is that day traders are not registered as professionals, and they are trading their own money, not the firm's capital. Day-trading firms typically expect their customers to trade many times per day.

More recently, brokers other than traditional day-trading firms have begun to offer services to very active traders through the Internet. Using the Internet, brokers can provide sophisticated services to active traders who can then trade from their own homes rather than use a trading salon. As a result, day trading is less distinct as a firm class than it has been historically. Figure 1.2.1.1.2 shows the traditional activities of a day-trading firm.

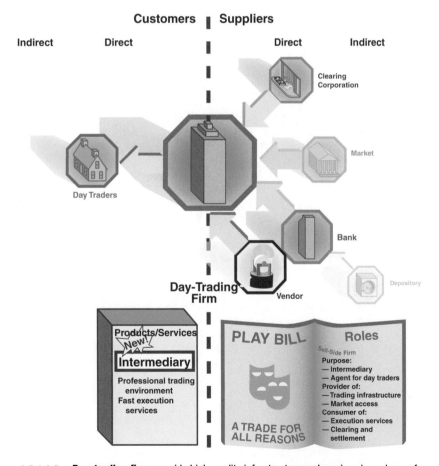

Figure 1.2.1.1.2 **_Day-trading firms_** provide high-quality infrastructure and services in exchange for the promise of frequent trades (and many commission fees) for individuals who are not registered as professionals but who trade full time.

Institutional Firms

Institutional brokers are firms that specialize in doing trades for investing institutions on an agency basis. For many firms, institutional agency business is only a part of the broker/dealer's services; however, other firms act only as an agent for institutions. Figure 1.2.1.2 shows two types of firms that provide primarily agency services to institutional investors.

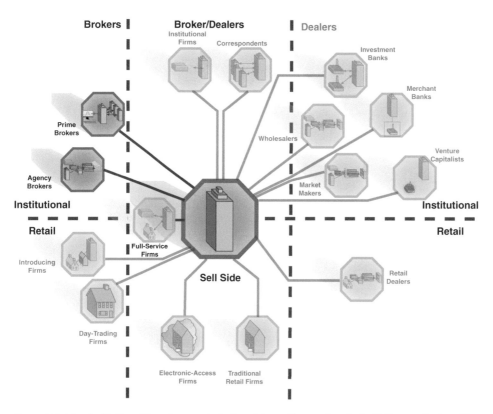

Figure 1.2.1.2   **Institutional firms** focus exclusively on intermediary services for institutions on the buy side.

AGENCY BROKERS

The term **agency broker** generally refers to a class of firms (and divisions of larger firms) that service institutional clients only as an agent. This widely used term is somewhat redundant because a broker is by definition an agent. Agency brokers help trade very large orders known as **blocks** and participate in other orders where the investing institution is interested in keeping costs low and/or when the institution wants to keep knowledge of the order as limited as possible (see Figure 1.2.1.2.1).[4]

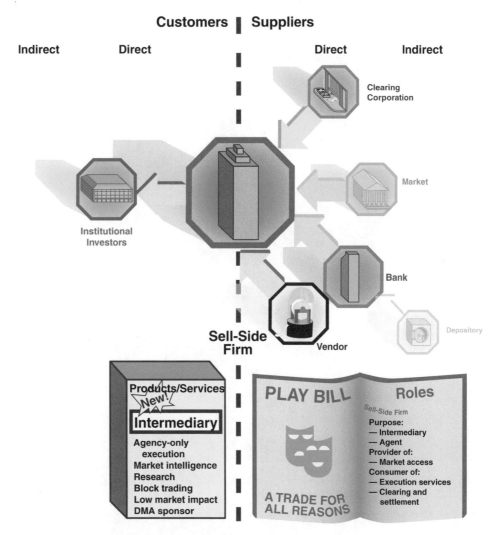

Figure 1.2.1.2.1 **Agency brokers** serve only as agents to lower market impact, to avoid conflicts of interest, and to keep execution costs low for institutional customers.

---

4 Book 2 provides a more complete description of the motivations for buy-side trading and the reasons institutions are concerned with widespread knowledge of pending orders.

PRIME BROKERS

A *prime broker* is a firm that provides specialized services for hedge funds. Prime brokers provide execution services for hedge funds, but they also consolidate trades done through other broker/dealers. Prime brokers often provide sophisticated trading tools known as *order management systems* (OMS) both to appeal to their hedge fund customers and to ensure adequate risk controls on a class of customers who have the potential to cause major capital problems if the hedge fund makes imprudent trades. Figure 1.2.1.2.2 shows the products prime brokers offer and roles they play.

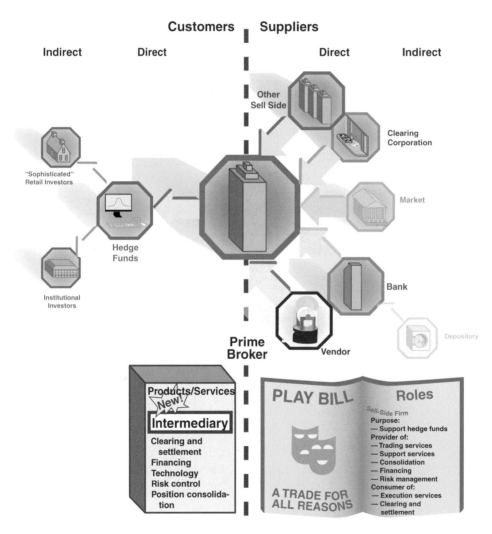

Figure 1.2.1.2.2 **Prime brokers** provide financing, processing services, risk management, and trade consolidation to hedge funds.

Brokerage Business Models

Brokers traditionally depend on commissions as their primary revenue source. **Fixed commissions** have been abandoned in most markets for years, and commission rates for most types of orders are quite low. The key to profitability for commission-based businesses is to handle large numbers of trades and to keep costs as low as possible. Alternatively, firms can provide ancillary services to supplement commission revenues, and/or firms can develop different revenue models. (In Book 2, we examine how the method by which different types of retail customers access the markets has a dramatic impact on their frequency of trading.)

One key method for retail firms to handle customers that do not trade frequently is to charge fees based on **assets-under-management** and fees in addition to commissions on trades. When firms charge for assets-under-management instead of commissions, the service is often referred to as **wealth management**.

Day-trading firms usually profit mainly from commissions, but day-trading firms demand that their customers trade frequently. Day-trading firms are reported to require as many as 25 trades per day. In addition, many day-trading firms and electronic-access broker/dealers (described later) that offer discounted commissions "sell" orders to dealers in a process known as **payment for order flow**. (Payment for order flow is discussed in more detail in Book 2.) Introducing firms often cater to wealthy customers and/or active traders and therefore are able to profit either from assets-under-management or from high volumes that generate large commission volumes.

Institutional agency brokers provide many different supporting services with the goal of generating more commissions and/or supplemental fees. For example, some agency brokers are built around very strong research departments. The trading activities provide a mechanism for paying for the research. Other agency brokers offer soft-dollar services. Soft dollars are a means of providing investment-related services to institutional customers in exchange for commissions; they are described in more detail in Book 2. Finally, other institutional brokers specialize in their ability to execute large or difficult trades for customers discreetly.

The biggest advantage of acting only as a broker is that all revenues are positive. Unlike dealers, which we consider in the next section, brokers do not risk their capital and are not subject to trading losses. Although brokerage revenues are positive and have low risk, in most situations brokerage profits are limited by pressure on commissions from customers. Figure 1.2.1.3 illustrates the business models for brokers.

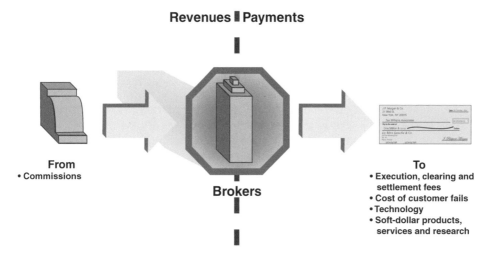

Revenues ▌ Payments

From
• Commissions

Brokers

To
• Execution, clearing and settlement fees
• Cost of customer fails
• Technology
• Soft-dollar products, services and research

Figure 1.2.1.3   ***Brokerages*** depend on revenues from fees and commissions and pay the costs of their personnel and infrastructure as they provide intermediary services.

DEALERS (PRINCIPALS)

An individual or organization that owns or is buying an instrument is known as a princi-pal. An intermediary that acts as a principal is known as a dealer. Dealers do not profit from a commission but from buying securities at lower prices and then reselling them at higher prices as a service for other investors. Dealers provide trades on demand (known as ***immediacy***) at a guaranteed price (see Figure 1.2.2).

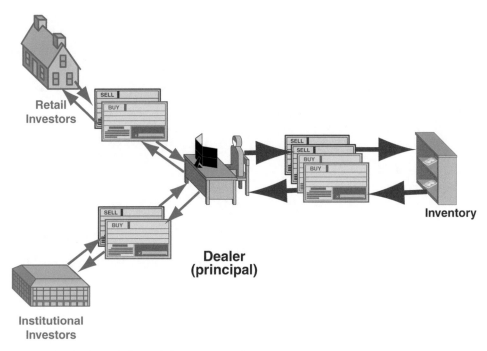

Figure 1.2.2 ***Dealers (principals)*** buy for and sell from their inventory as principals providing immediacy and guaranteed transaction prices for their customers.

Retail

Firms in the bond markets sometimes service the retail market, and because most bonds are sold from dealer inventory, there are retail dealers in this market. Prior to Nasdaq converting to an electronic trading system in the United States in 2002 and subsequently becoming an exchange with an automated market, there were retail deal-ers in equities. Some of those firms continue with the dealer business model, but most are brokers as well. Therefore, the role of retail dealer firm that is not also a broker is limited mostly to fixed income. Figure 1.2.2.1 shows the category of retail dealer. There are no subcategories.

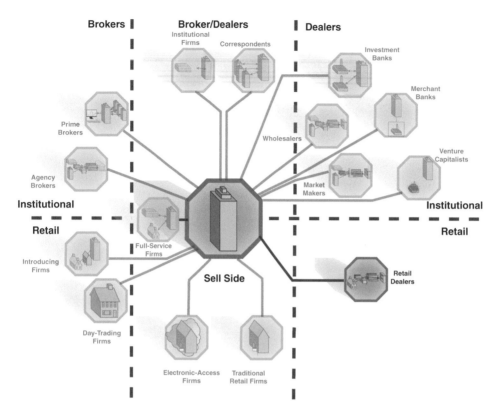

Figure 1.2.2.1 The **retail dealers** category services customers primarily in the fixed income and currencies areas.

Dealers serving only retail customers make markets that do not require huge inventory positions. Also, retail dealers must be assured that they can sell their positions quickly or price their market to reflect the possibility of holding positions for extended periods (see Figure 1.2.2.1.1).

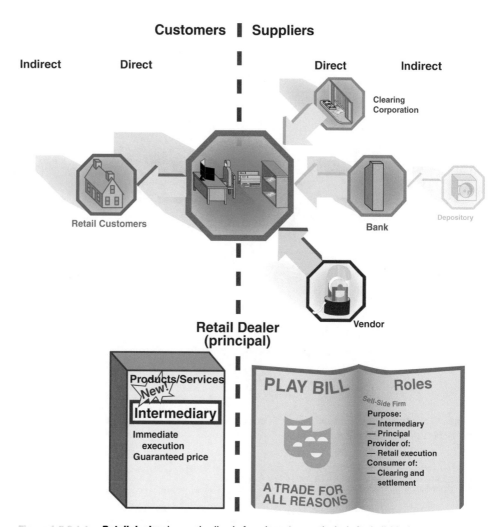

Figure 1.2.2.1.1 *Retail dealers* buy and sell only from inventory exclusively for individuals.

Institutional Firms

Although only a limited number of firms or divisions within firms are focused on retail customers in the role of dealer, there are many institutional dealer activities. We are primarily distinguishing activities in which a firm must risk its capital in the course of providing its primary service. Figure 1.2.2.2 shows the different types of institutional dealer activities.

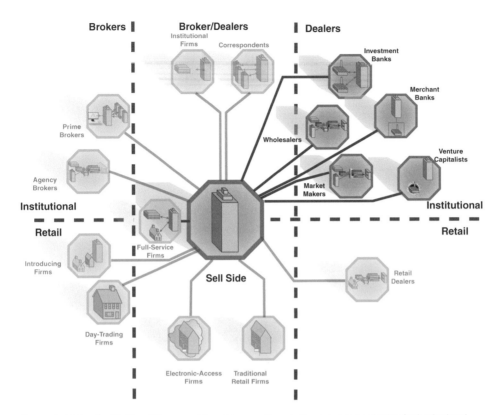

Figure 1.2.2.2 *Institutional firms* provide quick executions and/or a guaranteed price for institutional customers in five different formats.

MARKET MAKERS

Most markets, particularly those registered as exchanges or dealer associations (see Part 3), have a group of members or participants with special responsibilities that are known as market makers. A market maker has the responsibility of supplementing liquidity in the market by acting as a ***trader of last resort,*** or by providing immediacy when a trader wishing to use the market cannot find another trader on the opposite side (i.e., a buyer cannot find a seller or a seller cannot find a buyer).

Unlike other dealers, market makers are often required by rules to trade even in situations when trading is a disadvantage to the market-making firm. Market makers usually have better access to information than other traders and may get special financing advantages (see Figure 1.2.2.2.1).

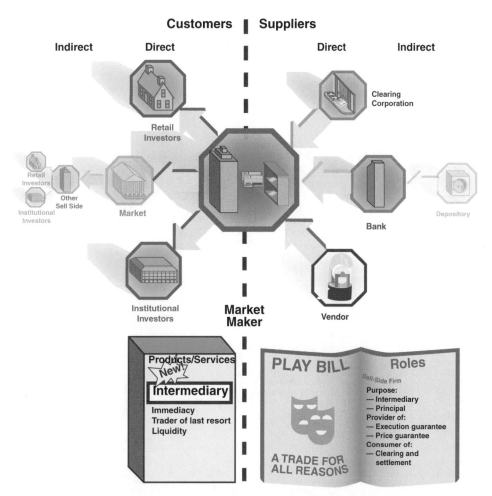

Figure 1.2.2.2.1   *Market makers* are empowered by markets with special rights and obligations to act as a guaranteed counterparty providing liquidity when no other traders are present for participants in the market.

WHOLESALERS

A few firms, known as ***wholesalers,*** specialize in acting as dealers for other firms out-side the exchange environment. Unlike market makers, wholesalers are not required to trade because of rules but do so because of their business objectives. These firms help other broker/dealers, both institutional and retail firms, by carrying an inventory of securities from which the other firms can buy or sell. This is particularly helpful for a firm acting only as a broker that needs to buy or sell a security for a customer when the other side for the customer's order in that security is not immediately available in the open market. Wholesalers are also helpful for firms that are themselves dealers but that may not have an inventory in every security that is of interest to their customers. Because wholesalers deal primarily with other firms, we categorize them as institutional firms (see Figure 1.2.2.2.2).

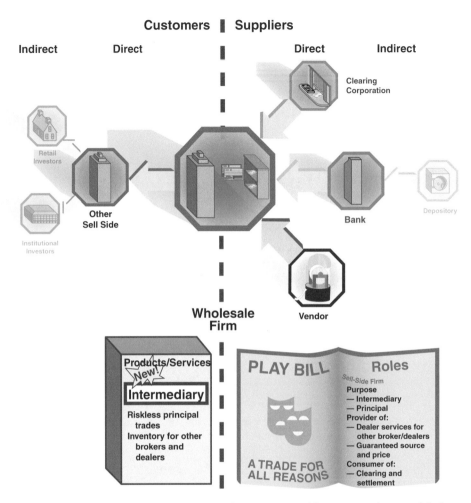

Customers | Suppliers

Indirect Direct | Direct Indirect

Clearing
Corporation

Retail
Investors

Other
Sell Side

Bank

Depository

Institutional
Investors

Wholesale
Firm

Vendor

Products/Services
New!
Intermediary
Riskless principal
trades
Inventory for other
brokers and
dealers

PLAY BILL   Roles
Sell-Side Firm
Purpose
— Intermediary
— Principal
Provider of:
— Dealer services for
  other broker/dealers
— Guaranteed source
  and price
A TRADE FOR   Consumer of:
ALL REASONS   — Clearing and
                   settlement

Figure 1.2.2.2.2   ***Wholesalers*** deal in a wide range of instruments providing an assured source of dealer transactions for other brokers and dealers.

INVESTMENT BANKS

Investment banks are firms that perform the investment banking functions. Most investment banks have divisions that act as most of the other types of firms described in this part, and several are part of, or have become, commercial banks as well. However, the category of investment bank refers to those organizations that are active in helping firms raise money in the primary market described in Part 3. The role of investment bank requires that the firm buy securities into inventory when an underwriting is consummated, and thus an investment bank acts as a dealer in that moment (see Figure 1.2.2.2.3).

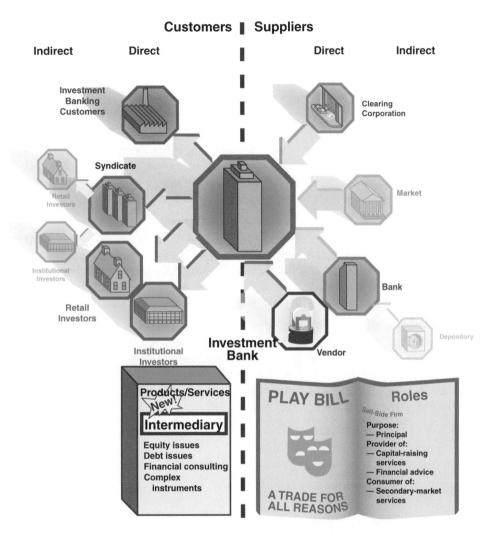

Customers | **Suppliers**

Indirect   Direct   Direct   Indirect

Investment Banking Customers

Clearing Corporation

Syndicate

Retail Investors

Market

Institutional Investors

Retail Investors

Bank

Institutional Investors

Investment Bank

Vendor

Depository

Products/Services
New!
Intermediary
Equity issues
Debt issues
Financial consulting
Complex
    instruments

PLAY BILL   Roles
Sell-Side Firm

Purpose:
— Principal
Provider of:
— Capital-raising
    services
— Financial advice
Consumer of:
— Secondary-market
    services

A TRADE FOR
ALL REASONS

Figure 1.2.2.2.3   ***Investment banks*** are dealers that specialize in raising capital for nonfinancial customers.

As we have noted repeatedly, terms in the trading markets are often used without precision. Many commentators use the terms "full-service broker/dealer" and "investment bank" interchangeably. We use the term "investment bank" here to mean firms (or divisions of firms) engaged in investment banking as described in Part 4, "Functions," of this book and in Part 4, "Processes," of Book 2. We use the term "full-service broker/dealer" (described later) to represent firms that service both retail and institutional customers and act as both a broker and dealer. Many of these full-service firms have divisions that act as investment banks.

MERCHANT BANKS

Merchant banks and their descendents **private equity firms** buy and sell companies or **controlling interests** in companies rather than just invest in the securities that companies issue. The firms described to this point only buy and sell securities or other instruments to benefit from short-run trading profits or longer-term investment returns.

Typically, investors and traders are not interested in companies as economic entities except to the extent the companies issue securities or other instruments that can be underwritten and traded. In contrast, "merchant banks," a British term, invest in companies, some of which are not publically traded, to profit from the ongoing operations of the company. In time, the merchant bank might sell the company at a profit.

Private equity firms more often acquire some or all of a company that is publically traded and that has gotten into financial difficulty or that has very depressed market value. The private equity firm may break up the company and resell the pieces. In some cases, the divisions of a publically traded company may be worth more separately than the market value placed on the combined.

When a situation such as this occurs, the private equity firm buys the publically traded firm (or a *controlling interests* in it) and breaks up the company into pieces to be resold individually. These firms engage in other investment strategies, many of which are created for each specific investment opportunity. Merchant banks and private equity firms may be subsidiaries of other financial organizations. Figure 1.2.2.2.4 shows the products and roles of merchant banks.

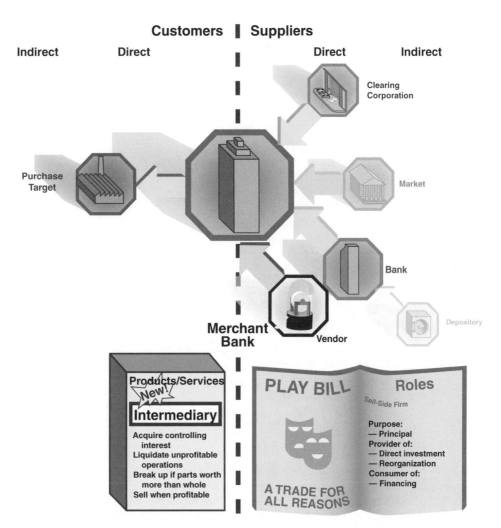

Figure 1.2.2.2.4 **_Merchant banks_** or private equity firms take long-term controlling positions in firms, eventually selling the firm or its components to profit on behalf of their shareholders or partners.

VENTURE CAPITAL FIRMS

In addition to investment banks that help with public offerings, a group of entities called **_venture capital firms_** or **_venture capitalists_** help to finance companies not yet mature enough to raise money in the public markets. Venture capital firms often provide substantial managerial support in addition to financing in exchange for an equity interest in the small company. The goal of the venture capital firm is for the small firm to **_go public_**, and the venture capitalist is then able to sell its equity interest in the **_secondary market_** (see Figure 1.2.2.2.5).

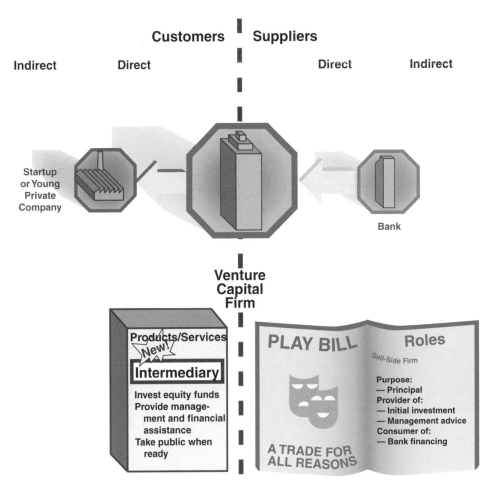

Figure 1.2.2.2.5   *Venture capital firms* provide specialized financing and management advice to young companies needing capital, eventually taking the companies public for the profit of partners or shareholders (in the venture capital firm).

Dealer Business Models

Dealer firms profit by risking their capital to buy instruments or even whole firms, and dealers subsequently resell what they have purchased, presumably at a profit. Figure 1.2.2.3 shows the revenues and major costs for firms operating as dealers.

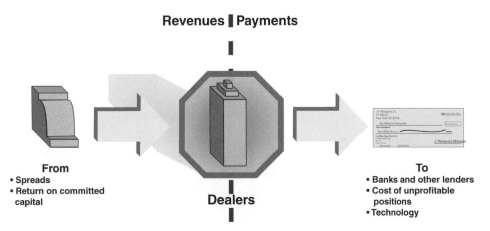

Revenues | Payments

From
- Spreads
- Return on committed capital

Dealers

To
- Banks and other lenders
- Cost of unprofitable positions
- Technology

Figure 1.2.2.3   ***Dealers*** profit from spreads between their bid and offer prices and may profit or lose money on instrument positions in their inventory as market prices fluctuate.

BROKER/DEALERS

A broker/dealer is a firm that is permitted by regulation to act as both a broker and a dealer. Most firms elect to be broker/dealers even if they specialize in one function or the other (see Figure 1.2.3). Prior to Big Bang in London, firms were not permitted to act as brokers and dealers (also known as jobbers). This policy, known as **single capacity**, was an attempt to limit conflicts of interest but had the effect of keeping the majority of both brokers and dealers small and unable to compete with larger foreign competitors that were permitted to provide both capacities.

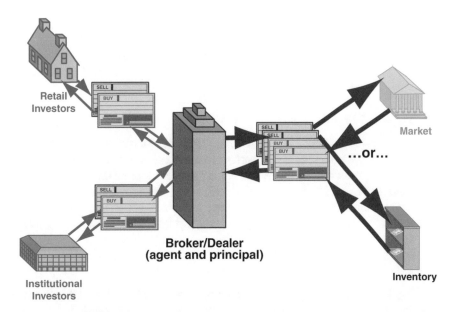

Retail Investors

Institutional Investors

Broker/Dealer (agent and principal)

Market

...or...

Inventory

Figure 1.2.3   ***Broker/dealers*** act as either principal or agent to satisfy the particular needs of their customers.

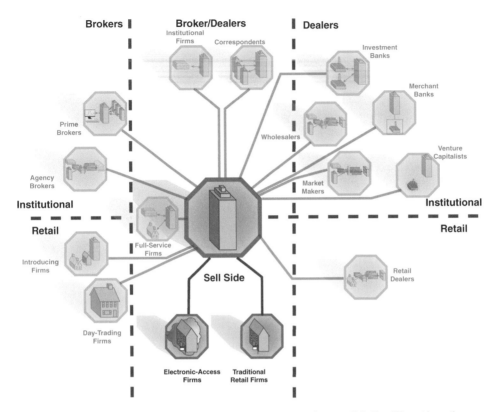

Brokers | Broker/Dealers | Dealers

Institutional Firms

Correspondents

Investment Banks

Merchant Banks

Prime Brokers

Wholesalers

Venture Capitalists

Agency Brokers

Market Makers

Institutional

Institutional

Retail

Retail

Full-Service Firms

Introducing Firms

Retail Dealers

Sell Side

Day-Trading Firms

Electronic-Access Firms

Traditional Retail Firms

Figure 1.2.3.1   **Retail broker/dealers** use different delivery strategies to satisfy the different investing and trading styles of their chosen customer segment(s).

Retail Broker/Dealers

We see in Book 2 that distinctions among retail customers is highly dependent on how they access the markets. Therefore, we distinguish among the firms that service retail customers by their distribution channels (see Figure 1.2.3.1).

TRADITIONAL RETAIL BROKER/DEALERS

We use the label **traditional retail broker/dealers** to mean firms that provide customers with a wide variety of research, asset management, and trading services. Sales agents for full-service firms are known as **financial consultants** or **registered representatives**. The sales agent is usually paid a commission for a customer's trades executed through the firm when that customer trades actively. For customers who do not trade actively, the firms and sales agents are paid from fees for managing the customers' assets. As we noted earlier, with the transition from commissions to assets-under-management fees, the industry has coined the term "wealth management," which is perceived to sound better than "retail broker."

Traditional retail broker/dealers employ branch offices located in shopping centers and on high streets as the delivery channel to provide services to customers. Financial consultants employ personal interactions with customers through either in-person meetings or telephone discussions. Figure 1.2.3.1.1 shows the roles, products, and direct relationships of traditional retail broker/dealers.

ELECTRONIC ACCESS BROKER/DEALERS

We define a second distribution strategy as **electronic access**. Many of these firms used to be part of a segment known as **discount brokerage**. Discount brokers evolved following the end of fixed commission rates in the 1970s and 1980s. They offered limited services at very low commissions. The sales representatives of discount firms are usually paid salaries instead of a portion of the commissions, and these firms encouraged automation to reduce the labor cost of providing services to customers (see Figure 1.2.3.1.2).

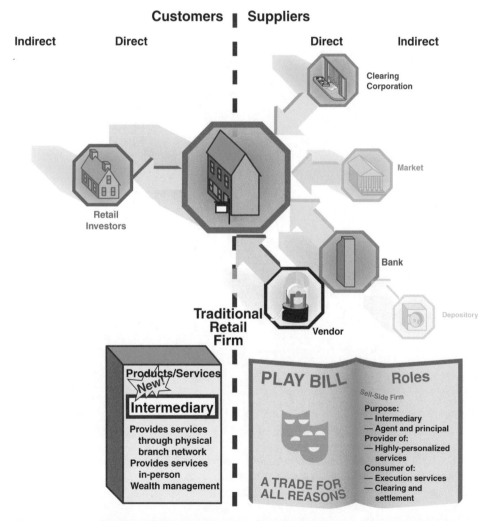

Figure 1.2.3.1.1 **Traditional retail broker/dealers** employ licensed financial consultants operating from physical branches to provide direct personal service for their customers.

Discount firms began their business dealing with their customers using the telephone instead of having branch offices. Next, discount firms began to use telephone keypads to enter orders[5] and request instrument prices. Increasingly, most discount brokers used the Internet as a primary delivery channel to keep costs low. To support customers who interact with the markets through the Internet, a help desk replaces financial consultants. As a result, we believe "electronic access" is a better description of these firms than "discount broker/dealer."

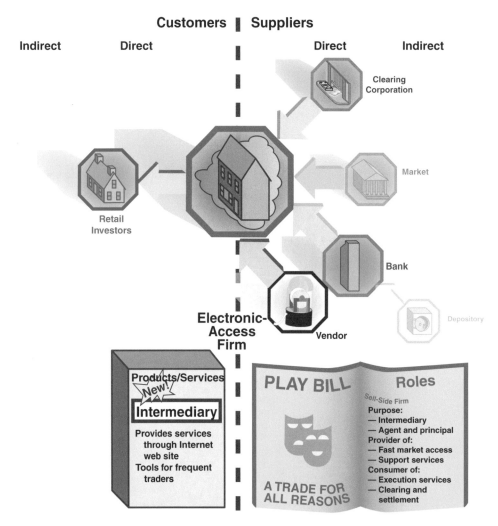

Figure 1.2.3.1.2   **_Electronic access broker/dealers_** employ Internet sites and electronic trading tools that facilitate frequent trading to satisfy aggressive customers.

---

5   Discount firms quickly learned that customers who entered orders using the telephone keypad traded much more frequently than customers who interacted with sales representatives over the phone. We return to this point in Book 2.

Institutional Broker/Dealers: Category

Institutions have increasingly dominated the trading markets over the past 50 years. As a result of this domination, specialized firms have developed to service institutional customers. Although institutional investors are demanding customers, they are concentrated in major financial centers and have the advantage that they do not require an expensive, geographically extensive branch network.

Many institutional firms have merged into other organizations and have lost their identities. However, firms still specialize in offering services only to institutions, and many large full-service broker/dealers (described later) maintain functionally independent institutional divisions. Figure 1.2.3.2 shows the members of the category of institutional broker/dealer. Note that institutional broker/dealer is both the name of the category and also the name of a member of the category.

Institutional Broker/dealers: Purpose

Institutional broker/dealers are a class of broker/dealer whose only customers are institutions. These firms may also have investment banking operations and other

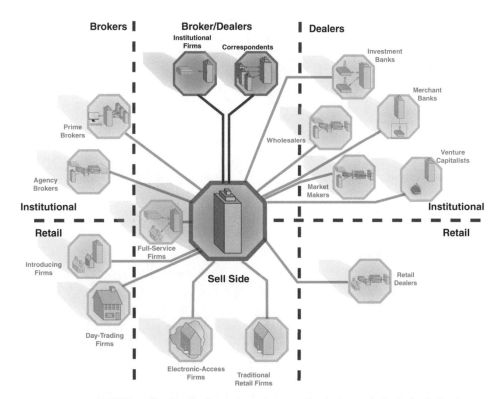

Figure 1.2.3.2   **Institutional broker/dealers** (category) act as either broker or dealer for institutional customers exclusively.

services. Institutional broker/dealers do not have the cost of serving retail customers or the regulatory burden of dealing with unsophisticated customers. They also have the capacity to provide the roles of both broker and dealer in the same transaction, acting as an agent for all the shares that can be comfortably executed in the markets and then purchasing any leftover quantity to complete the order (see Figure 1.2.3.2.1).

CORRESPONDENTS OR FCMS

Correspondent firms are a class of broker/dealer whose primary business is to provide services to other broker/dealers (see Figure 1.2.3.2.2). In the futures markets, the same function is provided by **Futures Commission Merchants** (FCMs).

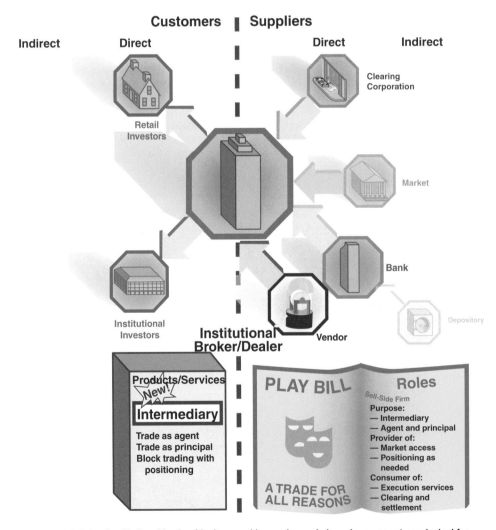

Figure 1.2.3.2.1   **Institutional broker/dealers** provide any demanded service as agent or principal for institutional customers.

Correspondent[6] firms may provide only the securities processing services or customer accounting or both. Correspondents are helpful with new firms because they enable a new broker to begin business without the costs of setting up a separate processing capability. Moreover, if a correspondent or FCM **carries the customer accounts** (described in Book 2), there are lower capital requirements for the firm using the correspondent. Correspondents also permit a broker/dealer to operate in a geographic

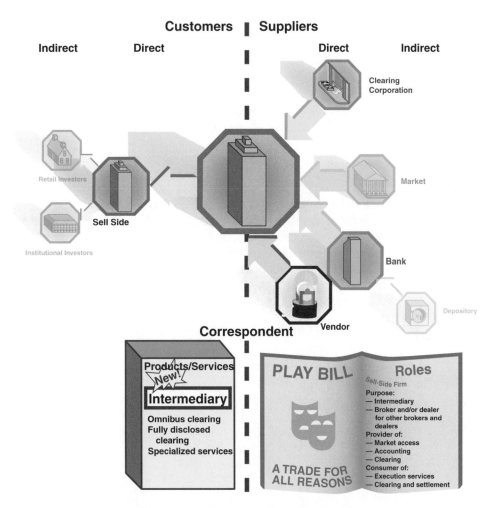

Figure 1.2.3.2.2 *Correspondents* assume the function(s) of broker, dealer, facilitator of market execution, clearing, settlement, and/or processing as requested for other sell-side firms.

---

6   Technically, a correspondent relationship is reciprocal. That is both the small firm such as an introducing firm and the larger firm carrying the introducing firm's accounts are each other's correspondent. Here, however, we use "correspondent firm" only to mean the firm providing correspondent services.

region that is remote from markets because the correspondent can trade for the remote firm and provide supporting services.[7]

Full-Service Firms: Category

Some firms, known as **full-service firms,** have grown both internally and/or through acquisition and merger to provide most or all of the different functions described for the sell side to this point (see Figure 1.2.3.3). Moreover, most full-service firms are owned by or have created commercial banks to become **universal banks**. These firms straddle the retail and institutional categories and provide broker, dealer and broker/dealer services.

Firms in the United States where the term "full-service firm" originated were not permitted to provide both investment banking and commercial banking services because investment and commercial banking were split during the Depression. In Europe and Asia, except Japan,[8] the dominant investment firms were always universal banks because investments and commercial banking were never separated. Full-service firm is the term we use for the category and also the name for the only member within the category.

Full-Service Firms: Purpose

Full-service firms act in the roles of both broker and dealer, and usually have both a strong retail customer base as well as institutional customers (see Figure 1.2.3.3.1). Some of these firms developed investment banking operations by leveraging their **distribution capacity** to become investment banks. In contrast, investment banks began primarily as underwriters of securities and have developed or acquired sales and trading capabilities. Many investment banks and full-service broker/dealers have further evolved into, or have been acquired by, universal banks.

7　The functions of a correspondent are introduced in Part 4, and the processes or services offered by a correspondent are described more fully in Book 2.

8　After World War II, the United States imposed U.S.-styled separation of banking and investment services on the Japanese financial market. As in the United States, the distinctions in Japan have gradually blurred during the intervening period.

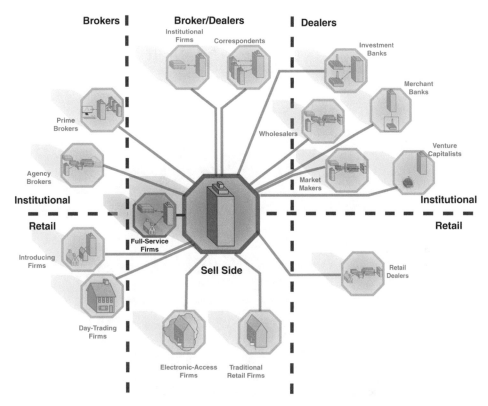

Figure 1.2.3.3   **Full-service firms** (category) includes entities that service both retail and institutional customers providing all sell-side services.

Broker/Dealer Business Models

Broker/dealers profit from commissions for the agency business and from acting as a dealer. They profit as investment banks from underwriting securities. They may have both institutional and retail customers, and they may sometimes profit from direct investments in companies (see Figure 1.2.3.4). Broker/dealers have, for the most part, benefitted from the strong trend over the past 50 years for **_bespoke_** financial transactions to be transformed into securities through a process known as "securitization." Securitization is described in more detail in Book 2.

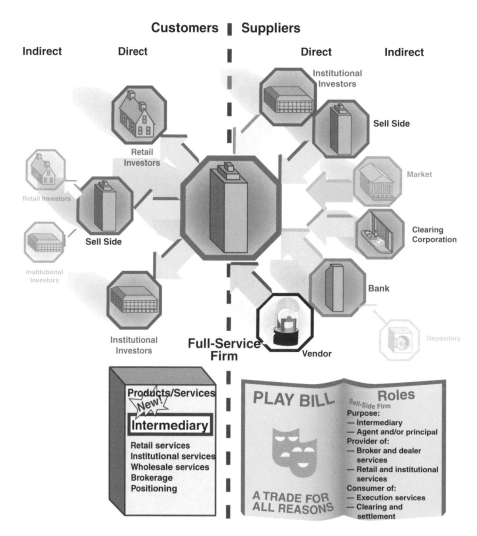

Figure 1.2.3.3.1 **_Full-service firms_** provide substantially all buy-side services as both broker and dealer for both institutional and retail customers.

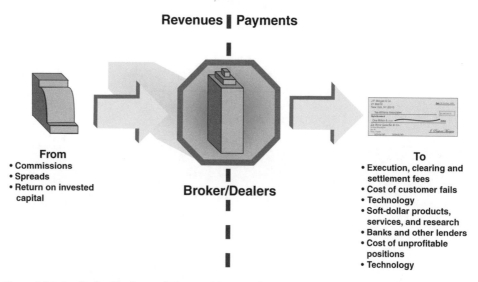

Revenues | Payments

From
- Commissions
- Spreads
- Return on invested capital

Broker/Dealers

To
- Execution, clearing and settlement fees
- Cost of customer fails
- Technology
- Soft-dollar products, services, and research
- Banks and other lenders
- Cost of unprofitable positions
- Technology

Figure 1.2.3.4 ***Broker/dealers*** profit from a wide array of potential services, but may also have substantial costs because of the breadth of services they offer.

Markets 3

Markets are places, both formal and informal, where securities and other instruments can be traded between owners of instruments who wish to sell their instruments and prospective buyers who want to purchase the securities. In this chapter, we focus only on the entities that provide market services. Figure 1.3 shows the roles performed by any market or trading venue however it is organized.

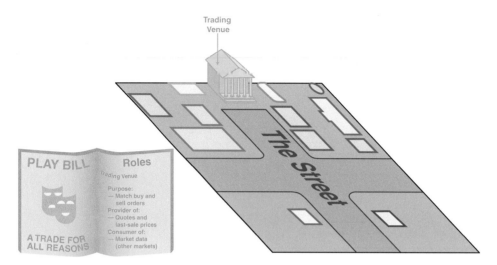

Figure 1.3   **Markets** provide a facility (either physical or electronic) for matching buy and sell orders for market participants.

Markets operate using rules that have developed through custom, the interests of those individuals and organizations that trade in the market, and by governmental laws and regulations. The structure of markets owes much to local custom. However, markets have actively copied one another throughout history. As the world economy becomes more globalized, there are important similarities among national markets, and these similarities are constantly increasing in frequency and importance.

We consider the functions performed within markets in Part 4, and we examine the processes employed in different types of market mechanisms in Book 2. Figure 1.3.0 illustrates the three primary organizational forms most often employed by trading venues.

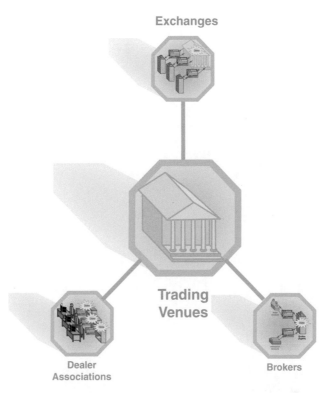

Exchanges

Trading
Venues

Dealer
Associations

Brokers

Figure 1.3.0   ***Markets*** are organized as exchanges, brokers, or dealer associations to satisfy the execution needs of differing constituencies.

EXCHANGES

Exchanges are a special category of market created for the specific purpose of trading securities and liquid derivative instruments. Exchanges typically trade equities, futures, and/or options although some exchanges list other instruments as well. Many exchanges permit only broker/dealers as members although a growing number of exchanges permit investment institutions to route orders directly to the exchange under the sponsorship of a member. (This service, known as ***direct-market access***—DMA—is explained in more detail in Book 2.)

When most exchanges were ***membership corporations***[9]—in essence, ***mutualized*** facilities run on behalf of the broker/dealers that were members of the exchange—most of the functions associated with operating the exchange were focused on satisfying the members. Many exchanges have become shareholder-owned corporations with publically traded shares seeking to make a profit. Now they more frequently resemble other for-profit organizations, and in their pursuit of profits the exchanges are sometimes at odds with the broker/dealers that use them (see Figure 1.3.1).

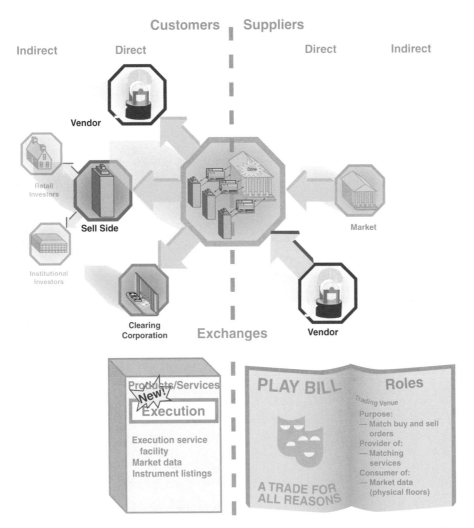

Figure 1.3.1   **Exchanges** are dedicated execution venues organized as member associations or for-profit companies to facilitate trading on behalf of sell-side intermediaries.

9   Membership in exchanges is generally a form of equity investment and is therefore a perpetual security. (Equity securities are described in Part 2 and again in Book 2.) Many exchange memberships are traded in private markets because only broker/dealers are permitted to be members. Memberships should not be confused with equity shares in those exchanges that are publically listed. Shares in for-profit exchanges convey ownership of the exchange but not the right to trade on the exchange. Interestingly, membership corporations have the same organizational form as country clubs, a fact that has created more than a few arch comments.

DEALER ASSOCIATIONS

A number of instruments trade in professional markets among competing dealers. Another term for this type of market is an ***over-the-counter market***. Currencies and bonds typically trade in dealer markets. A dealer market, then, is a group of independent dealers that come together to trade and establish either formal or informal rules to govern trading, much as an exchange develops trading rules. Often national regulators officially sanction these associations (see Figure 1.3.2).

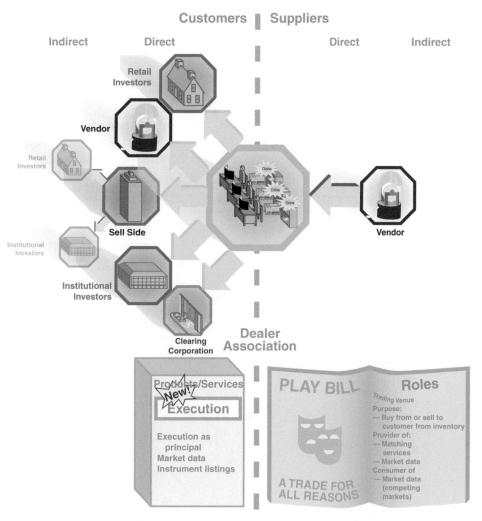

Figure 1.3.2   ***Dealer associations***, whether formal or informal, provide rules and procedures to streamline trading among participating dealers.

MARKETS ORGANIZED AS BROKERS

A number of markets or trading venues are registered as broker/dealers. The earliest examples of markets created as brokers were **interdealer brokers** (IDBs), sometimes called **brokers' brokers** or **voice brokers.** IDBs are widely used in both the bond markets and in foreign exchange markets. In both of those markets, dealers do not want other dealers to know that they have a large position in a bond issue or currency.

To disguise their positions, dealers trade with one another using the services of IDBs that match the buyer and seller while disguising their identities from one another. The IDBs are registered as brokers because the magnitude of the transactions would overwhelm those that are much smaller entities than the dealers they trade with for transactions in both the bond and ForEx markets.[10]

Beginning in the late 1990s in the United States and following the implementation of MiFID[11] in Europe, a number of special-purpose brokers have developed as **alternative trading facilities** that compete with traditional exchanges and dealer associations. These firms are variously known as alternative trading systems (ATSs), **electronic communications networks** (ECNs in the United States), or **multilateral trading facilities** (MTFs in Europe). Generally, they are organized as brokers, but cannot be dealers because of the conflict of interest that would occur if they had an incentive to profit from orders entered by their customers. Also, acting as a dealer would create much higher **market risk** for the entity.

Organizing a market as a broker has other advantages. In many jurisdictions, it is easier, quicker, and cheaper to create a new broker than to create an exchange. Also, a broker may be able to accept orders from institutions directly, but in many countries exchanges are not permitted to take orders directly from the buy side. Figure 1.3.3 illustrates both the products and roles of markets organized as brokers.

10   In a project working with an IDB in the 1980s, we inquired what would happen if one of the dealers engaged in a trade brokered by an IDB failed before the trade settled. The official for the IDB said that he did not know for sure, and to the best of his knowledge, this had never happened.
11   **Markets in Financial Instruments Directive** (MiFID) is a set of financial regulations implemented by the European Union in November 2007.

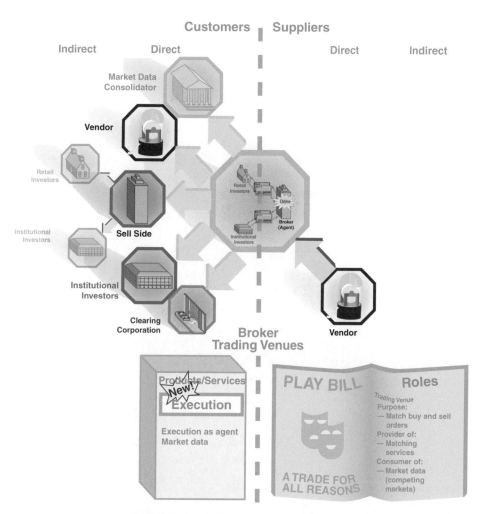

Figure 1.3.3 ***Markets organized as brokers*** offer agency execution services in many countries to the buy side directly, to other brokers, and to dealers.

MARKET BUSINESS MODELS

Markets for most of the history of trading were organized as exchanges or dealer associations. Because exchanges and dealer associations were primarily member corporations with the sole purpose of serving their members, they charged only enough for services to cover the costs of operation. In the sidebar "How Trading Venues Make Money," we explain the revenue sources based on a group of major exchanges.

HOW TRADING VENUES MAKE MONEY

Market centers depend on seven possible sources of revenue. The four primary revenue sources for markets are trading fees, clearing and settlement revenues, market data, and listings.* Investors and traders that use the market are asked to contribute most of the fees for trading and market data. (Listings are fees paid for the right to trade shares on a market and are paid by companies and other entities that issue equities and sometimes bonds.) Other revenue sources tend to be specific to individual markets. In the following sections we will describe each of these revenue sources, and we will describe the prospects for each. The figure here** shows the averaged revenue sources for major exchanges.

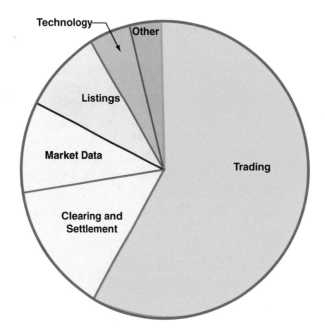

Not all these fees are available to every exchange, and what they mean differs from exchange to exchange.

---

* Not all exchanges have listings and a few exchanges benefit from licensing copyrighted or patented services such as contract design as well as proprietary information services beyond market data. However, the three primary revenue sources sustain most exchanges and other trading venues.

** This information is based on data from Mondo Visione. We took this information showing the percentage breakdown for 19 important exchanges worldwide and constructed a consistent set of categories. We made a few assumptions because exactly comparable revenue categories did not exist among the exchanges. Finally, because some markets did not have all revenue sources (i.e., Clearing and Settlement and Listings), we constructed median percentages rather than averages. This approach also limited the impact of size. We elected to exclude actual numbers because our purpose is to show relative portions of income and not to focus on details, which varies in absolute amounts year to year.

More recently, many exchanges and dealer associations have become for-profit corporations, and their pricing incentives have changed accordingly.

As a general rule, exchanges and dealer associations charge fees for each transaction. In contrast, markets organized as brokers charge some variation of commissions, which are usually charged per share. Historically, large exchanges had a broad mix of large and small transactions. For trades involving many shares, it is usually possible to make more money as a broker than as an exchange.

The reason is that traders are usually more comfortable paying per-share fees, where costs are purely variable, than per-transaction fees, which are fixed across wide ranges of trade sizes. However, as more trading has become automated, the average size of transactions has decreased. As a result, profit potential from per-share fees has fallen into line with per-transaction charges. In competitive markets where more than one trading venue competes for the order flow from firms using trading services, complex pricing models have evolved and change dynamically. Incentives and rebates are offered to lure traders.

ORGANIZE AS A BROKER OR AN EXCHANGE?

As we noted, when the number of shares per trade is large, it is usually easier to make money as a broker. In the figure on the next page, we examine trading costs assuming a brokerage model involving €0.01* per share. For trades of 100 shares to 1000 shares, a comparable per-transaction fee would range from €1.00 to €10.00, which could be an acceptable range. At 100,000 shares, a per-transaction fee would have to be €1000.00 per transaction to equal a per-share fee.

Although €1000.00 might be acceptable for a trade of 100,000, it would not be for a trade of 50,000 or 10,000. The exchange fee could be broken into more ranges (e.g., from 1 to 1000, from 1001 to 10,000, etc.), but it still lacks the flexibility of a per-share fee for large trade sizes.

---

* We choose €0.01 per share for mathematical simplicity and not to suggest that this is a good price. Transaction fees are highly volatile because of competition, and the definition of a "good price" is a transient concept.

Continued

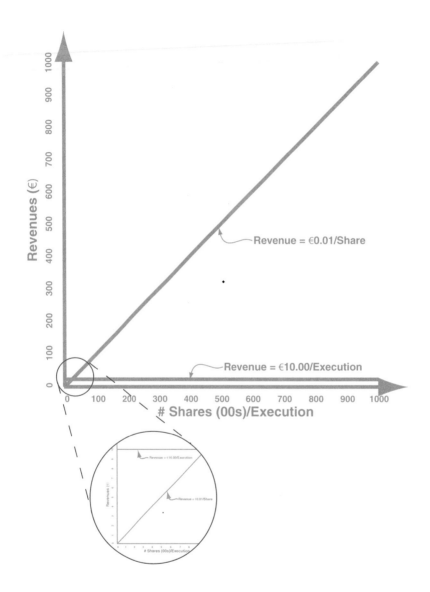

Very early in the creation of automation of the equity markets, two attempts at automation of the Weeden Holdings Automated Market (WHAM) and Instinet market took different paths to regulatory approval. WHAM became an exchange by purchasing the exchange registration of the very small Cincinnati Stock Exchange. By contrast, Instinet registered as a broker. These two approaches to creating new trading venues remain viable forms of organization.

Figure 1.3.4 shows the primary sources of revenue and costs for exchanges.

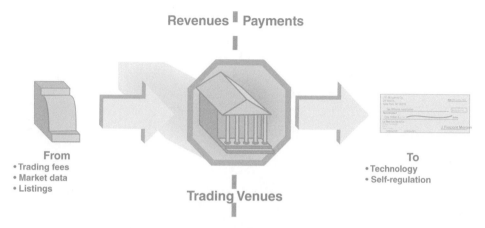

Revenues ▌ **Payments**

From
- Trading fees
- Market data
- Listings

Trading Venues

To
- Technology
- Self-regulation

Figure 1.3.4   ***Trading-venues*** depend on trading, listings, and market data as major revenue sources and other sources as well, while spending money on staff, marketing, and technology for business operations.

Support 4

A number of different entities are required to support the trading markets. Some of these organizations are divisions of other entities that are actively engaged in trading. Other organizations are purpose-built for the support functions they provide. Figure 1.4 highlights the types of entities that support the trading markets.

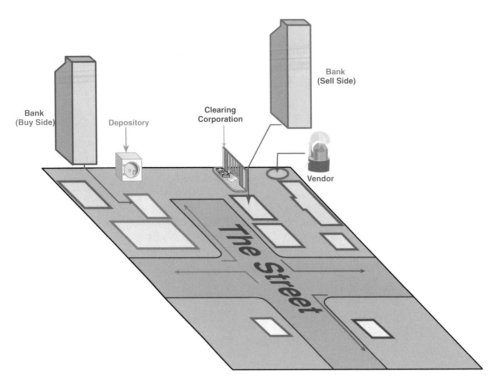

Support entities provide clearing, settlement, safekeeping, financing, and technology products and services to facilitate the operation of the trading markets.

CLEARING CORPORATIONS

Clearing corporations serve the function of "insuring" transactions between the time the trade is complete and the point when funds are formally exchanged for the securities on settlement. Most clearing corporations originated as part of exchanges, but many are now independent and are frequently responsible for clearing tasks for a number of different exchanges.

In the United States, for example, there are only three clearing corporations: one each for equities, futures, and options. In Europe, by contrast, two different clearing models compete, each with different structures and each with different exchanges that endorse their methods. In Asia and much of the rest of the world, clearing is tied directly to the exchange of which it is a part (see Figure 1.4.1).

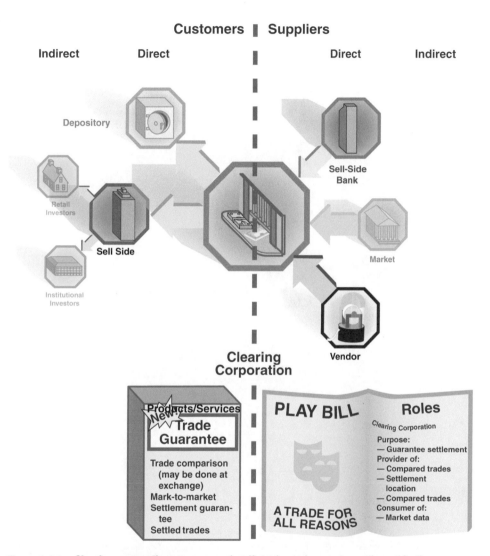

Figure 1.4.1 *Clearing corporations* compare and verify trades and guarantee settlement for those executions in the trading markets.

DEPOSITORIES

Depositories are facilities for warehousing and/or managing the official ownership records of instruments. The depository, in one of two ways, permits the transfer of ownership by bookkeeping entries rather than by physical movements of certificates, and physical re-registrations of securities certificates. The depository generally maintains a master list of which person or entity owns all traded instruments (see Figure 1.4.2).

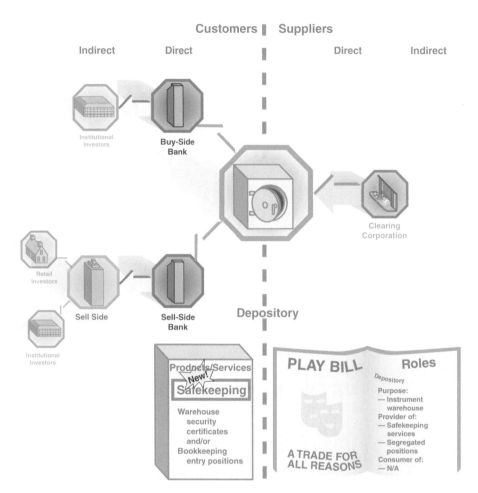

Figure 1.4.2   **_Depositories_** warehouse stock certificates and/or maintain electronic ownership records for most or all of the instruments in specific trading markets.

Depositories are usually separate from markets, and in some markets they are owned by the banking system rather than by the sell side.

BANKS

Many banks, such as Citibank, HSBC, Deutsche Bank, and UBS, are major participants in the trading markets through both investment management and broker/dealer subsidiaries. However, banks participate in the securities markets through their commercial banking operations as well. Banks are critical to the trading markets because they provide services that only entities chartered as banks are permitted to provide. For example, banks are the only entities in many markets that are permitted to be direct participants in depositories. They provide warehousing services for the securities owned by buy-side entities. These services are known as ***safekeeping*** or ***custody.*** Banks are also the only entities permitted direct access to ***funds-transfer mechanisms*** and are therefore necessary for every instrument settlement (see Figure 1.4.3.a). For the sell side, banks also provide financing for dealer positions (see Figure 1.4.3.b).

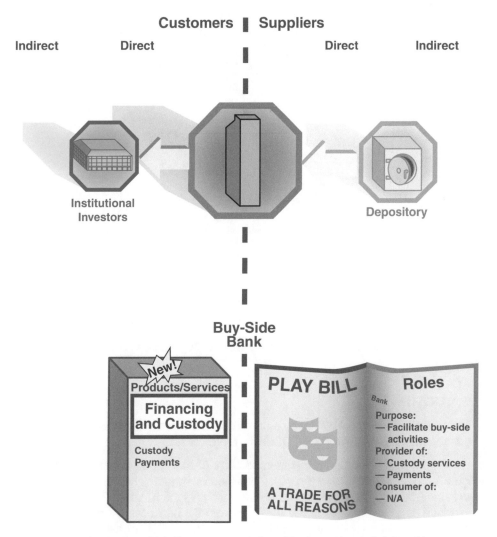

Figure 1.4.3.a   ***Banks (buy side)*** offer payment, custody, and trustee services to their buy-side customers.

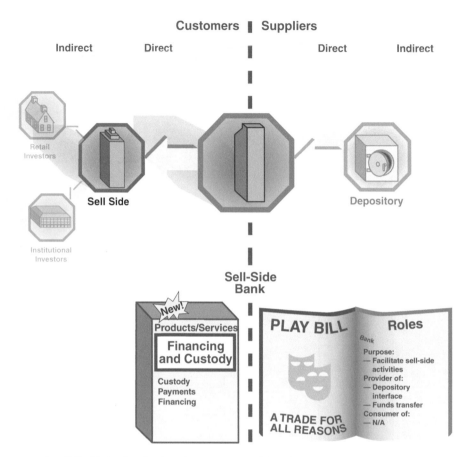

Figure 1.4.3.b **Sell-side banks** offer financing, payments, safekeeping, and services to their sell-side customers.

VENDORS

The trading markets are serviced by a number of firms that provide all manner of services to other market participants. These firms are collectively referred to as **vendors**.

Vendors service participants in all parts of the traded-instruments markets. Figure 1.4.4 shows some of the services provided by vendors and firms that sell to the markets. When we describe vendors, we are talking primarily about firms not required to register as a member of the buy or sell side or as a bank. Market participants provide services to one another (e.g., banks, correspondent broker/dealers, and the like); and in the role of service providers to the trading process, market participants might be considered vendors.

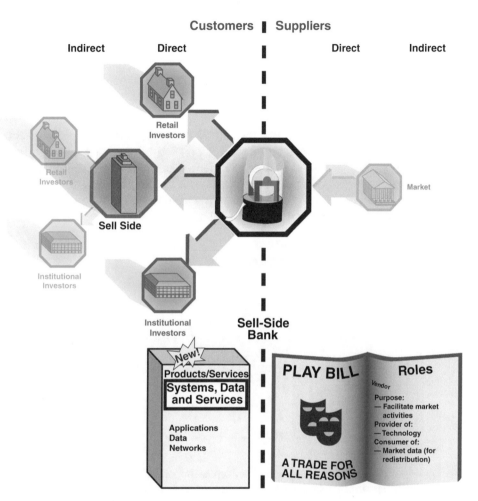

Figure 1.4.4   ***Vendors*** provide technology—systems, data, and networks—through products and bespoke services to any of the entities in the trading markets.

Vendors provide services that fall into three primary categories:

1. Processing and computational services

2. Data services

3. Network and communications services

We describe the services of vendors in more detail when we talk about the technical infrastructure of the industry in Book 3, *An Introduction to Trading in the Financial Markets: Technology—Systems, Data, and Networks*.

BUSINESS MODELS

Clearing corporations are created to protect the markets and do not serve a primary profit-making role. Nevertheless, clearing corporations represent significant portions of the revenues to their parent exchanges in markets where the clearing corporation is a part of an exchange, as illustrated in the figure in the sidebar, How Trading Venues Make Money, earlier.

Clearing corporations charge fees for all the transactions they process. They also maintain margin funds posted to protect pending transactions although most clearing corporations allow the interest income on securities posted with the clearing corporation to flow through to the firm that posts margin. Because of the volumes involved, significant income can be earned on the *float* on funds left on deposit overnight at the clearing corporation (see Figure 1.4.5.a).

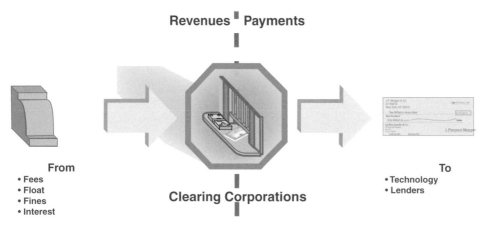

Revenues Payments

From
• Fees
• Float
• Fines
• Interest

Clearing Corporations

To
• Technology
• Lenders

Figure 1.4.5.a   ***Clearing corporations*** provide their services for established fees but also profit from float while paying for their staff and infrastructure to guarantee settlement for traded instruments.

Depositories earn revenue from the positions they maintain, and they charge fees for the services they provide. Moreover, depositories earn truly significant income

THE VALUE OF FLOAT

Bradford Trust Company was an early competitor to The Depository Trust Company in the United States. Bradford proposed to charge nothing for the depository services it would offer, believing that it would make enough money from the float on various pools of funds it would manage to cover its costs and make a profit.

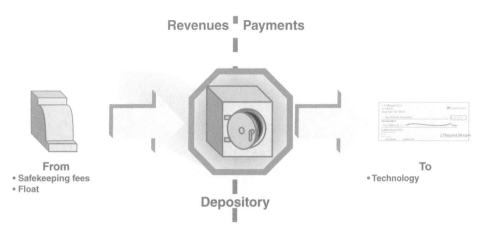

Revenues ■ **Payments**

From
- Safekeeping fees
- Float

To
- Technology

Depository

Figure 1.4.5.b   ***Depositories*** charge established fees and receive float income while paying for staff and infrastructure costs to provide safekeeping for traded instruments.

because of huge volumes of funds that flow through the depository in the form of interest and income payments. Moreover, depositories profit from dividend and interest payments that the depository holds for extended periods of time when the beneficial owner of securities in the depository cannot be identified (see Figure 1.4.5.b).

For the services banks[13] provide to the trading markets, banks make money from three primary activities. Banks take deposits from market participants and lend those securities out to other customers just as they do for other commercial and retail segments. Banks charge fees for access to the payments system and for services they provide as custodians for invested assets. Finally, banks lend money to market participants (see Figure 1.4.5.c).

---

13   Obviously, banks provide many services not of interest here. Commercial and retail banking could easily require an entire book. We are concerned only about services in support of the trading markets.

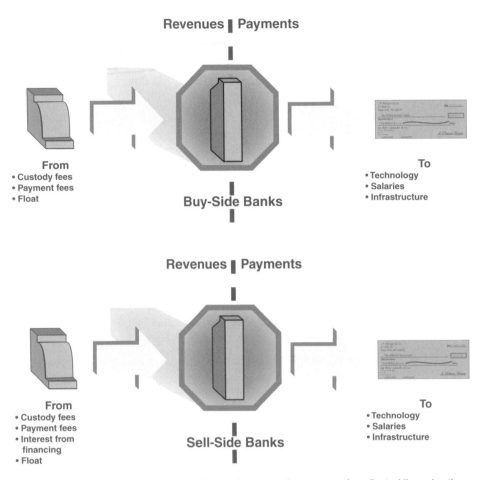

Figure 1.4.5.c   **Banks** charge fees, receive interest income, and earn money from float while paying the staff, infrastructure, and technology costs to provide unique banking services to the trading markets.

Vendors of data have two primary business models for the content they sell. Per-user fees have largely replaced per-device fees as personal computers have replaced **dumb terminals** or display devices. User fees cover information viewed by individuals. Quantity or connection charges are the primary fee structure for bulk data, depending on the format of the information and how it is delivered. Most data is licensed instead of sold. Users pay for the right to access the data and are constrained from transforming and reselling the data without permission (see Figure 1.4.5.d).

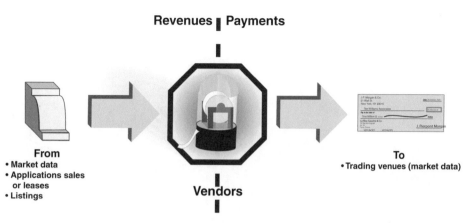

Figure 1.4.5.d   ***Vendors*** sell products and/or receive lease income while paying for their staff and infrastructure to provide systems, data, and network services to entities in the trading markets.

Software and applications are charged as software packages either sold or licensed for use. In addition to the charge for the application, vendors often charge for maintenance and application updates. Alternatively, many users pay a vendor to operate the software on the users' behalf. Many users have begun to outsource whole activities to vendors who undertake the activities of departments or divisions rather than just operating software.

Market data and reference data are major products delivered by vendors. Ownership of data most often resides with data creators such as exchanges and news organizations. The creators primarily lease the right to use the data, but ownership does not transfer to the user. In addition to delivering data, vendors help data creators track usage and frequently invoice for data usage on behalf of the data creators.

Network vendors charge a combination of volume-based fees, often for the number of messages transmitted, and for the number and importance of the connections they offer. Message rates may differ based on the type of message transmitted (see Figure 1.4.5.d).

We explain these services of most supporting entities in more detail when we describe the processes they perform in the trading markets in Book 2. As noted, the activities of vendors are covered in Book 3.

Regulators 5

Nearly every trading market in the world has at least one and sometimes several national regulators. A few markets have no regulator because of tradition or, more frequently, because the market spans several national boundaries. Often when nations compete for control of a market, the result is little or no regulation. Even in markets with little governmental regulation, the market participants regulate themselves formally or informally. Figure 1.5 identifies regulators in the trading markets.

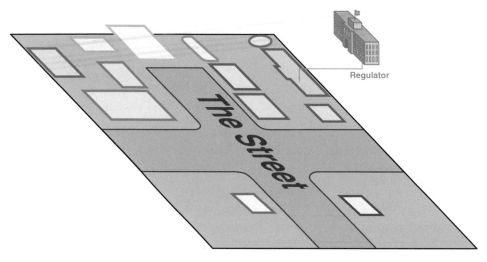

Figure 1.5   **Regulators** supervise markets for governments and/or for market participants.

REGULATORS: PURPOSE

Unregulated markets depend on collective or **self-regulation.** "Self-regulation" is the term used when the members of a market voluntarily choose to adopt regulation without being forced by a government regulator. Even in markets where there is a national regulator, self-regulation is often present to propose rules that are then approved by the national regulator, and a self-regulator may provide the day-to-day enforcement of regulations (see Figure 1.5.1).

National regulators have three primary obligations:

1. Protect and ensure the fairness of the national market
2. Protect citizens of the country that regularly trade in the markets
3. Provide an important mechanism of national economic growth

Regulation is described briefly in Part 6 and more fully in Book 4, *An Introduction to Trading in the Financial Markets: Global Markets, Risk, Compliance, and Regulation.*

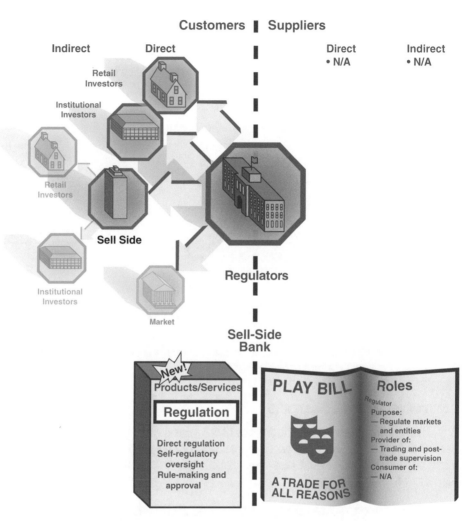

Figure 1.5.1   **_Regulators_** enforce rules to ensure the fair and efficient operation of markets and monitor the financial strength of participants for the markets.

BUSINESS MODELS

We do not think of regulation as a business, but regulation must be funded. Self-regulatory oversight is usually an overhead expense paid for out of other revenues of the entity managing the self-regulation. National tax revenues may fund national regulation, but regulators often add a small fee to transactions that often pays for direct regulation of trading. When transactions are taxed, the fees for regulation are paid by those who receive the benefit of the regulation; however, taxes on transactions, sometimes known as **stamp duties,** may have the effect of shifting trading activity to competitive markets where the taxes are not present (see Figure 1.5.2).

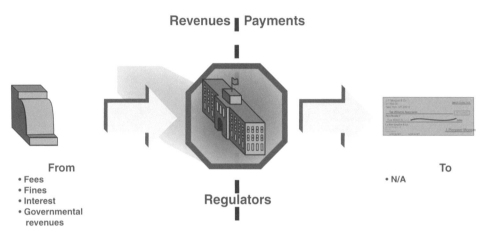

Revenues ▮ Payments

From
• Fees
• Fines
• Interest
• Governmental
  revenues

To
• N/A

Regulators

Figure 1.5.2   **Regulators** may be subsidized by national governments or charge transaction fees to cover the cost of supervision of the market under their control.

ENTITIES NOT INCLUDED

We have not included some important entities that support the trading markets. In particular, specialized lawyers, accountants, and consultants help in the process and might be included. However, these organizations are beyond the scope of our exploration of the trading markets.

RELATED INFORMATION IN OTHER BOOKS

Entities are not covered directly in any other part of any of the books in this set. However, the entities defined in this book are referenced in all the other books, and the definitions presented in this part are used throughout. Related information that can be found in other books is indicated in Figure 1.6.

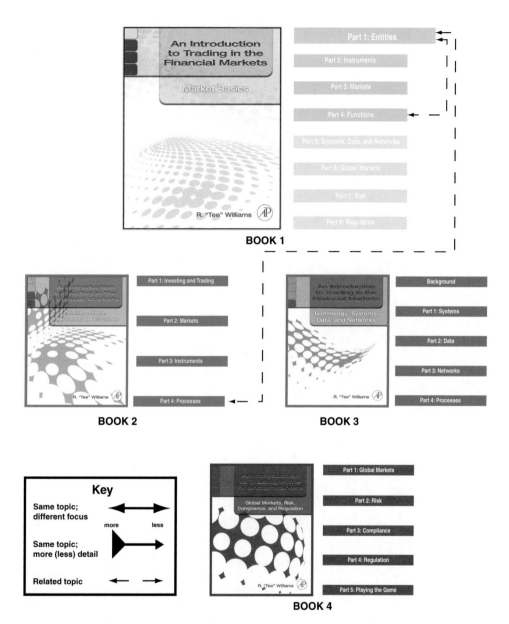

Figure 1.6   Related information in other books in the set.

Instruments

Instruments are the products traded in the markets we are exploring. We define three major categories of instruments: cash, derivative, and packaged instruments. Several characteristics of instruments differ among categories. For example, cash instruments convey ownership of something. Securities, a subcategory of cash instruments, convey to the purchaser ownership of a financial asset. Currencies represent ownership of actual cash, and commodities trading results in ownership of physical goods.

Derivative instruments are generally standardized **contracts**. The contract usually obligates one party to the contract to undertake specific actions under certain circumstances defined in the contract. Figure 2 provides an overview of traded instruments.

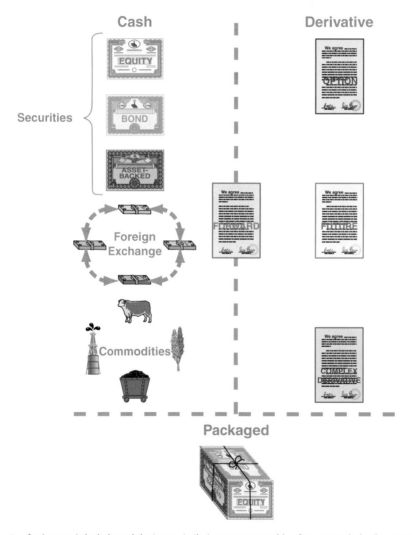

Figure 2   *Instruments* include cash instruments that convey ownership of an asset, derivative contracts that obligate the writer of the contract to perform specified actions, and packaged instruments that permit ownership of a portion of a diversified pool of instruments for traders or investors.

As a result of discussions and research, we have found that the formal distinctions among different types of instruments are not precise. For example, we separate securities from derivatives, but in the United States, options (derivative instruments) are categorized as securities because the Securities and Exchange Commission regulates options. We take care to explain our definitions and follow them in these books.

In many countries because of custom and/or law, physical certificates were originally required to prove ownership of securities. Laws and customs certificates are embedded in company charters, commercial codes, and governmental laws and regulations. However, paper certificates are an anachronism in the world of computers and are not needed as proof of ownership. In fact, physical certificates are expensive to maintain and cause processing problems. (See the discussion of the "Backoffice Crisis" in the "History" section.)

Therefore, most markets seek to eliminate certificates, and certificates have no meaning in those countries where securities are **dematerialized**. (See Book 2, *An Introduction to Trading in the Financial Markets: Trading, Markets, Instruments, and Processes*.) We should warn you to make sure of what is meant by "securities" or "derivatives" or "instruments" when others discuss them.

Cash 1

The cash markets include securities, currencies, and physical commodities (see Figure 2.1). The unifying characteristic is that the purchaser is buying the asset that is traded. The securities subcategory includes instruments commonly referred to as "stocks and bonds" but more accurately labeled as "equities and fixed income" (U.S.) or "fixed interest" (U.K.). Currencies and physical commodities are included because they are traded in liquid markets, and the asset (a currency position or a quantity of a commodity) is actually purchased.

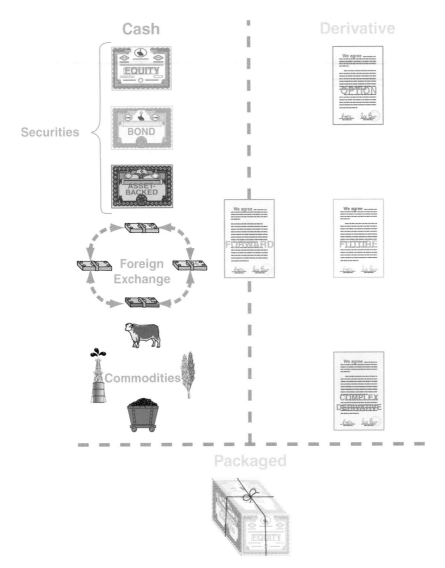

Figure 2.1 **Cash instruments** are financial and commercial assets that provide specific value to investors, to commercial entities, and to producers.

EQUITIES

Equity securities are *shares* in the ownership of corporations. The purchaser of an equity security is entitled to a portion, or "share," of the benefits that come from owning a portion of the company. An equity owner profits from the change in the value of the security and possibly from *dividends* paid from the company's profits.

Although other types of entities (such as governments, *nongovernmental organizations* (NGOs), educational institutions, and charities) often issue bonds, it is very rare for organizations other than corporations to be publically owned. Equities come in different forms. *Common shares* or *common stocks* confer regular ownership. *Preferred shares* offer limited ownership rights but usually offer a first right to dividends. Other details of equities and other instruments are covered in more detail in Book 2.

When a company raises capital by issuing new equities, the money from the initial sale of the issue flows to the company net of fees and a spread paid to the investment bankers. (This process is described in Book 2.) After the equity is issued, it continues indefinitely unless it is canceled or liquidated as happens when a company becomes bankrupt, is merged into another company, or the company buys back its shares in the open market. With outstanding shares, income generated by the company may be paid to shareholders in the form of dividends. Sometimes companies issue stock dividends, *stock options*,[1] or *warrants* that entitle the holder to convert the holding into equity shares at a predefined price.

The cash flows from an equity security are shown in Figure 2.1.1.

---

1 These stock options are functionally similar to options described in the "Derivatives" section later in this part, but the company that issues the equity shares also issues the stock options described here. These options are written against shares the company holds that are not being publically traded. Traders create the derivatives described here in the secondary market. (In fact, those options are sometimes referred to as *traded options*.) The stock options referenced here are frequently issued to corporate employees as part of their compensation.

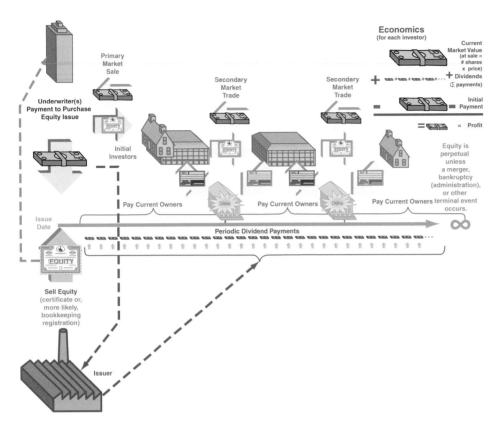

Figure 2.1.1 **Equity instruments** convey ownership in the entities that issue them, never mature, and may pay dividends (income) periodically to investors and to traders who wish to participate in the firm's ownership and its future economic benefits.

FIXED INCOME (INTEREST)

Bonds and other **fixed income** securities (known as **fixed interest** in the United Kingdom), represent a loan and convey ownership of an income stream. The income most often comes in the form of **interest**. Most fixed income has a finite life, and at the end of its life, the amount borrowed is returned to the lender or to a subsequent holder who has purchased the security in the secondary market.

Some fixed income is said to be **securitized**, which means that financial assets that cannot be traded easily have been converted into a security with a liquid trading market. Examples of securitized assets include mortgages and credit-card debt. (Book 2 describes securitization in more detail.)

Rather than going to a bank and borrowing money, a company can issue bonds in fixed units, usually 1000.00 pricing increments (e.g., dollars, pounds, or euros). Although some companies are big enough to issue bonds directly with very little help from investment bankers, most bonds are underwritten in a process described in detail in Book 2. After an underwriting, the funds that have been raised go to the issuing company after fees are paid to the investment bankers. The bond has a fixed life, or **term**.

For example, 30 years is a common term for a bond, although shorter-term instruments also are issued. At the end of its term, the bond **matures**, and the bond owner or holder is repaid the **face value** of the bond, which is usually the amount borrowed initially.

Many bonds pay interest to the holder every quarter. The amount of interest paid is known as the **coupon rate**[2] or interest rate. The coupon rate is expressed as a percentage, and that percentage is multiplied by the face amount of the bond holdings to compute the interest payment. (Actually, most interest pays quarterly. The coupon rate is usually stated as an annual percentage, and so payments are one quarter of the yearly amount.)

Some fixed-income instruments are purchased at a **discount**. Discount instruments are issued at an amount that is lower than the amount that will be paid back when the instrument matures. The difference between the amount borrowed and the amount paid back is the discount or interest rate.

For example, if a one-year bond with an interest rate of 5% were sold at discount, the investor would pay $950 for the bond and receive $1000 back at maturity.[3] (Book 2 provides more detail on fixed-income instruments.) Figure 2.1.2.a shows the cash flows that result from an interest-bearing fixed-income instrument.

Figure 2.1.2.b shows the cash flows that result from a discount fixed-income instrument.

---

2   The term "coupon" comes from the time before the widespread use of computers when most bond certificates represented the loan and had to be presented when the bond matured to receive the principal. Bonds often had small, perforated coupons on the bottom of the certificates. Each coupon was dated for an interest payment during the life of the bond. The holder of the bond would have to detach a coupon and present it to a paying agent to receive an interest payment on each date when the interest payment was due.
3   The mathematics of interest rates can be complicated, and anyone interested in understanding how to calculate bond interest, bond prices, and yields (the effective return to a bond holder as a result of the payment of interest rates) should find a book that is dedicated to bond calculations.

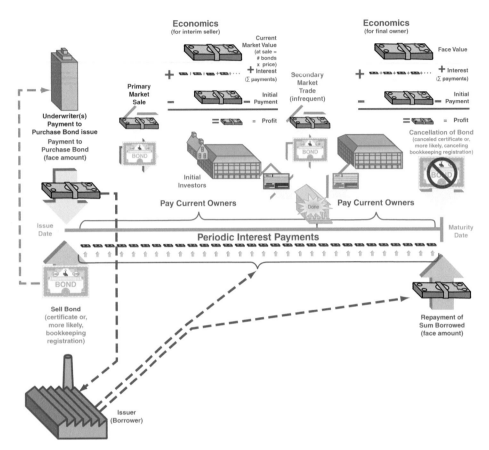

Figure 2.1.2.a   *Interest-bearing fixed-income instruments* pay income periodically, repay the face value when the instruments mature, and may be easily traded during their life to investors willing to lend funds.

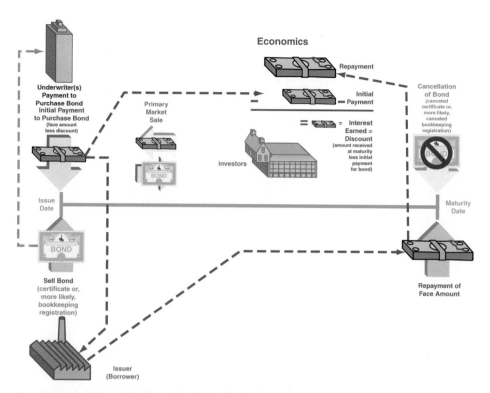

Economics

Figure 2.1.2.b   *__Discount fixed-income instruments__* provide less money than must be repaid (the face value) when the instrument matures, with the difference representing the income (interest) earned by investors willing to lend.

THE TIME-VALUE OF MONEY

Interest calculations are actually a bit more complicated than simple percentage calculations. The difference arises because that interest earned can be reinvested, and in effect the interest paid early in the life of the instrument in turn earns interest, which is known as **compounding**. As a result, for many calculations the value of a bond's repayment at the end of the life of a fixed income instrument reflects the fact that the use of the money from the repayment is postponed and therefore is worth less than the same amount of money at the present. The lower current value of a payment that will be received in the future is known as the **present value** of the future payment. Present values can be computed using the following formula:*

Simple interest $\qquad$ $PV = FV * 1/(1+i)$
Compound interest $\qquad$ $PV = FV * 1/(1+i)^t$

where: $\qquad$ $PV = $ The **present value**
$\qquad$ $FV = $ The **future value**
$\qquad$ $i = $ The **interest rate**
$\qquad$ $t = $ The **time**

Note that if the time period is one period (usually a year), the two calculations provide the same result.

Alternatively, present values can be found in published interest tables and from calculations programmed into financial calculators and spreadsheets. Present value and other interest calculations are straightforward but can be complex. Most good books on fixed income securities and/or financial calculations provide detailed descriptions of a wide variety of present value and interest calculations.

---

*Moorad Choudhry, *The Bonds & Money Markets: Strategy, Trading, Analysis* (Oxford: Elsevier Ltd., 2003).

CURRENCIES

Banks, governments, corporations, and individuals need to be able to transact in **currencies** other than that of their home location. To do this, they need to be able to sell the currency of their location and buy currency in the location where the transaction has to take place. The need to buy and sell currencies is quite common, and the market for these transactions is well developed and efficient. The market for currencies is known as **foreign exchange**, **FX**, or **ForEx**.

Currencies are issued by national governments; the process of issuing currencies is beyond the scope of these books, however. (In Book 2 we mention briefly the process by which national banks and other monetary agencies sometimes use the bond markets to add or remove liquidity from the banking system.) Therefore,

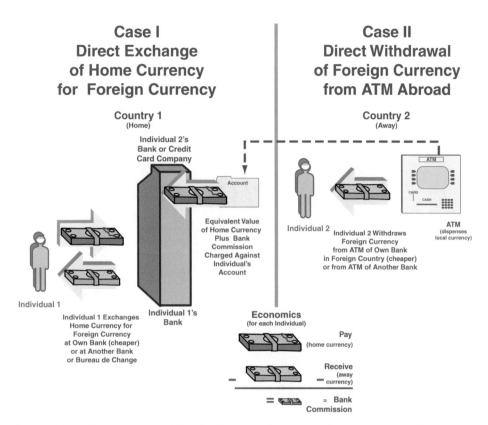

Case I
Direct Exchange
of Home Currency
for Foreign Currency

Case II
Direct Withdrawal
of Foreign Currency
from ATM Abroad

Country 1
(Home)

Country 2
(Away)

Individual 2's
Bank or Credit
Card Company

Account

ATM

CARD   CASH

Equivalent Value
of Home Currency
Plus Bank
Commission
Charged Against
Individual's
Account

Individual 2

Individual 2 Withdraws
Foreign Currency
from ATM of Own Bank
in Foreign Country (cheaper)
or from ATM of Another Bank

ATM
(dispenses
local currency)

Individual 1

Individual 1 Exchanges
Home Currency for
Foreign Currency
at Own Bank (cheaper)
or at Another Bank
or Bureau de Change

Individual 1's
Bank

Economics
(for each Individual)

Pay
(home currency)

Receive
(away
currency)

−

=   = Bank
Commission

Figure 2.1.3.a   *Foreign exchange* (FX or ForEx) employs the currency of one country to buy the currency of another for individuals, investors, and commericial entitites.

the only cash flow we are concerned with in currency trading is the creation or exchange of **demand-deposit accounts, time-deposit accounts**, or loan accounts, as shown in Figures 2.1.3.a, 2.1.3.b, and 2.1.3.c.[4]

Although we discuss foreign exchange in the part of this book describing instruments, it is in fact a transaction and not an instrument. Currency transactions always involve the money of two different countries. It is not reasonable to think of buying or selling euros without simultaneously selling or buying dollars, pounds, or yen. The ForEx market is commonly thought of as buying and selling currencies, but bank deposits and short-term, fixed income (or fixed interest) instruments are also widely traded in the ForEx market.

---

4   Figures 2.1.3.b and 2.1.3.c show different foreign exchange processes used primarily by businesses and investors. Figure 2.1.3.a shows the mechanics for retail customers.

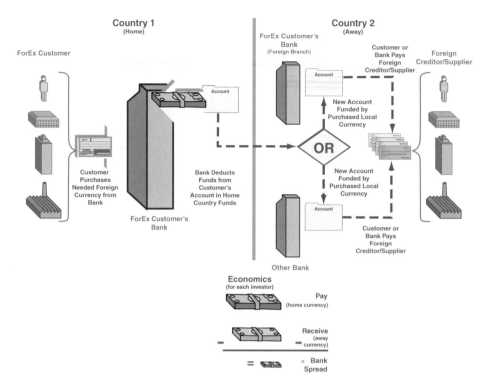

Country 1 (Home)

ForEx Customer

Country 2 (Away)

ForEx Customer's Bank (Foreign Branch)

Customer or Bank Pays Foreign Creditor/Supplier

Foreign Creditor/Supplier

Account

New Account Funded by Purchased Local Currency

Customer Purchases Needed Foreign Currency from Bank

ForEx Customer's Bank

Bank Deducts Funds from Customer's Account in Home Country Funds

OR

New Account Funded by Purchased Local Currency

Account

Customer or Bank Pays Foreign Creditor/Supplier

Other Bank

Economics (for each investor)

Pay (home currency)

Receive (away currency)

= Bank Spread

Figure 2.1.3.b

The most common reasons for foreign exchange trading are commercial movements of goods and international financial trading and investments. Although individuals need to make foreign exchange transactions when they travel abroad, the size of these transactions is very small. Moreover, with credit cards and bank cards, many people travel getting only the cash they need from ATMs in the countries they visit. The banks and credit-card companies handle the foreign exchange transactions required.

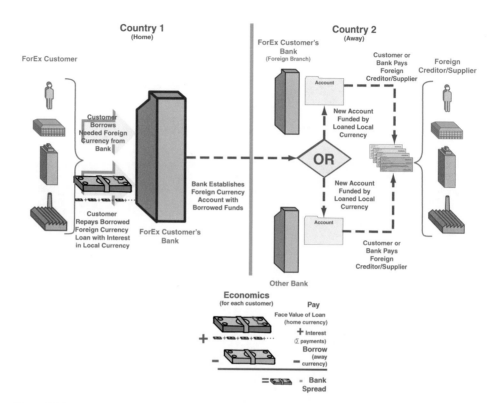

Figure 2.1.3.c

COMMODITIES

Commodities are the basic input to most industrial processes; however, the only commodities that are widely used have markets that trade with the liquidity of securities and other traded instruments (see Figure 2.1.4).

Representative examples of commodities with liquid markets include the following:

Agricultural commodities   Any type of basic agricultural product is subject to trading provided that there is sufficient volume to justify active trading. Trading can involve negotiated contracts, or more commonly local markets establish standardized quantities and quality grades.

Metals   Most metals widely used as components of industrial processes can be actively traded. In some cases, processed materials such as beams, rolls, and plates may be actively traded.

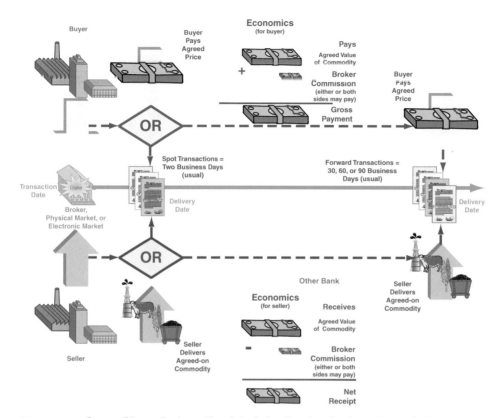

Figure 2.1.4   **Commodities** are fixed quantities of physical produce from farming, mining, and other commercial processes sold onward at competitively established prices, and are used by producers and consumers usually for further processing.

Energy   Oil, natural gas, and (recently) electricity are actively traded.

Lumber and building materials   Standard sizes of lumber, plywood, and other commonly used building materials are traded in a market that permits distributers to satisfy unanticipated demand and producers to reduce excess inventory.

Stamps and coins   Collectors actively trade coins and stamps for both hobby and investment. In particular, coins are graded by recognized entities that permit both buyer and seller to transact without necessarily having to meet to evaluate the coins.

Gems   Gems, both cut and uncut, are traded actively. As with coins, there are recognized institutes that grade gems, particularly diamonds.

Other instruments   Other commodities may have active trading markets provided that they can be delivered in recognized quantities and grades are available for active trading.

A majority of commodities are bought and sold directly between the producer and manufacturer with long-term contracts. However, most production processes result in periodic needs for product that cannot be satisfied by normal supply agreements. In these situations, the trading markets provide a way to supply or acquire additional quantities quickly. Thus, building supply companies can buy standard quantities outside their normal supply agreements, and producers can sell excess inventory. Any commodity that can be sold in standard quantities and recognized grades benefits from active trading.

Many commodity markets have established financial arrangements that determine the process for managing transactions. Nevertheless the primary procedure is for agreed quantities of the commodity to be exchanged for acceptable payment that may be checks or funds transfers. Usually, the active side of the transaction (i.e., the party that contacted the broker to initiate the search either for a buyer or for a source for needed commodities) pays the commissions, but other arrangements may be common (e.g., commission splitting), or agreed as part of the transaction.

Derivative Instruments 2

Derivatives are instruments that derive their value from the value of another instrument or commodity (see Figure 2.2). Derivatives are created by a contract that obliges the parties involved to take certain actions depending on the terms of the agreement they make. Although derivatives may include bespoke contracts, derivative exchanges have developed to trade standardized contracts that are **fungible**.

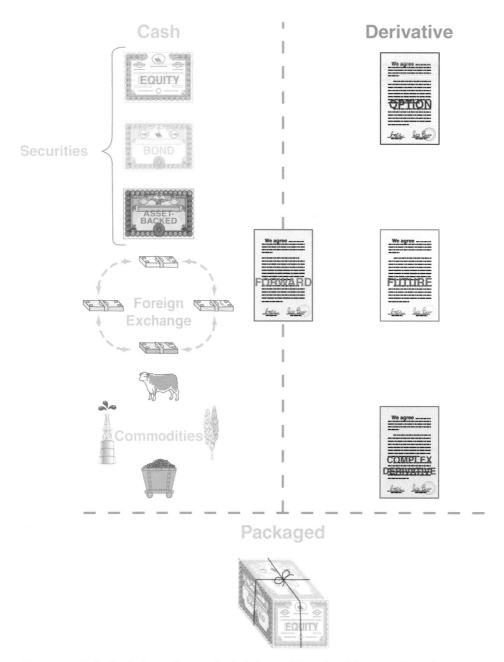

Figure 2.2   **_Derivative instruments_** are contracts that commit the writer of the contract to perform an act or service to investors or to traders who need the service.

OPTIONS

Options are contracts that permit the owner (**_holder_**) to purchase (known as a **_call option_**) or sell (a **_put option_**) a security or some other financial instrument from or to the individual or firm that wrote the option contract (the option **writer**) in the event that the financial instrument known as the **underlying** reaches a certain value. The amount the purchaser pays is called the options **premium.** Option contracts have a fixed life, and at the end of that life the contract **expires** without value if the holder does nothing.

The set date on which the option contract expires is known as the **expiration date** or **expiry date**. There are two styles of options contracts. **American-style options** can be exercised at any time during the life of the contract.[5] **European-style options** can be exercised only on a fixed **exercise date** that is stipulated in the contract. The exercise date is usually one or two days before the expiration or expiry, and the exercise date is the only date when a European-style option can be exercised or is the last date when an American-style option can be exercised.

The financial instrument on which an option is written is known as the underlying. For each underlying security, commodity, or instrument, there is typically an option contract expiring every three months for at least a year. For every **expiration month**, there are a number of active contracts at differing prices based on how much the price of the underlying security has moved over the length of the contract. Each of these prices, known as **strike prices** or **strikes**, trades separately. Depending on the price of the underlying instruments, strikes are a fixed number of pricing units apart. For example, a market might choose to give the lowest-priced underlyings (perhaps including underlyings with prices lower than 20 pricing units) strikes with 2 pricing units separating each higher strike. For underlyings from 20.01 pricing units to 50 pricing units, the market might separate successive strikes by 5 pricing units. Finally, underlyings of 50.01 and higher would have strikes that are 10 pricing units apart. (Each market defines the pricing of strikes with possible input from regulators. If multiple exchanges are trading the same contracts, the strike increments would be common for all.)

In many markets, new strikes are generated automatically when the price of the underlying moves up or down by the pricing increments used to determine the strikes. In our example, if the price of an underlying for a call option moved from 18 units to 20 units, a new strike would be created and be open for trading at 25 units and perhaps at 30 as well.

Anyone can write an option contract, but market makers on the various options exchanges are actively engaged in writing contracts. The writer receives a one-time payment of the premium. Investors purchase options to protect their investment portfolios against unexpected changes in price, and **speculators** use options to bet on price movements in the underlying security, commodity, or currency with a lower overall investment than the speculator would have if he or she had purchased the underlying instrument. Figure 2.2.1 shows the cash flows that occur with options contracts.

---

5   As a practical matter, most options are only sold very close to the exercise date. Prior to exercise, it is easier to liquidate a position or book a profit (or loss) by trading the contract.

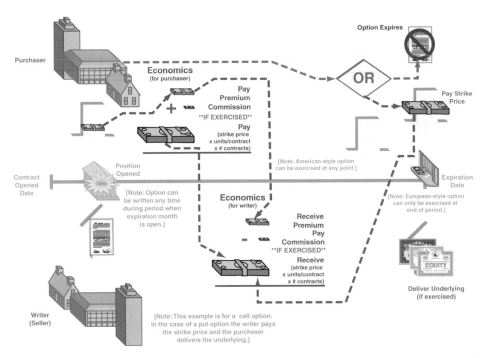

Figure 2.2.1 *An **option contract*** obligates the writer of the contract to perform a task (often to buy or sell an instrument at a specified price) to traders or to investors who may or may not invoke the obligation.

FUTURES

A ***future*** is a derivative contract that promises to ***deliver*** a specified good, instrument, or cash during a set future month known as the ***delivery month*** under the terms set forth in the futures contract. With a future, unlike an option, if nothing is done, the seller of the contract known as the ***short*** (the person or entity that sold the contract) is expected to deliver to the purchaser of the contract known as the ***long***[6] in accordance with the contract. Also unlike an option, futures do not have fixed strike prices. The price is established by contracts trading in the market at the time the future is traded. Market conditions also establish prices if an open contract is traded prior to delivery.

Futures contracts are designed to provide a hedge against price movements. As such, the goal of the contract is not primarily to deliver either physical or financial instruments, but rather as a way to bet or ensure against undesirable price movements. (Forward contracts described later are intended for actual delivery.) Therefore, many

---

6 "Long" and "short" are terms used in the trading markets to indicate a person or entity who owns a security or instrument (long) or who has a position in an instrument or security that the investor does not own (short). A ***short position*** is created when a trader borrows the instrument or security for sale. To liquidate the short position, the investor must purchase the security (at a lower price, it is hoped) at a later date to cover or liquidate the position. Effectively, a short position is a bet that the price will go down.

futures contracts are designed to permit a cash payoff at the time of delivery rather than actual delivery of a physical commodity or security. This is known as **cash delivery**.

Futures contracts are different from the corresponding cash commodities or instruments on which the future is written. Futures delivery is for fixed amounts and very specific delivery quantities, grades, and locations (if physical delivery is even possible). These standard terms make the futures contracts fungible. Therefore, all contracts are the same and can be purchased and then resold without having to link the original short with the long position.

Through the delivery date, the long can liquidate his or her **position** by either selling it to another trader, or by buying the short position from someone else who has sold a contract and has an open position. Selling the long position or buying a short position has the effect of liquidating the long position, but if the long purchases a short position, the contract is effectively terminated.

One of the measures of futures contracts is the **open interest**, which is the sum of all the contracts for each delivery month that exist in a future at a given time. When a short position is created, the open interest rises by the number of contracts in the position, and when a position is liquidated, the open interest is reduced by the amount of the contracts in the position. Figure 2.2.2 shows the cash flows associated with a futures contract.

FORWARD CONTRACTS

A forward contract is not a derivative, but is a type of commercial transaction. Forwards are considered here because of their similarity to futures. A forward contract is a bespoke agreement between a buyer and seller of a commodity or financial instrument to make or take actual delivery of a commodity at a date in the future at a price that is agreed at the time the contract is created. (See Figure 2.2.3.)

Forwards may have many of the characteristics of a future such as standardized quantities and grades, but unlike most futures, most forward contracts are primarily commercial contracts that almost always result in physical delivery. Also, unlike futures that are highly standardized, forward contracts can be adjusted to meet the specific needs of the parties to the contract. Delivery dates, quantities, and payment terms may be modified as needed.

Forwards are prior agreements for subsequent transactions. Generally, there is no market price and limited trading of the contract after the initial transaction. They are considered in these books because of their similarity to futures and their use in currency trading.

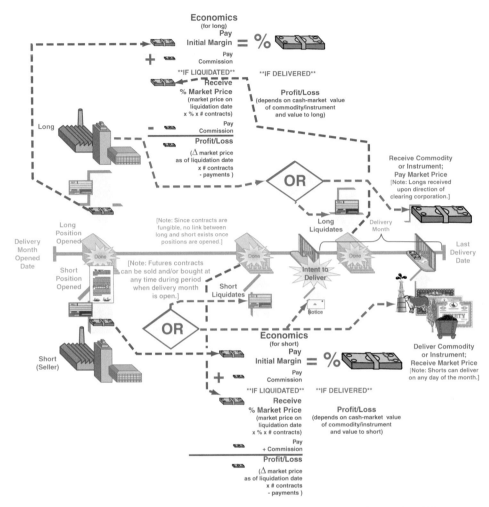

Figure 2.2.2 A ***futures contract*** creates a contractual obligation for one party (the short) to deliver a commodity, financial instrument, or sometimes cash (in lieu of commodity or financial instrument) during a defined future month to another party (the long) who agrees to accept its delivery.

COMPLEX DERIVATIVES

Complex derivatives are structured or engineered contracts constructed for a holder, usually a financial firm or industrial corporation, by a writer, usually an investment or commercial bank. Each instrument is constructed to meet a very specific financial need.

Often contracts are created to ***swap*** or to trade either ***risks*** or ***income streams***. One participant has an ***exposure*** or income that it finds unattractive to its business. The bank or broker/dealer tries to find another firm with different needs that is willing to accept the first firm's income stream or exposure. Thus, the two firms swap their income streams or exposures.

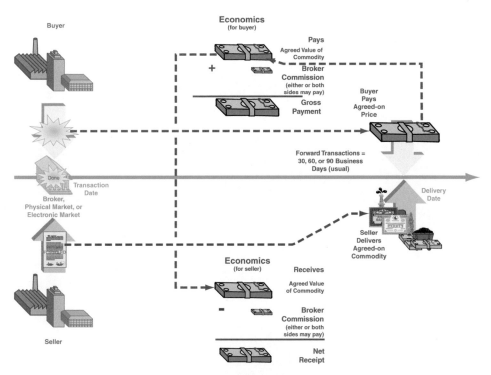

Figure 2.2.3   ***Forward contracts*** are bespoke contractual obligations to complete a financial or a commercial transaction at a defined future date and at a price that is established by the contract between two parties who may be investors, traders, producers, or consumers.

If a willing counterparty cannot be found, the bank or the broker/dealer may assume the first firm's risk or exposure. The bank or broker/dealer is betting that it will be able to find a counterparty later or even profit from the income stream if the exposure does not result in a loss.

In other types of transactions, broker/dealers and banks take bonds or other fixed income instruments and separate the promise to repay the loan obligation from the promise to pay interest during the life of the bond. This creates a cash flow for the life of the bond and a discount security with no interest payments. Institutional investors and insurance companies often find these specialty synthetic instruments attractive.

As with forward contracts, the details of complex derivatives are usually customized. However, as with futures, the primary purpose of complex derivatives is generally for risk transfer and not for commercial delivery.

Packaged Instruments 3

Packaged instruments are investment portfolios that permit an investor to participate in a diversified group of cash instruments without requiring the full outlay needed to purchase each of the fund's component instruments directly (see Figure 2.3). Packaged instruments have the advantage that they offer an investor with limited financial resources the ability to own a **diversified portfolio**. Typical packaged instruments include shares in a **mutual fund**, **units** of a unit trust, or shares in an **exchange-traded fund**.

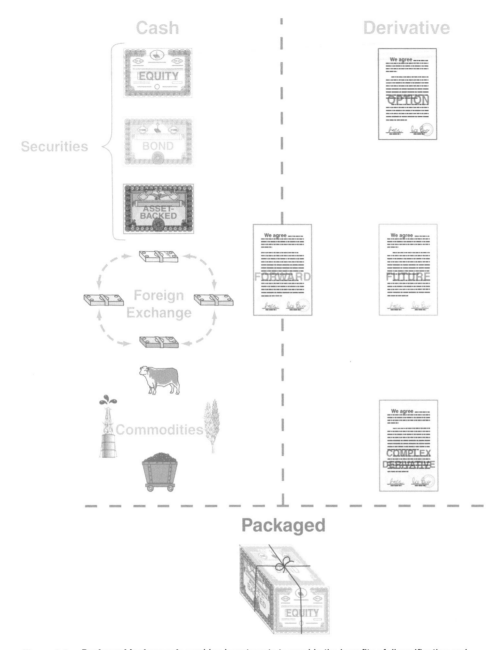

Figure 2.3   ***Packaged instruments*** combine investments to provide the benefits of diversification and professional investment management efficiency for individual investors.

MUTUAL FUNDS

Mutual funds are professionally managed investment portfolios that permit investors to own a share in the funds, not the securities within the funds (see Figure 2.3.1). To be able to sell shares, the fund is incorporated, and the corporation issues shares. For a relatively small investment, an investor can purchase shares in a mutual fund and then own a portion of a portfolio that is highly diversified. In contrast, the same amount invested in individual securities would buy only a few shares or bonds, and the resulting holdings would not be very diversified. By owning shares in several mutual funds, an investor can employ different *investment styles*, each in diversified portfolios. (We discuss investment styles in Book 2.)

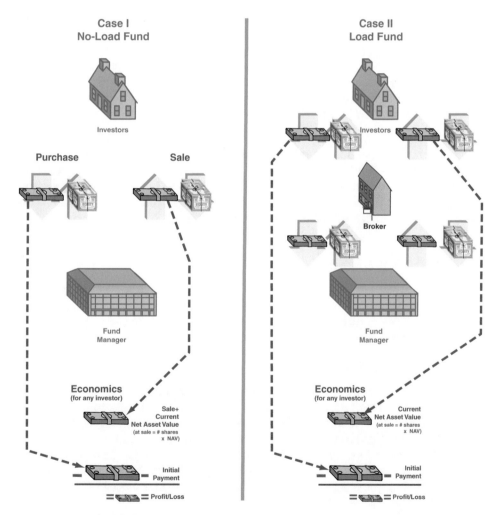

Figure 2.3.1   *Mutual funds* sell shares in diversified investment pools with defined investment objectives that must be repurchased on demand by the fund manager to individuals, who usually have limited funds to invest.

Mutual funds are managed by mutual fund companies described in Part I, "Entities." Large mutual fund organizations and other buy-side organizations that have mutual fund management subsidiaries establish funds employing different investment styles. For example, one mutual fund may search out small companies with strong potential to grow quickly. Still other funds may seek seasoned companies that consistently pay dividends. Other funds may focus on companies in different geographic regions. Another type of fund may specialize in specific types of securities such as bonds. There are many different categories of investment styles for funds and even more variation in how they are promoted and sold.

Mutual funds are typically sold directly to investors either by the company that manages the funds or by broker/dealers. If an investment company sells directly to an investor, the company has the cost of a sales staff and marketing costs. The marketing costs are included in the management costs of the mutual fund company. Alternatively, a mutual fund company may sell its shares through broker/dealers who will charge a commission for the sale. Funds sold directly without broker/dealers are known as *no-load funds*. Funds sold through broker/dealers are called *load funds*.

Mutual funds trade based on the value of the portfolio divided by the number of shares issued. Values are updated at the end of each trading day based on the *official price* or *net asset value* (NAV) of the securities in the portfolio times the number of shares owned. Unlike most companies, the shares in these mutual funds are not traded among investors, but are created on a purchase and liquidated on a sale.

UNIT TRUSTS

Unit trusts are similar to mutual funds, but differ in that the funds are not incorporated. Firms that manage unit trusts create a fund, and its value swells or falls based on market performance. As in the case of mutual funds, investors purchase or sell units to the fund manager either directly or through brokers.

EXCHANGE-TRADED FUNDS

Exchange-traded funds, or EFTs, are investment portfolios usually managed as *index funds* (see Book 2 for a description of index funds) by investment companies for which shares are issued and traded on exchanges. Like mutual funds, exchange-traded funds are incorporated and issue shares. Unlike mutual funds, the shares in exchange-traded funds are traded among investors on exchanges. Because the value of the shares of an EFT are not derived completely from the value of the securities in the portfolio,[7] the values of ETFs can vary from the exact value of the underlying portfolio. (See Figure 2.3.2.)

---

[7] Because shares in an EFT trade freely in a secondary market, supply and demand can cause the price of the EFT shares to diverge from the actual value of the underlying portfolio.

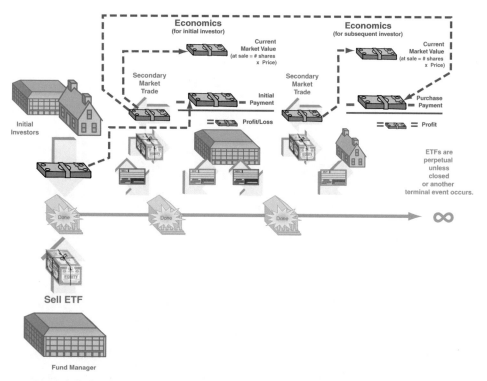

Figure 2.3.2 ***Exchange-traded funds*** are managed funds that track important indexes and issue shares that are traded like stocks on major exchanges with market-established share prices for investors and for traders.

RELATED INFORMATION IN OTHER BOOKS

This book introduces instruments, explains something about their characteristics, and explains cash flows that occur over their life. We return to instruments in Book 2, where we examine the elements that comprise instruments, the common measures used to evaluate instruments, the participants in the markets (both investors and frequent traders) for different instruments, and the nature of the markets in which instruments are traded. For information about forthcoming books, see Figure 2.4.

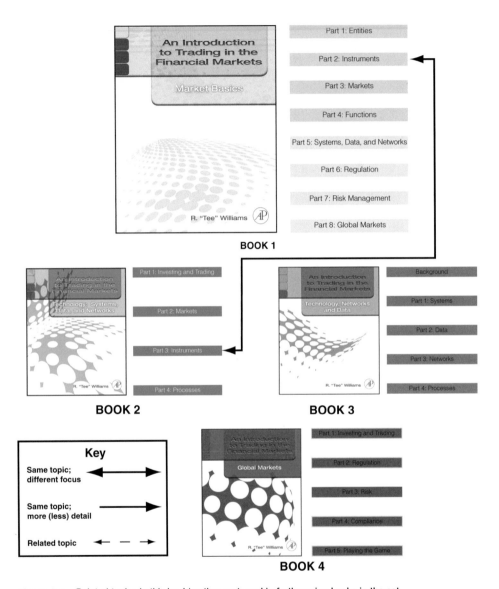

Figure 2.4 Related topics in this book's other parts and in forthcoming books in the set.

Markets and Marketplaces

Part **3**

We use the term "markets" to refer to the creation and trading of securities and other traded instruments. Marketplaces are the venues where instruments that have been created and issued to the public are exchanged between buyer and seller. We can categorize markets in several different ways, but there are two basic types of markets for traded instruments.

The primary market is where securities are created. The secondary market is where instruments are traded after they have been issued. Figure 3 contrasts the primary market that raises capital for entities that need financing by issuing securities primarily, with the secondary market that permits holders of instruments to purchase or sell instruments that are already outstanding.

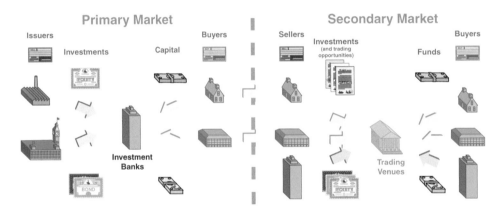

Figure 3 **Primary and secondary markets** create new securities and then permit trading in the created securities and other instruments among traders and investors.

We sometimes use the term "marketplace" because, as we saw earlier in the "History" section, until relatively recently the buying and selling of instruments in markets had to be conducted at a physical location. However, beginning in 1976 with the Toronto Stock Exchange, trading has become increasingly automated, and now much—maybe even most—trading occurs in a virtual marketplace.

The Primary Market 1

The primary market is where securities get created. Unlike the secondary markets described next, primary markets raise money on behalf of companies or governments. Figure 3.1 shows the purpose of the primary market.

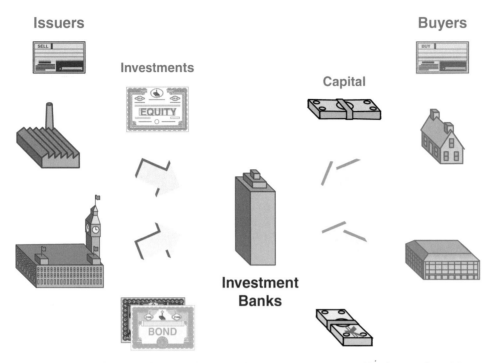

Figure 3.1 The **primary market** allows investment banks to acquire new securities from nonfinancial companies, governments, and others and sell them onward to traders and investors.

There are a number of different processes that can be used to raise capital in the primary market. These processes are explored in Book 2, *An Introduction to Trading in the Financial Markets: Trading, Markets, Instruments, and Processes,* where we create a process flow illustrating capital-raising activities and discuss each of them. This flow is analogous to the trading process presented in Figure OV.1 in the "Overview" at the front of this book.

Secondary Markets 2

Secondary markets do not raise money for the companies or governments that issue securities (see Figure 3.2). Instead, the secondary markets provide the facility to allow a current owner of a security to sell it if the owner no longer wants the security. In contrast, someone else who would now like to own the security can buy it from the seller in the secondary market.

When an outstanding security or instrument trades, no money goes to the company or government that issues the security. Instead, ownership passes between investors with no effect on the issuing entity. However, firms that issue securities benefit when their securities and other instruments are actively traded. An active secondary market makes the process of offering new issues simpler because prospective investors are more willing to invest if they know they can *liquidate* their position whenever they want.

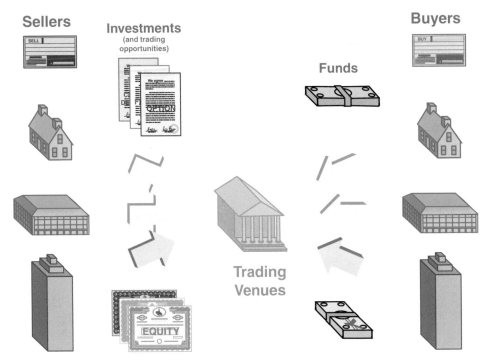

Sellers   Investments   Buyers
           (and trading
            opportunities)

Funds

Trading
Venues

EQUITY

Figure 3.2   *The secondary markets* permit securities created in the primary markets, and other instruments created in other ways, to be exchanged among investors and traders.

RELATED INFORMATION IN OTHER BOOKS

Part 3 describes how markets can be organized, owned, and registered in the various countries where they operate. Here, we explore the purposes of both the primary and the secondary markets. In Book 2, we examine the structure and mechanics of different markets, characteristics of markets for different types of instruments, and processes that occur in primary and secondary markets (see Figure 3.3).

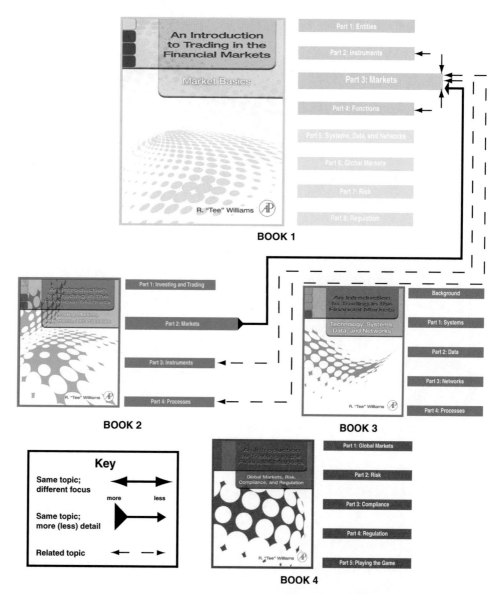

Figure 3.3   Related topics in this book's other parts and in forthcoming books in this set.

Functions
(Activities)

Part 4

Within the entities described in Part 1, there are many roles or functions[1] performed by individuals and departments within the firms. As with entities, these functions can be grouped into buy-side, sell-side, market, and support functions. Almost every one of these roles has unique, dedicated technology support described in Book 3, *An Introduction to Trading in the Financial Markets: Technology—Systems, Data, and Networks*. Figure 4 depicts these functions. As with entities, many large financial firms perform most of these functions under a single umbrella corporation.

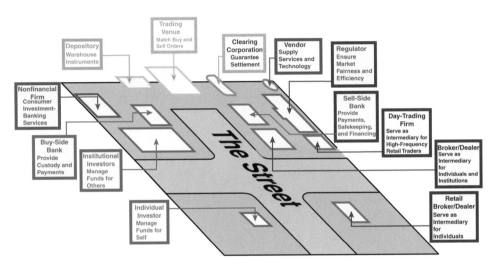

Figure 4   The various **functions** of the participating entities within the trading markets on the Street are required to create trades or support the trading process.

In Book 2, *An Introduction to Trading in the Financial Markets: Trading, Markets, Instruments, and Processes,* we explore how the functions we define here interact in the processes required for both the primary and secondary markets.

---

1   As we were researching Book 4, we encountered the concept of "functional regulation." The idea of functional regulation is somewhat related to our definition, but the correspondence is not exact. Functional regulation as revealed in a quick web search of several definitions seems to be halfway between what we define as an "entity" and the way we use the term "function." The concept of functional regulation is that supervision of banks and other financial entities would occur at a level that would have banking regulators monitor commercial banking regulations and securities regulators controlling activities such as trading and investment banking. We are comfortable with our use of the term "function," but you should understand it is sometimes used in other ways.

The trading markets can generally be divided into individuals acting on their own behalf and organizations operating as professionals for others. Investors, both individuals and institutions managing money, are commonly called the "buy side." Intermediaries are typically referred to as the "sell side."

The terms "buy side" and "sell side" do not mean that one group is exclusively buying securities and the other side is exclusively selling. Rather, the terms refer to the fact that one group (the buy side) is buying or consuming the services of an intermediary, whereas the other group (the sell side) is providing or selling those services. We are not sure of the exact origin of these terms, but they are either in common usage or at least are understood in most of the world.

We look primarily at the activities of institutional investors, broker/dealers, banks, and trading venues. Similar discussions could be written for clearing corporations, depositories, corporations, and vendors, but these specific functions are not covered in detail here.

One final note, functions are activities that firms must perform to make the trading markets work and are not necessarily specific job titles. Although some of the functions we describe may refer to an actual job title in some organizations (e.g., "buy-side trader" or "position manager,") other functions (e.g., "customer accounting" or "securities movement and control") are group functions that require multiple job types to complete.

Categories 1

For both the buy and sell side, the terms *front office*, *middle office*, and *backoffice* are often used, usually without great precision (see Figure 4.1). We use these terms as well, but we employ fixed definitions as described in the three subsections that follow. We use these categories to group functions in the buy and sell sides.

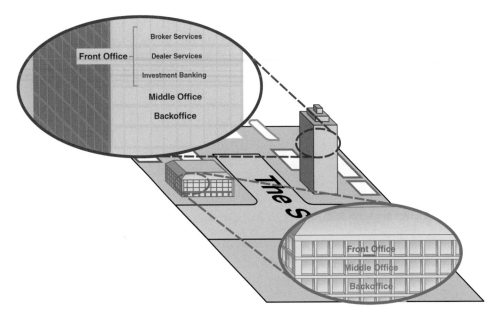

Figure 4.1.1   ***Functions on the Street*** are grouped into three major categories to distinguish the target of each function within buy-side and sell-side firms.

We believe that we use these terms in a way that is in keeping with common usage, but we do not know of any fixed definitions we can adopt. Therefore, as with all the definitions we employ, you should verify what others mean when they use these terms.

FRONT OFFICE

When we refer to the "front office," we mean both functions that are primary lines of business for an organization and customer-facing activities. Therefore, in referring to

LEAVE CLEARING TO US!

In the late 1980s, the vice chairman of the Johannesburg Stock Exchange returned from a meeting with the banks. (At the time, the relationship between the banks and the brokerage community in South Africa was very strained as was the case in many markets around the world. Both groups thought they had the right to control the local trading markets.) He was very amused, and when asked what was so funny, he described a situation that had occurred in the meeting that day. For several months, a joint committee of banks and brokers had been deadlocked over which of the two groups should control clearing. Each group thought it should control the process.

In the meeting on the day in question, it became evident that when the banks used the term "clearing," they meant clearing checks and bank drafts. The brokers wanted to clear securities and derivatives. In fact, the entire problem turned on each group misunderstanding what the other meant by the terms used in the meetings. This case was more extreme than most but illustrates the confusion that definitions can create.

"broker/dealers," we include trading activities that are not necessarily customer facing, but that are primary lines of business.[2] We also include the customer-facing function of sales and customer support (see Figure 4.1.1.a).

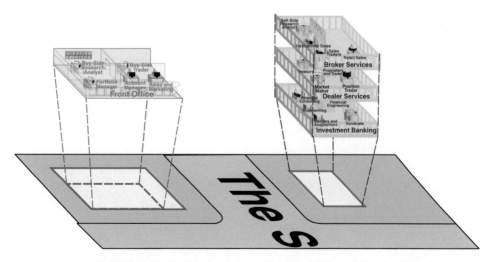

Figure 4.1.1.a   *Front office* refers to the primary lines of business and/or activities that interact directly with customers for buy-side and sell-side firms.

---

2   For example, proprietary trading (described later) is not an activity that involves customers, but we include it in the front office because it is usually a primary line of business.

MIDDLE OFFICE

When we use the term "middle office," we talk about the activities that support front-office activities, support customers, and account for customers. Examples might include customer accounting in a buy-side firm or compliance for a sell-side firm (see Figure 4.1.1.b).

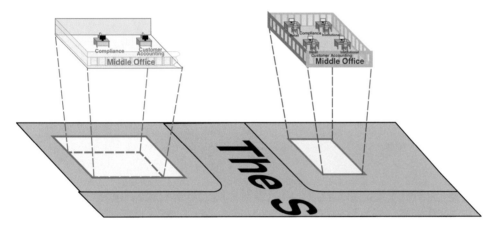

Figure 4.1.1.b   **Middle office** refers to activities that support the front office or produce information required by customers for both buy-side and sell-side firms.

BACKOFFICE

We use the term "backoffice"[3] to mean those activities that relate to securities and the markets. Therefore, backoffice activities include those that support securities activities after a trade as well as clearing and settlement (see Figure 4.1.1.c).

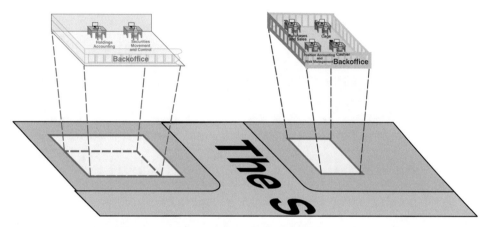

Figure 4.1.1.c   ***Backoffice*** refers to basic activities that support the front and middle offices and interact with the post-trade processes for both buy-side and sell-side firms.

---

3   As we noted in the Preface, we write "backoffice" as a single word because the term is becoming widely used both inside the trading markets as well as in the larger economy.

Buy Side 2

Buy-side functions relate primarily to investing in traded instruments for profit, whether for one's self or as a service for others. The activities of the buy-side front office include investing, supporting customers directly, and acquiring new customers. The middle-office activities of the buy side include accounting for customers and their holdings as well as regulatory reporting and compliance as it regards customers. The backoffice manages securities positions and supports the completion of trades. These functions are shown in Figure 4.2.

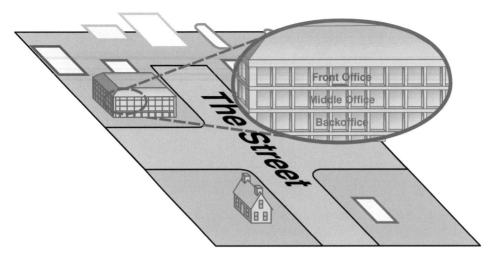

Figure 4.2 The **buy side** provides investing and trading services for itself, for the firm, and for customers.

INDIVIDUAL INVESTORS

Individuals trading in the markets do not have "functions" in the strict sense of the term although they do perform most of the functions of institutional investors to a limited extent (see Figure 4.2.1). We describe three primary categories of individual investors in Book 2. The most significant distinction among retail customers is how the individual interacts with the markets. We describe the sell-side functions that support these individuals later.

INSTITUTIONAL INVESTORS

We look at the functions of the buy side without regard to the investment philosophy of the firm or how the firm is registered with regulators. (The structure of firms required to comply with regulations—that is, the type of entity a firm has elected to be—was considered in Part 1. In Book 2, we address trading motivation and buy-side processes in more detail.)

Many institutional investors have subsidiaries that represent more than one of the entity types from Part 1, and most have different funds that are managed using multiple strategies described in Book 2. Whatever the type of entity and however funds are managed, most firms have individuals or departments performing the functions described later. As shown in Figure 4.2.2, the functions performend by buy-side firms can be grouped into front office, middle office and backoffice.

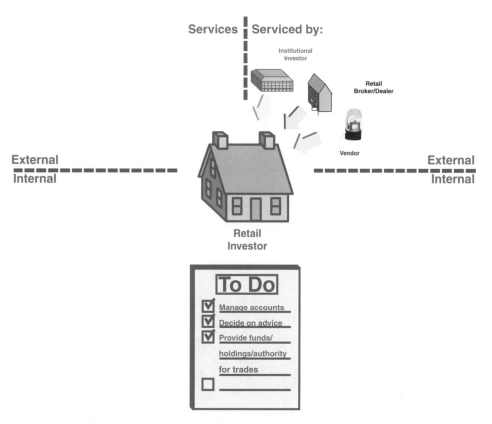

Services | Serviced by:

Institutional
Investor

Retail
Broker/Dealer

Vendor

External
Internal

External
Internal

Retail
Investor

To Do

☑ Manage accounts

☑ Decide on advice

☑ Provide funds/
  holdings/authority
  for trades

☐ _____

Figure 4.2.1   *Individual investors* perform their own investing and trading functions aided by intermediaries who help them participate in the trading markets.

Front-Office Functions

The primary buy-side front-office functions include **account management**, portfolio management, **sales and marketing**, **research**, and **trading**. These represent all the functions needed to acquire accounts, manage portfolios, service customers, and execute trades (see Figure 4.2.2.1).

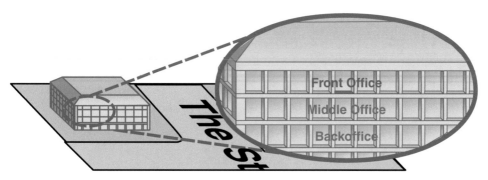

Figure 4.2.2 **Institutional investors** require investing and trading functions from the front office, and support functions from the middle office and backoffice to be able to provide investment products and services to individuals and corporate customers.

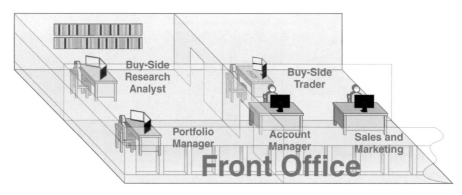

Figure 4.2.2.1 The institutional **front office** manages investments, executes trades, and delivers customer support to satisfy the investment needs of its customers.

PORTFOLIO MANAGER

Portfolio managers are responsible for investing customer funds in accordance with broad principles established for the fund they manage. Portfolio managers often have a wide variety of objectives that must be balanced. The following descriptions examine only a few of the portfolio managers' decisions.

Figure 4.2.2.1.1 shows that portfolio managers have a number of primary tasks and services to perform and are serviced by a number of functions, both internal to the investment manager and by outside functions.

Portfolio managers usually have existing security holdings, and from time to time they may decide that one security has lower prospects than they expect of holdings they wish to maintain. When this occurs, the managers must sell the security that has fallen from favor. With the money obtained from the sale, the managers

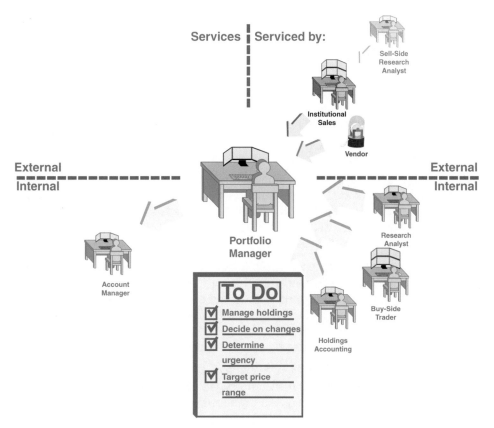

Figure 4.2.2.1.1 **Portfolio managers** control the assets entrusted to them, deciding what to buy or sell to be able to implement the investment strategy established for the funds they manage.

must decide whether to select a new security to add to the portfolio, to increase the quantity of an existing holding, or to leave the funds resulting from the sale in cash in anticipation of more attractive investments later.

Other decisions may include deciding how to handle new infusions of cash and planning for anticipated and unanticipated requirements for cash to be withdrawn from the portfolio.

Portfolio managers decide what to buy or sell in part based on investment research provided by broker/dealers in anticipation of trades executed through them and by internal research analysts.

Portfolio managers also participate in the marketing of the services of the firm by describing investment philosophy and processes to prospective customers of the firm.

A portfolio manager may employ a variety of different analytical tools to analyze securities, assess the market risk of the portfolio, and analyze such things as diversification and **asset allocation**. We explore investment motivation in more detail in Book 2 and investment tools in Book 3.

BUY-SIDE TRADER

When a portfolio manager decides what to buy or sell, in most firms the order placement decision is not made by the portfolio manager, but rather by a **buy-side trader** whose responsibility is to manage the transaction process so as to minimize the cost of the transaction. The use of buy-side traders is particularly common for equities and other exchange-traded securities (see Figure 4.2.2.1.2).

A buy-side trader takes an order to purchase or sell an instrument or group of instruments from a portfolio manager. The portfolio manager may provide instructions on how time sensitive the transaction is and perhaps even broad ideas on what price range would be acceptable. The buy-side trader has the responsibility to decide which marketplace to use, what broker/dealer to employ, and what instructions to use. We describe the buy-side trading process in detail in Book 2.

In collaboration with portfolio managers, buy-side traders may also have the responsibility to ensure that any research obligations[4] are met and to measure the performance of broker/dealers in executing securities transactions.

---

4   Research obligations are created when sell-side firms provide useful information and services to the buy side. Examples include investment research created by the sell-side firm and also so-called **soft-dollar services** described in Book 2, *An Introduction to Trading in the Financial Markets: Trading, Markets, Instruments, and Processes.*

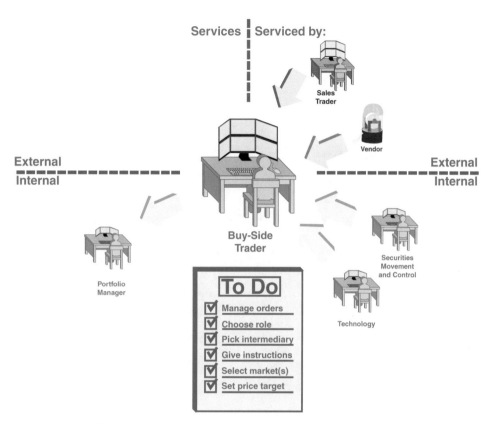

Sales
Trader

Vendor

External
Internal

External
Internal

Buy-Side
Trader

Portfolio
Manager

Securities
Movement
and Control

To Do

☑ Manage orders
☑ Choose role
☑ Pick intermediary
☑ Give instructions
☑ Select market(s)
☑ Set price target

Technology

Figure 4.2.2.1.2   **Buy-side traders** decide how, when, where, and at what price to implement the buy
and/or sell decisions of portfolio managers.

Buy-side traders often employ **order management systems** (OMSs) that
accept orders from portfolio managers and then track orders as they are completed
in whole, or in part, or are fully or partially cancelled. The functionality of OMSs is
described in Book 3.

Many buy-side traders come to their jobs from positions on the sell side.

RESEARCH ANALYSTS

Research analysts for buy-side firms typically have the responsibility of presenting
research information to portfolio managers in a comprehensible form. This task often
includes doing original research, but more importantly buy-side analysts synthesize
the research reports and ideas received from broker/dealers (see Figure 4.2.2.1.3).

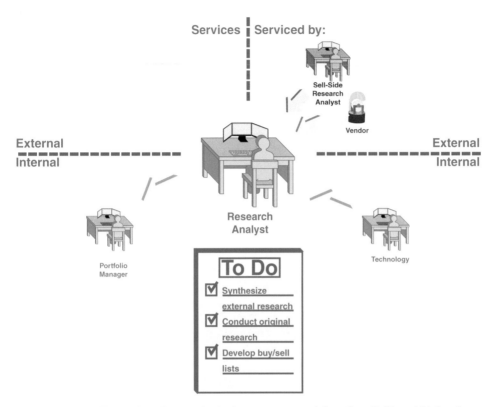

Figure 4.2.2.1.3 *Research analysts* synthesize investment research from the sell side and third parties, and conduct original research to support the decision making of portfolio managers.

Buy-side analysts in some firms assist the senior investment personnel in the firm in establishing a so-called **buy list** that tells portfolio managers which securities are permitted to be owned in portfolios managed by the firm. Other broad instructions from investment committees where research analysts have an input include asset allocation, which suggests the percentages of portfolios that should be allocated to different instrument categories.

SALES AND MARKETING

All types of investment management firms need to market their services although the way each is regulated can have a distinct impact on the type of promotion that is permitted. Regulators generally try to ensure that promotional and marketing practices are not deceptive and present true descriptions using accepted measurement practices (see Figure 4.2.2.1.4).

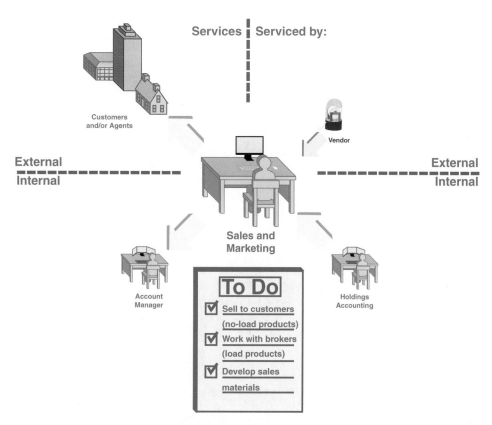

Figure 4.2.2.1.4 *Sales and marketing* attracts new customers and additional funds and/or supports intermediaries that attract new customers for the firm's investment services.

Those funds that distribute their services directly to customers typically have a dedicated sales force that may use print publications, direct mailing, the Internet, and sales offices to solicit customers. Funds that use the services of broker/dealers call on and are called on by the broker/dealers who do or might promote the products. Those firms that are not permitted to actively sell their services depend on maintaining relationships with accountants and lawyers as well as word of mouth through existing customers to attract new business.

Most management companies produce brochures that describe their various funds' investment philosophies and describe past performance. As a general rule, investment funds tend to compare their investment performance against comparable funds. A number of companies maintain **universes** that track the historical performance of funds with similar characteristics. Brochures commonly compare the historical performance of funds to the performance of the universe of funds with similar characteristics. Firms use these comparisons in marketing materials.

ACCOUNT MANAGERS

A critical function for an investment firm is managing the relationship with clients. Mutual fund companies maintain help desks and customer service organizations responsible for handling customer questions and issues. Customers with large portfolios usually have a dedicated account manager although the account manager may deal with many individual customers (see Figure 4.2.2.1.5).

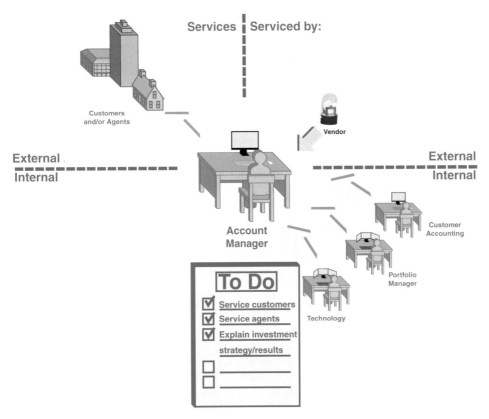

Figure 4.2.2.1.5 **Account managers** provide support and explain their firm's actions and strategies to customers who interact directly with the firm

For organizations that manage money directly for individuals and trust departments, there is a staff dedicated to managing individuals' accounts. These account managers meet with customers to explain the structure and performance of their accounts. For trust customers, account managers help with specific problems such as taxes and personal problems.

ABOVE AND BEYOND OR UP, UP, AND AWAY

Account managers from a well-known trust firm are purported to have arranged to have a helicopter land in a Central American prison to extract a client who was imprisoned on supposedly baseless charges. Most account management functions are less dramatic.

Middle Office

As we noted, middle-office functions support customer-facing activities. These functions include **customer accounting** and **compliance** (see Figure 4.2.2.2).

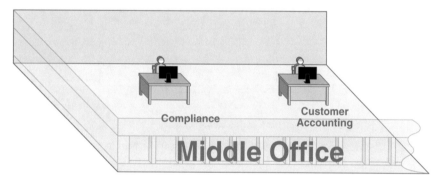

Figure 4.2.2.2   The **middle-office functions** for institutional investors include providing support related to customer accounts to the front office.

CUSTOMER PROCESSES

The term "customer processes" refers to the accounting and reporting functions required to service a customer. Customer reports include valuing and reporting customer holdings, accounting, reporting, and distributing as-needed income arising from securities transactions and positions (see Figure 4.2.2.2.1).

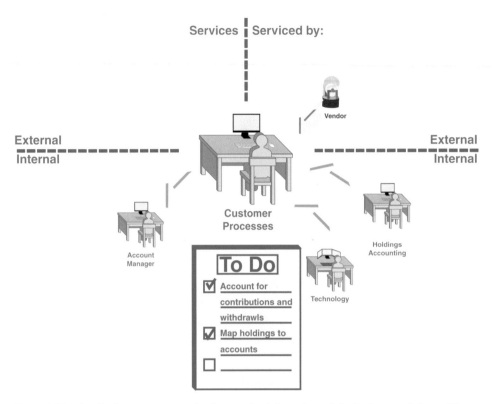

Services | Serviced by:

External
Internal

Vendor

External
Internal

Customer
Processes

Account
Manager

Holdings
Accounting

To Do
☑ Account for
   contributions and
   withdrawls
☑ Map holdings to
   accounts
☐ _____

Technology

Figure 4.2.2.2.1   ***Customer processes*** develop reports, statements, and electronic presentations of the holdings of customers.

The customer accounting process is described in Book 2. Moreover, many buy-side firms manage investments through investment products sold to customers and internal ***comingled funds*** that are in effect internal mutual funds used to manage customers' investments. Thus, customers hold positions in the products or comingled funds, and those products or funds in turn have holdings in instruments. We examine this issue in more detail in Book 3.

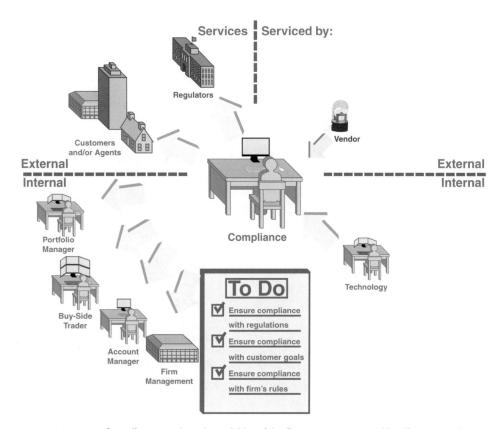

Figure 4.2.2.2.2 *Compliance* monitors the activities of the firm to ensure acceptable adherence to the rules, wishes, and policies of regulators, customers, and the firm.

COMPLIANCE

The compliance department of an investing institution is responsible for ensuring that the firm adheres to all regulations to which the firm is subject. In addition, clients and the firm itself sometimes place restrictions on the way accounts are managed as a part of a charter. Typical restrictions might involve certain instruments the fund cannot own for reasons of conscience, such as instruments associated with companies or things not considered to be socially or morally responsible. The compliance department ensures that these instructions are followed (see Figure 4.2.2.2.2).

Compliance is described in more detail in Book 4, *An Introduction to Trading in the Financial Markets—Global Markets, Risk, Compliance, and Regulation*.

Backoffice

Among the backoffice functions are **securities valuation**, **securities movement and control**, and **regulatory accounting** (see Figure 4.2.2.3). These functions are needed to support the activities of the firm, satisfy the demands of regulators, and manage securities transactions and positions.

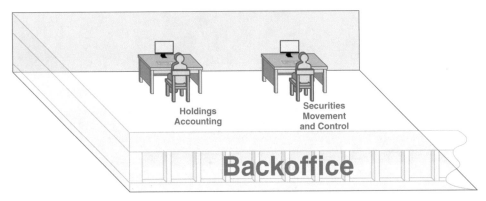

Figure 4.2.2.3   The **backoffice** manages interactions with the Street and accounts for non-customer holdings in support of customers and the firm.

HOLDINGS ACCOUNTING

The way a firm accounts for holdings is often constrained by the way it is registered. In particular, income may affect the taxes of beneficiaries for some types of accounts and not for others. All firms must monitor the status of investment holdings to ensure that the holdings are consistent with the best interests of the firm's customers and represent sound investment strategy. Accounting may also need to satisfy specific reporting requirements from regulators (see Figure 4.2.2.3.1).

For example, some funds are required to report all their securities positions on a quarterly basis. Mutual funds must report their fund values at the close of business each day. Buy-side firms may also be asked to demonstrate their efforts to achieve best execution for their securities transactions. (**Best execution** is described in Book 2.)

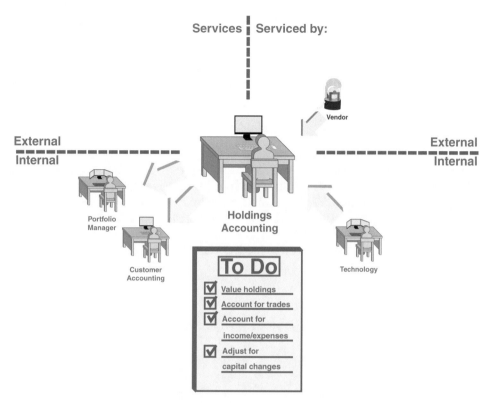

Figure 4.2.2.3.1 *Holdings accounting* tracks cash and instrument positions for the investment firm and indirectly for its customers.

As a part of its accounting, an investment institution must periodically, and in some cases continuously, value the securities it manages and provide valued securities positions to various accounting processes. For equities and other instruments traded in liquid markets, valuing is usually simple. For bonds that do not trade often, and for other instruments such as complex derivatives, valuation can be very difficult. Instruments that are not properly valued can create risks for the firm that owns or trades them.

During the time the institution holds the instrument, it must manage the income produced by the instrument through dividend or interest payments, and manage any changes in the value or quantity of the instrument. Fluctuations in market value cause changes in the value of holdings. Changes in quantity often result from so-called **capital changes**, which include events such as **stock splits**, in which the number of shares in a position changes (usually, an increase in the number of shares); stock dividends (the holding becomes entitled to extra shares instead of receiving cash); or a bond that is **called** (the bond is paid off prior to maturity). For bonds, maturity requires surrendering ownership in exchange for money equal to the face value of the bonds in the position. Other related activities are also involved in tracking holdings.

Securities Movement and Control

When an institution trades, its securities movement and control department is responsible for conducting a number of activities to complete and settle the transaction. The firm must affirm the details of the trade, and then the firm interacts with its **custodian bank** and the broker/dealer that executed the trade to arrange settlement, ensuring that either the funds (purchase) or security transfer instructions (sale) are positioned for settlement. After the trade is settled, the department passes control of the instruments purchased or funds received to holdings accounting (see Figure 4.2.2.3.2).

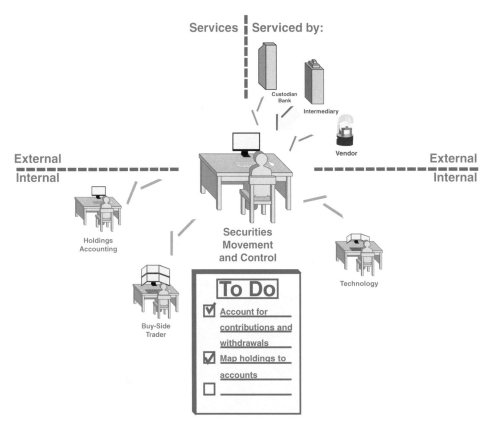

Figure 4.2.2.3.2 **Securities movement and control** monitors completed trades prior to settlement and other movements of instruments for a firm.

Technology

A dedicated staff at large institutions is responsible for managing the systems employed by the firm. They find the sources of all the information used in investment analysis, trading, clearing and settlement, and customer and regulatory reporting; and manage the networks that the firm employs. The data used is a particularly large issue for investment firms and includes data from the markets, such as prices, news, and research; reference data used to manage and value investment positions; and process data created during the investment and trading processes (see Figure 4.2.2.3.3).[5]

In addition to finding the information, the data departments must also manage the contractual requirements of the information's creators and manage the quality of information being used within the organization. This function may also require that the data management staff understand the assumptions employed in the creation of the data and the exact requirements of different users of the data.

More detail on the systems, data, and networks used in institutional investment firms and the processes employed to manage it are presented in Book 3.

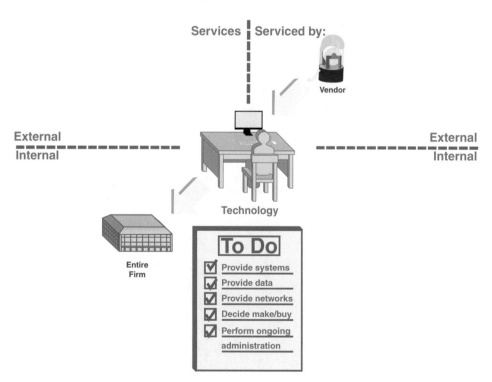

Figure 4.2.2.3.3 **Buy-side technology** builds or buys systems, data, and networks required for the operation of the firm.

---

5 We do not classify technology as a "Backoffice" function specifically, and thus it does not appear in Figure 4.2.2.3. Nevertheless, technology is critical to the front office, middle office, and backoffice.

Sell Side 3

As we noted in Part 1 on entities, the activities related to intermediating between investors and the markets are generally referred to as the "sell side." As illustrated in Figure 4.3 this includes primarily broker/dealers, although as we have seen the broker/dealer may be part of a larger financial organization.

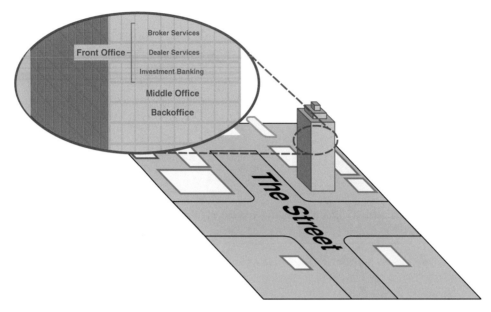

Front Office
Broker Services
Dealer Services
Investment Banking
Middle Office
Backoffice

The Street

Figure 4.3   The **sell side** requires the functions that permit it to serve as an intermediary between the investors and the market.

BROKERS, DEALERS, AND BROKER/DEALERS

We have described the overall functions of brokers, dealers, and broker/dealers that act as intermediaries standing between the customer and the markets.

The functions of broker/dealers can be categorized in three primary ways:

1. Customer activities or **customer-side activities** that relate to the service of customers, and market activities, or **street-side activities** related to the markets;

2. **Retail services** for individual investors, and **institutional services** for institutional investors; and

3. Broker services versus dealer services.

After introducing these important distinctions, we provide a functional breakdown using the front, middle, and backoffice as we did in describing the buy side. We further separate functions into those where a firm acts as a broker and those as dealer. A broker/dealer simply uses these two functions together as needed. Although there is coordination and decision making to determine which role to play in a given situation, we do not distinguish an independent broker/dealer function.

FRONT OFFICE

Within what we call the broker/dealer front office—the primary lines of business and customer-facing activities—there are three major groups of activities (see Figure 4.3.1). Brokerage services include sales and agency trading. Dealer functions control the commitment of the firm's capital to trading activities. Investment banking involves the activities required to help finance corporate customers and place newly created securities with investors.

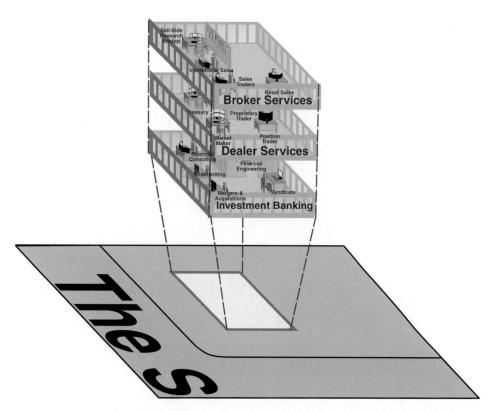

Figure 4.3.1   The *sell-side front office* refers to primary lines of business and customer-facing activities of broker/dealers.

Brokerage Functions

Broker/dealers acting as brokers or agents provide a service to their customers by acting as the customers' representative in the marketplace. As such, a broker is supposed to represent a customer's best interest at all times, and the customer pays for this service with a commission that is usually an established amount per unit of the instrument that is bought or sold (e.g., a commission might be £0.03 per common share purchased or sold). When acting as an agent, the firm has a fiduciary obligation to the customer to get a good price. Figure 4.3.1.1 shows the brokerage (agency) functions for a sell-side firm.

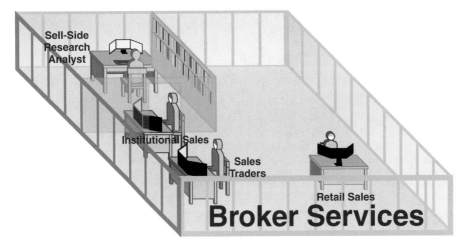

Figure 4.3.1.1 The **brokerage front office** provides access to the markets as an agent and provides support to customers.

The services of a broker are provided to two different customer categories— retail customers and institutional customers—and a number of different activities are performed for each group.

RETAIL SALES

Broker/dealers that service retail customers (individuals) have departments dedicated to sales. Retail sales involves two major sales channels. *Direct sales* involve a salesperson calling on customers directly and by phone. *Indirect sales* are primarily conducted through web sites on the Internet and, less frequently than in the past, using automated telephone systems. Most retail firms employ both direct and indirect channels at least to some extent (see Figure 4.3.1.1.1).

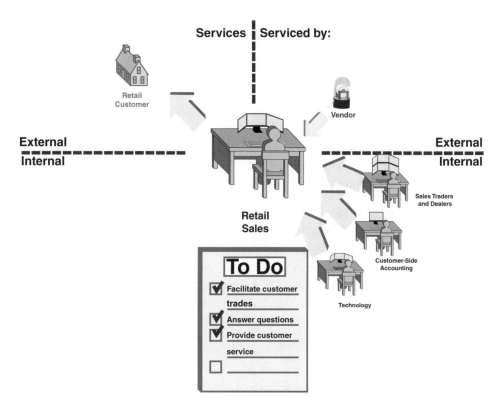

Figure 4.3.1.1.1 *Retail sales* markets the firm's products and services directly and indirectly to individuals.

The salespeople operating from offices close to customers perform the direct sales function. In addition to suggesting securities for customers to purchase or sell, sales personnel provide customer support in resolving account issues and in delivering and explaining customer statements. Retail firms provide research information on companies to support sales and to explain investment products the firms sell. Investment products include mutual funds, unit trusts, college savings, and retirement accounts. These products may be created by the firm or may be created and packaged by other organizations. Retail brokerage is increasingly becoming known as "wealth management," which reflects the increasing use of assets-under-management instead of commissions on transactions to pay for services.

Indirect sales may involve many of the same services offered by a sales force, but delivered indirectly through the Internet. Firms that specialize in Internet delivery often provide highly sophisticated web sites with tools that facilitate trading, as well as research and analytical tools. Indirect sales typically charge lower commissions than are charged when a direct salesperson is involved.

Customers who trade very frequently tend to prefer Internet access for trading, both because they can reduce the time required to enter orders and because they often do not like the perceived interference of a salesperson. A major concern for a firm is that a customer trading without a salesperson for guidance may engage in risky trading practices. Thus, Internet trading sites have sophisticated monitoring tools to oversee customer trading, and firms attempt to protect themselves by requiring customers who choose to trade online to sign disclaimers stating that the customer understands the risks and is willing to assume them.

Retail sales personnel focus primarily on their customers. Customer orders are passed on to traders and systems that manage the orders. Some very large customers deal directly with specialized traders in trading rooms who place orders while the retail sales personnel act as account managers.

INSTITUTIONAL SALES

Institutional sales[6] differs from retail sales primarily in scale, and because the "customer" is an organization rather than an individual (see Figure 4.3.1.1.2). However, scale alone does not suggest all the differences. Institutions, as we saw in Part 1 on entities, are governed by a number of different regulatory requirements, and the broker/dealers that serve them must be aware of and help customers comply with these regulations. Also, except for very active retail traders, most retail customers

---

6   As with other terms in the trading markets the distinctions among functional terms such as "institutional salespeople," "sales traders," "traders," "dealers," and "position managers" vary from firm to firm and region to region. For clarity this book will use the term institutional sales to refer to those individuals who have customer responsibilities for institutions, and who are not involved in placing orders. We use the term trader or sales trader to refer to those who handle securities transactions on behalf of the customer, and who manage customer trades on an agency basis. We use the term dealer to refer to those who buy and sell securities in order to profit from holding short-term positions, and/or profit from the spread between the bid and offer prices. We define those who manage the firm's inventory positions in securities determining how much or how little to hold and at what price to acquire or sell positions as **position managers** or **position traders**.

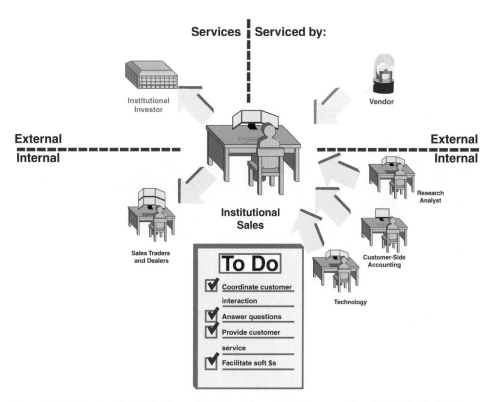

Figure 4.3.1.1.2 **Institutional sales** performs the sales and service support functions for institutional customers.

have only one or a dominant brokerage relationship. Institutions, by contrast, have many broker/dealers competing for the **order flow** generated by the institution.

Institutional salespeople are responsible for one or possibly a few customers. Salespeople must know their customers well and support the demands for reporting and trade allocation. Historically, sales personnel would have actively pushed specific securities to portfolio managers. Now the salespeople are mostly responsible for serving buy-side traders who manage the customer's trading process.

Although the role of sales personnel has changed, institutional sales personnel, sales traders, and research analysts still actively push ideas to their customers. Now, however, instead of phone calls, trading ideas are more often promoted using Twitter and instant messaging. The overall goal of encouraging customers to trade through the firm remains.

Institutional salespeople focus primarily on customers. Institutional sales personnel perform account management functions and leave orders to sales traders and others.

FUNCTIONS IN A TRADING ROOM

A trading room at a major broker/dealer houses most if not all of the trading and dealing functions described in this section. Simply looking at different people, most of whom are sitting at large workstations with multiple screens, is no indication of what each is doing. Within the room, people performing both agency and dealer functions work in close proximity. Traders and sales personnel work closely with position traders. Indeed, as we describe in Book 2, on complex trades the activities of those positioning orders and those dealing with customers are highly coordinated.

A dramatic change in trading has occurred as more and more traders use algorithms to initiate orders sent to the markets. Although large trading rooms still exist, now trading for some active trading firms takes place in smaller rooms where traders and model builders monitor applications that make the trading decisions and generate orders. These smaller automated trading rooms often generate many more orders than huge trading rooms where people do the trading. This change in approach has had a profound influence on the economics of trading, the volumes of orders and other messages generated, and the status of traders in the trading markets.

SALES TRADER

Sales trading involves managing agency orders for customers. In an agency trade, the customer calls or uses a routing facility to send an order through the broker/dealer to the market(s). The individual performing the function of sales trader for the broker/dealer may help in selecting where to send the order, choose the trading venue for execution, and manage the order if it is complicated until it is complete. Then the broker notifies the customer of the complete or partially complete order and allocates the executions to the customer's accounts in accordance with the customer's instructions (see Figure 4.3.1.1.3).

Sales traders have account responsibilities but handle orders. Agency orders they place directly with the markets. If the instruments in the customer's order are traded in a dealer environment, the sales trader may route the order to dealers within the firm or to wholesalers.

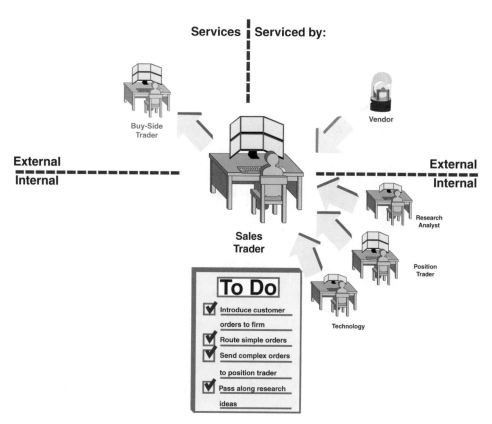

Figure 4.3.1.1.3   *Sales traders* handle orders; that is, execute simple orders and pass complex orders to position traders for customers of sell-side firms.

The process of managing a customer's agency orders was historically the role of sales traders and was a critical function in a trading operation. Now much of the order placement function has become automated. Institutions often send orders directly to markets using **direct market access** (DMA). Most markets throughout the world are beginning to permit DMA.

Firms provide software known as **execution management systems** (EMS) that customers can use for sophisticated order placement using a variety of different rule sets to control how, when, and in what quantities the order is sent to the market. Sales traders still play an important role in helping manage the execution of complex orders and blocks. A sales trader can quietly "shop" an order to other customers using a special message type known as an **indication of interest**. The trading process is described in more detail in Book 2, and indications of interest are described in Book 3.

RESEARCH ANALYST

Research analysts who work for sell-side firms have the responsibility of providing investment ideas to retail and institutional customers. The intent of these ideas is to encourage transactions. A research analyst may work with institutional sales personnel and traders to help evaluate instruments the customer may own or may be considering for purchase, and together they may tailor recommendations to the customer's special circumstances and needs (see Figure 4.3.1.1.4).

In addition, firms' research helps to create interest in companies that have been or could be investment-banking clients. Periodically sell-side firms are accused of providing information that is biased by investment-banking relationships. Although these failures to be objective in analyzing firms can create problems, most experts agree that the presence of competing analysts trying to generate information causes instrument prices to accurately reflect available financial information.

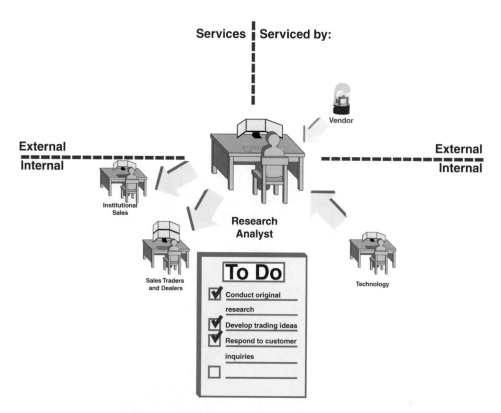

Figure 4.3.1.1.4 **Sell-side research analysts** generate investment ideas by analyzing companies and industries for retail and institutional customers.

Research analysts have responsibility for the industry or industries and instruments they cover and do not have direct customer or trading responsibilities. Analysts are often drawn into meetings with customers and may contact customers directly when they believe they have hot news customers need to know.

Dealer

A dealer is an individual or firm that makes money by buying and selling securities from its inventory to provide liquidity in the market and to profit from the process. A dealer is a principal and trades for his or her own benefit. The dealer makes money by buying securities at prices lower than the price at which he or she sells them (see Figure 4.3.1.2). Some dealers have special responsibility and authority granted by the market. These dealers are known as market makers.

A market maker is often required by the exchange or marketplace in which he or she is functioning to provide both the price at which he or she is willing to buy, known as a **bid**, and the price at which he or she is willing to sell, or the **offer**, along with a **size** for both the bid and the offer. The combination of a bid price with size and an offer price with size is known as a **quote**. The difference between the bid and offer price is known as the **spread**, and the spread is the theoretical profit the dealer makes from buying and selling. The quoting process is described in Book 2.

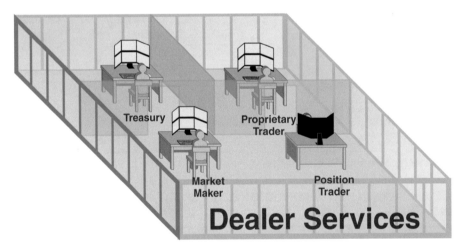

Figure 4.3.1.2   **Dealers** trade using the firm's own capital to provide immediacy and a guaranteed price for customers.

The role of dealer implies the broker/dealer is risking the firm's capital to service a customer, or acting as a principal for profit. If the firm does not employ its capital carefully and well, it may not be adequately compensated for its services and risks losing its capital.

POSITION TRADER

Any activity in which a dealer acquires a position in a security as a service for a customer with the firm's own money is referred to as **positioning**. Firms generally have very strict rules on when the firm can take a position and how large that position can be. Some firms insist that the firm carry no positions overnight (i.e., when the market is closed). This is referred to as being **flat**.

Position managers or **position traders** are responsible for a firm's positions in securities and for setting prices for securities sold to customers from the firm's inventory (see Figure 4.3.1.2.1). In the case of orders placed through exchanges and other dealers, the salesperson is responsible for the relationship with the customer, whereas the sales trader is responsible for placing the order and the relationship with "the Street"—exchanges and other dealers.

During this process, the position trader is responsible for what positions the firm is prepared to take—either long or short—and determines prices at which the firm is prepared to buy or sell. The position trader therefore determines how and when the firm commits its capital, for how long, and at what prices.

Often, in the process of helping a customer with an order, a firm will take a position to complete the order. When this occurs, the firm generally plans to

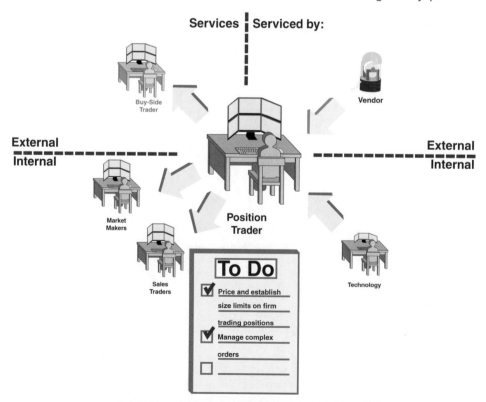

Figure 4.3.1.2.1 **Position traders** manage a firm's position, set guidelines for pricing dealer quotes, and set limits on the size of trading positions that can be acquired from the firm's customers.

liquidate the position as soon as possible, without a loss, it is hoped. These trades are known as ***accommodations*** and are done to help a customer, not as a continuous business activity. Other firms actively take positions as a business strategy, betting they can profit from the positions they take.

MARKET MAKERS

When a firm decides to continuously have positions as a business, the function is often known as market making, or dealing. A frequent reason that a firm might elect to be a market maker is to support an investment-banking customer's securities. By supporting the security, we mean that the broker/dealer will help to stabilize the price in the secondary market and make sure that investors in the security have a place where they can buy and sell the securities in all market conditions. Thus, the broker/dealer is providing liquidity for the securities of its investment-banking customers.

While a *dealer* is a general description for a firm that is risking its capital as a business strategy, some firms elect to be market makers. A *market maker* elects to make markets in specific instruments in continuing support of an exchange or trading venue. Figure 4.3.1.2.2 shows the specific case of a market maker but this applies to the more general case of a dealer as well.

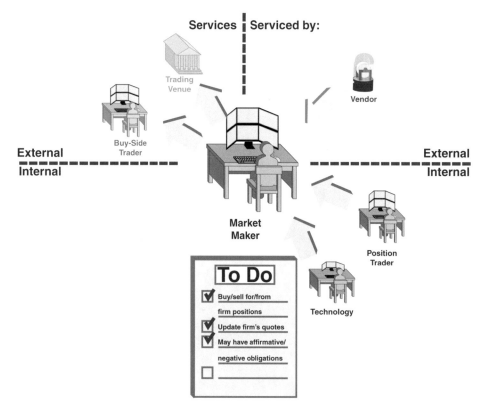

Figure 4.3.1.2.2   ***Market makers*** are a special case of the function of dealer who sometimes have special rights and obligations granted by markets in which they trade with all customers using the market.

Some marketplaces have a specific role for market makers, and firms that elect to perform this function must do so in accordance with the rules of the marketplace. This function is referred to variously as a **specialist**, market maker, **registered market maker**, or similar terms.

The role of market maker is recognized as an important function by regulators, and market makers often get access to information that is not widely disseminated. Also, market makers sometimes receive access to credit at highly favorable interest rates, and may be allowed to take larger positions than regular traders.[7]

PROPRIETARY TRADERS

Firms also choose to take advantage of the information they acquire from their activities in the markets to trade for profit with their own capital, often very aggressively. This is known as **proprietary trading** or **prop trading** (see Figure 4.3.1.2.3).

---

7 **Leverage** permits market makers to take large positions in their role of providing liquidity on demand. Without leverage, market makers would be limited by the amount of capital they could commit. Lenders find security positions attractive as collateral for loans because securities are more liquid than most other assets.

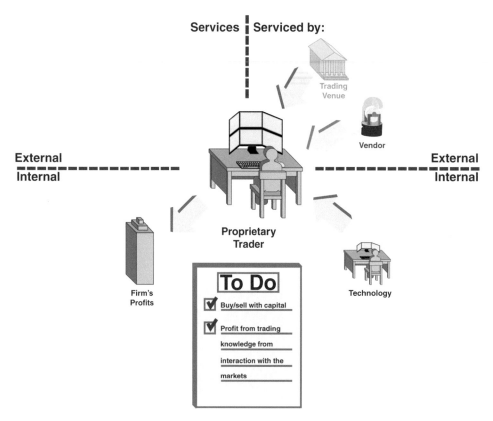

Figure 4.3.1.2.3   ***Proprietary traders*** speculate with a firm's own capital to profit in the market for a firm's direct profitability.

By being members of various marketplaces, broker/dealers can often trade for costs that are lower than those for retail and institutional customers. Also, broker/dealers, as a result of their normal trading activities, have access to information that permits them to trade with detailed information on supply and demand. Most other investors are not aware of this information because they are not constantly in the market. Having good information on supply and demand does not necessarily mean the broker/dealer knows more about the long-term prospects for the entity that issues the instrument, but information on supply and demand can permit the broker/dealer to make money on short-term price movements.

Broker/dealers are usually not permitted to use information on the specific trades by a customer to profit to the disadvantage of the customer, but the firm is usually not prevented from using its overall "sense of the market" to trade for its own account.

TREASURY

An important factor in the distinction between broker and dealer is the following: If a firm acts only as an agent, it is not required to have any excess capital other than that required for its operations. For a broker, "enough capital" means sufficient capital to cover the exposure created by its customers' transactions during the settlement process (see Figure 4.3.1.2.4).

If a firm is a dealer, it takes positions, and those positions require that the firm maintain reserves of capital to cover the positions it carries. The function within a sell-side firm that manages required capital is generally referred to as the ***treasury department***, or perhaps the treasury function in the ***capital markets division***.[8]

Managing this capital is an active process. When a firm has more capital than is required at any moment, the excess capital is put to work quickly. When the firm is short of capital, the treasury must arrange financing or liquidate positions to remain in compliance with its regulatory obligations.

---

8   From observation, "treasury" seems to be more of a banking term, whereas "capital markets" seems to be more commonly used by broker/dealers and investment banks.

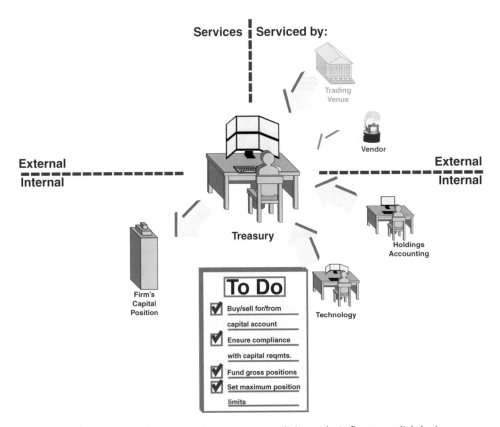

Figure 4.3.1.2.4 The **sell-side treasury** invests excess capital or seeks to finance capital shortages as necessary for regulatory requirements and/or risk management.

Whatever the situation that causes a firm to adjust its capital position, the process spans all the activities of the firm and must ensure that the firm has sufficient capital to remain in business. Capital adequacy may be under the oversight of exchanges acting as SROs and may be required by regulatory authorities as well. (The meaning and importance of capital to sell-side firms are considered again in detail in Book 4.)

One way to think of the difference between position trading and treasury is that position traders consider how to invest the firm's capital in trading operations, whereas the treasury department is concerned about managing capital in totality, including not only trading, but also other risky activities such as underwriting.

TRADERS TALKING

Periodically, there is a financial scandal, and among the revelations about what happened, quotes from traders during the course of the episode are made public. (The trading process is often recorded to help resolve disputes that arise about transactions.) The public revelations often reveal seemingly callous jokes and comments that become a source of outrage among politicians and the press. Although insensitive comments are regrettable, it must be remembered that trading is an extremely stressful activity. Anyone working around traders quickly becomes accustomed to jokes and a level of profanity. This behavior represents a means to relieve pressure more than true heartlessness.

Investment Banking

The process of helping companies raise new money is generally referred to as "investment banking" or **corporate finance** (see Figure 4.3.1.3). Investment banking for the most successful investment banks is one of the most profitable activities in the financial community. Investment banks become successful by having strong connections with large companies that need to raise capital frequently and/or in large amounts; the skills required to help customers choose the right instruments and determine the best price and timing to bring a new issue to the market; and the sales capabilities to distribute new issues when the instrument is ready for sale.

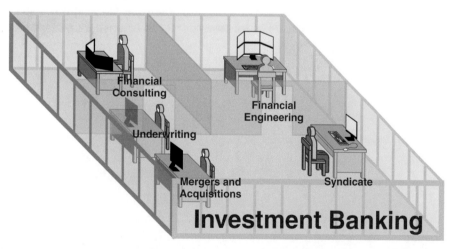

Figure 4.3.1.3   **Investment banking** refers to functions required to help commercial, government, and other customers raise capital in the primary market.

The relationship between a company that needs to raise capital and an investment bank often lasts for many years. The investment-banking cycle often begins with the investment bank providing advice on what types of securities are best and what timing is likely to raise the most money at the least cost to the firm.[9]

Major investment banks generally offer services to all types of companies and for all types of instruments. Nevertheless, most investment banks have specialties relating to either the type of instrument or the type of issuing company. For example, one firm may specialize in domestic equities issues and another in raising bonds and other types of instruments for city, provincial, state, or national governments.

Competition among investment banks is high, and banks strive to be known as the best investment bank. Publications such as *Institutional Investor, Euromoney,* and other magazines rank investment banks by type of underwriting (i.e., equities, corporate bonds, municipal underwritings, etc.).

These rankings are known as **league tables**, the term used for football (soccer) rankings in the United Kingdom. Positions in these tables help prospective investment-banking customers decide which underwriter to use. The league tables are very influential, and competition among investment banks to be at the top of the tables is intense.

FINANCIAL CONSULTING

An important service investment banks offer their corporate customers involves consulting to help determine the best financial structure (the mix of equities, bonds, and other financing instruments) for the corporation. The services also help the firm plan for the long-term mix of securities and rough timing horizon to keep the desired ratio of equity to debt. Although these services may involve fees, the long-run goal is to have the investment bank be the **lead underwriter** for the client's issues (see Figure 4.3.1.3.1).

---

9   This cost, known as the **cost of capital**, is described in more detail in Book 2.

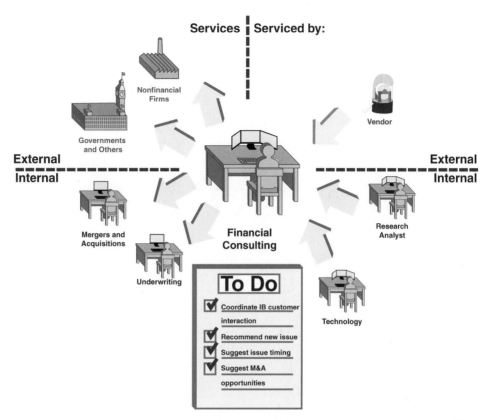

Services | Serviced by:

Nonfinancial
Firms

Governments
and Others

External
Internal

Vendor

External
Internal

Mergers and
Acquisitions

Research
Analyst

Underwriting

Financial
Consulting

To Do

☑ Coordinate IB customer
interaction

☑ Recommend new issue

☑ Suggest issue timing

☑ Suggest M&A
opportunities

Technology

Figure 4.3.1.3.1   ***Financial consulting*** helps investment-banking customers decide which types of securities to issue and when to issue them to support the customer's capital structure most effectively.

UNDERWRITING

Underwriting is the actual process that brings new instruments to market. Underwriting is the basic activity of investment banking, and most of the other functions support or feed underwriting (see Figure 4.3.1.3.2). Underwriting involves a multi-step process that has several variations described in detail in Book 2.

The underwriting process applies primarily to investment banks serving established companies. Another tier of investment banking focuses on smaller companies and those going public the first time. This often includes smaller investment banks that specialize in new companies raising money for the first time. These lower-tier underwritings are often done on a ***best efforts*** basis. Best efforts means that the underwriter does not guarantee a price for the underwriting and does not buy the entire issue from the company. Instead, the underwriter attempts to sell the securities at the best price possible and is paid by the firm for the selling effort.

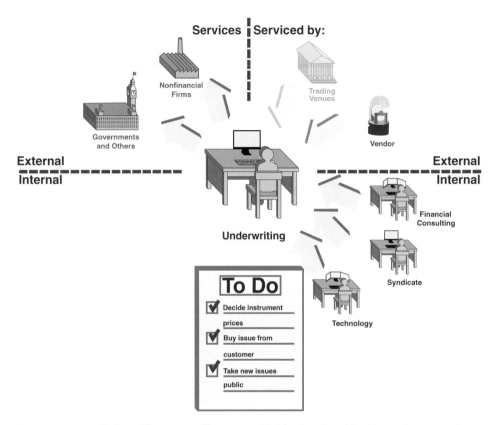

Figure 4.3.1.3.2   *Underwriting* manages the process of helping investment-banking customers create and distribute new securities that can be issued in the primary market.

SYNDICATION

The potential risks involved in underwriting securities have led to the process known as **syndication** (see Figure 4.3.1.3.3). The syndication function within an investment bank is responsible for managing and accounting for a group of other investment banks and broker/dealers known as a **syndicate**. Syndicates are assembled for each underwriting; however, continuing loose associations among potential syndicate members simplifies the process of assembling new syndicates.

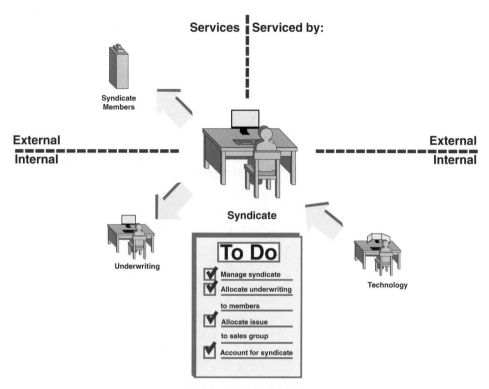

Figure 4.3.1.3.3   **Syndication** manages and accounts for the team (syndicate) of sell-side firms that help to underwrite new issues and distribute those issues to investors.

MERGERS AND ACQUISITIONS

Investment banks help their customers when the companies become interested in buying another company, merging with another company, or being acquired by another company. This activity for investment banking is commonly known as **mergers and acquisitions** (see Figure 4.3.1.3.4). When companies merge or acquire other companies, both parties hire investment bankers to help maximize the benefits or protect against possible harm from the transaction. The transactions can result in huge fees for the investment banks involved.

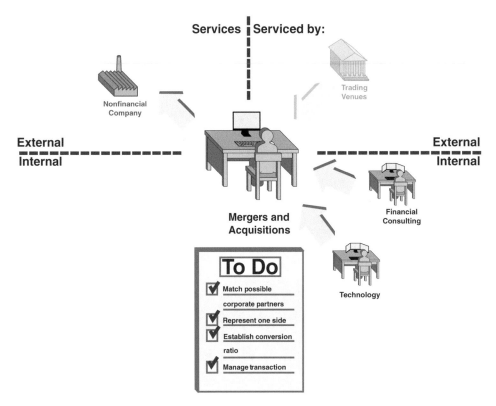

Figure 4.3.1.3.4 ***Mergers and acquisitions*** provides advice, financing, and trading services related to acquiring, being acquired by, or merging with other companies for investment-banking customers.

VALUABLE CUSTOMERS

Investment banking can be one of the most profitable parts of a sell-side firm. Firms such as utilities that raise money frequently have traditionally been highly prized as clients. This continues although, as we see in Book 2, new methods of raising funds are diminishing the role of investment banks for some large, well-known firms that raise capital frequently and can do so without much help.

Clients who actively engage in acquisitions are also highly prized by investment banks because of the fees they generate. Investment banks commonly suggest possible acquisition or merger candidates to their investment-banking clients and to other firms when they think a deal may make sense.

FINANCIAL ENGINEERING

Financial engineering is a term sometimes applied to the process of creating new financial instruments or new approaches to employing existing financial instruments (See Figure 4.3.1.3.5). Realistically, all investment-banking activities involve some "engineering," but what is generally meant by the term is the creation of new instruments. Complex derivatives are common products of these instrument-creation activities. In general, the term is applied to developing instruments with special characteristics to fit specific, unique financing or risk mitigation needs.

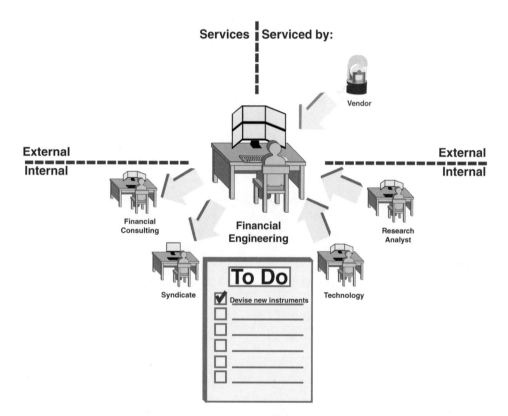

Figure 4.3.1.3.5 *Financial engineering* develops new investment and trading products to satisfy unique needs for investment-banking customers.

MIDDLE OFFICE

The middle-office departments of broker/dealers are responsible for managing all of the supporting activities directed to customers; that is, customer-side activities both to support the firm's customers directly as well as the functions required by regulators. Figure 4.3.2 shows the functions of the middle office for both retail and institutional customers.

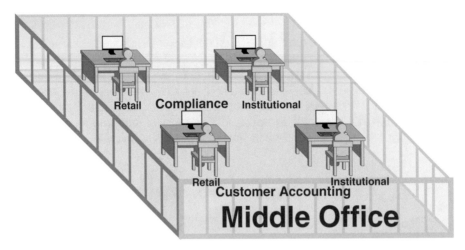

Figure 4.3.2   The **sell-side middle office** refers to functions that directly support the front office and/or customers of the broker/dealer.

Customer-Side Processes

Processing for customers requires two primary activities: managing positions in instruments and managing cash positions (see Figure 4.3.2.1). Accounting similar to that required for customers is also required for financial products that are packaged and resold to customers by the sell side. Customers have holdings, as do many financial products. What is unique is that financial products have holdings, but the packaged product may be among the holdings of customers in turn. We examine this topic in more detail in Book 3.[10]

---

10   While the specifics of customer processes for individuals and for institutions have different specifics, the primary purposes are similar. Therefore we will not repeat the general graphic.

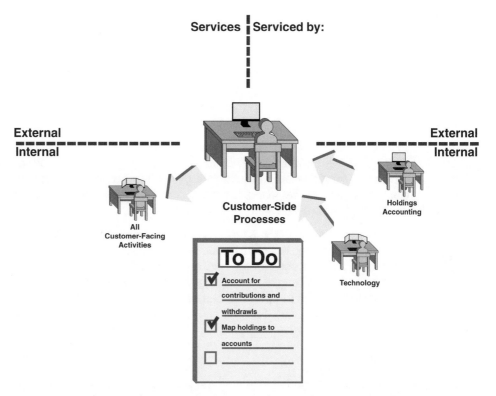

Figure 4.3.2.1 **Customer-Side processes** manage positions in instruments in addition to managing cash positions.

RETAIL

Customer processes for retail customers involve maintaining the count of all positions held in the customers' names. For each position, the firm must periodically value the position based on **official prices** for the instrument at the accepted time for the market where the instrument is traded, and report the combined value of all holdings to the customers. In addition to valuing holdings, the positions must be adjusted for what are known as capital changes. Capital changes occur when stocks split, when a stock dividend is declared, or when a bond matures or is called.

Customer reports were historically printed and mailed, but increasingly reporting is electronic through web pages.

INSTITUTIONAL

Institutional customers have requirements that are functionally similar to retail customers, but the details differ. Retail customer reports are presentations prescribed by regulation, and even when reports are presented electronically, the reports are designed for the customers to read. Institutional reporting is most often in electronic format and is passed from computers on the sell side to an institutional customer's computers for processing.

For institutional customers executing large orders through a broker/dealer, the broker/dealer takes responsibility for allocating executions back to the customers' internal accounts. Many different executions at different prices may be required to complete a large order. Moreover, a customer firm may have combined securities held in different internal (to the customer organization) accounts.

Combining orders from multiple accounts can reduce transaction costs and simplify order management for the buy-side trader. In the allocation process, the broker/dealer computes an average price for the total order and allocates both the average price and shares back to the original accounts within the customer firm. Because not all orders are fully completed, this process can be very complex. Trade allocation is so important that we have included it as one of the steps in the trade process. It is discussed in more detail in Book 2.

Compliance

Compliance in the financial markets includes three primary types of activities. First, firms and their officers are obligated to follow rules set down by regulators and may be subject to fines, sanctions, or criminal proceedings when those rules are violated. Second, customers place obligations on firms when the customers use a firm's services, and firms risk losing the customers and facing possible lawsuits if the customers' requirements are not met. Finally, most firms have strict internal procedures that all employees are expected to follow. The compliance departments of firms ensure that all regulatory, customer, and internal rules are followed (See Figure 4.3.2.2).[11]

RETAIL

Retail compliance is primarily focused around regulatory requirements that firms not sell products that are not suitable for individual groups of customers. **Suitability**

---

11   As with customer processes, compliance for individuals and for institutions differ in specifics but include similar general processes and the figure is not repeated.

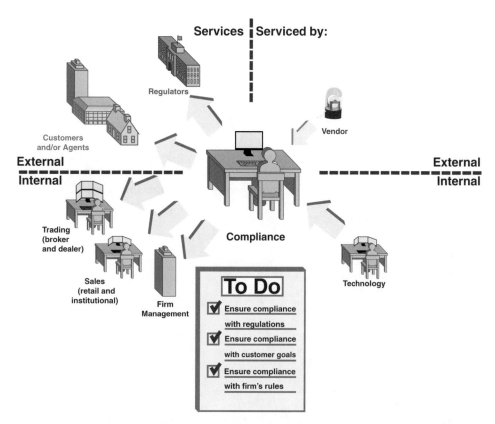

Figure 4.3.2.2 ***Sell-side compliance*** monitors the activities of the firm to ensure that those activities conform to the wishes and/or requirements of customers, regulators, and internal policies.

rules generally relate to whether the risk implicit in specific products or strategies is consistent with the customer's ability to understand the product and its risk, and whether the customer would be able to sustain potential losses that can be anticipated for the product or strategy. Retail compliance also ensures that the firm does not take unfair advantage of its customers as it tries to earn a profit.

INSTITUTIONAL

Institutions are generally considered able to protect themselves, so the nature of compliance is different. Many institutional investors are under the obligation to provide best execution for their customers, and under regulations, sell-side firms may be expected either to prove best execution or at least justify decisions on where orders were routed for execution. In addition, firms may be expected to help institutional customers enforce investment rules that forbid certain types of investments (e.g., liquor or gambling issues) or encourage others (e.g., environmentally conscious issues).

We describe the reporting process in more detail in Book 2 and the technology supporting the reporting process in Book 3. The overall process of compliance is described in Book 4.

BACKOFFICE

Backoffice functions include several street-side activities needed to settle trades and involve interacting with marketplaces, clearing corporations, banks, and agents for customers such as custodians (see Figure 4.3.3). The backoffice is charged with managing the settlement process to exchange money from the buyer with instrument ownership from the seller. The backoffice must also monitor the trading positions of the firm and assess the risk created by the firm's **capital commitment**.

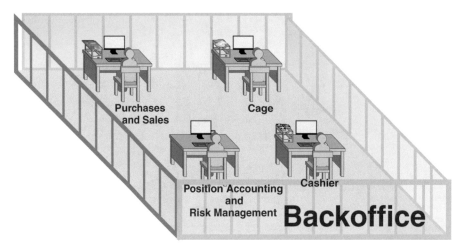

Figure 4.3.3   The **sell-side backoffice** refers to activities of broker/dealers related to trading and other activities with the Street.

Beyond agreeing to the details of an execution, the buyer's broker must make certain its customer provides necessary funds to complete settlement. Likewise, the seller's broker must ensure that either the physical certificates are present, or delivery instructions are issued to the depository or custodian in time to be presented for settlement. If, for any reason,the customer does not produce the funds or instruments for settlement, the broker/dealer is still required to deliver the funds or instruments even if they must be borrowed to do so. The broker/dealer can then resolve the problem with its customer, but settlement is accomplished in spite of the customer's failure.

Three primary functions comprise the sell-side backoffice. These terms may differ from firm to firm, but the functions are necessary. Firms must manage the processes following a trade, monitor positions in instruments, and control cash. In addition, those firms that create internal positions (i.e., invest the firm's own capital) must manage those positions and the risks involved.

Purchases and Sales

The **purchases and sales** (P&S) group is charged with receiving all **trade reports** from markets, matching all orders from customers and internal accounts with the trade reports (see Figure 4.3.3.1). The department must resolve any difficulties with the execution so that both the buyer and seller agree on the details of the trade. When physical trading occurs involving either trading on an exchange floor or trades completed over the phone, the details of the transactions must be verified and agreed on by both the buyer and seller or their broker/dealers before settlement can take place.

P&S must make sure that the customer has provided any funds or instructions necessary for settlement, and if the customer fails to provide necessary settlement information or funds, the P&S department must make sure that alternate arrangements are made to successfully settle the trade. Customer failures are sent back to customer-facing departments who are best positioned to resolve the problem and who will have the failed transaction on the department's **profit and loss** (P&L) account until the problem is resolved.

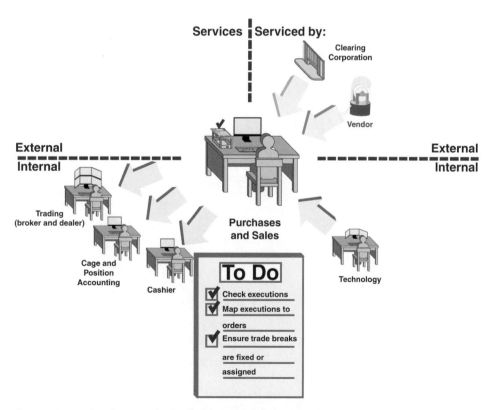

Figure 4.3.3.1   **Purchases and sales** tracks trades after execution, fixes or assigns trade breaks, and controls the clearing process for orders from customers and internal accounts.

In automated markets, there should be no problems with the details of the trade. Whatever order information is put into the automated execution system is what will settle. The parties to a trade can make a mistake in entering the information, but once entered, the information is acted upon as entered.

The Cage

The **cage** is responsible for managing security positions for a firm (see Figure 4.3.3.2). This task includes controlling securities positions that must be delivered during the period prior to settlement (for sales) and receiving securities positions following settlement (for purchases). In addition, the cage must manage **segregated** securities that are pledged for loans and for other purposes, arrange for securities that must be borrowed or that are available for loan, and manage customer holdings that are maintained in **street name**.

The term "cage" is a relic that comes from the time when secure rooms were used to temporarily house physical certificates at broker/dealer firms just prior to or following settlement. (Prior to depositories, long-term storage of certificates occurred at custodian banks.) The modern cage function tracks ownership records for instruments in the firm's account, for customer holdings left in street name or in the customer's name that are managed by the firm, and for instruments pledged for loans and for other segregated holdings.

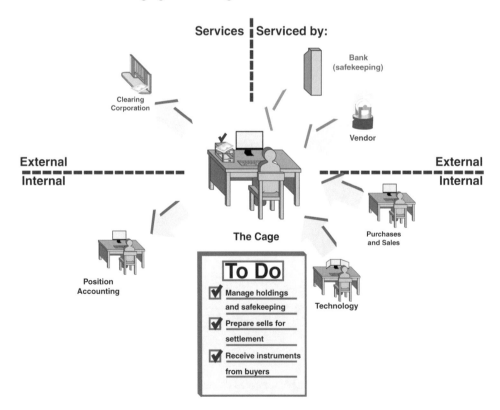

Figure 4.3.3.2   The **cage** controls instrument positions for customers and the firm's own accounts.

Cashier

The **cashier** at a broker/dealer is the department that manages the cash funds required for securities settlement (see Figure 4.3.3.3). In addition, the cashier is responsible for managing cash and/or short-term securities demanded to meet **margin calls** from an exchange or clearing corporation.

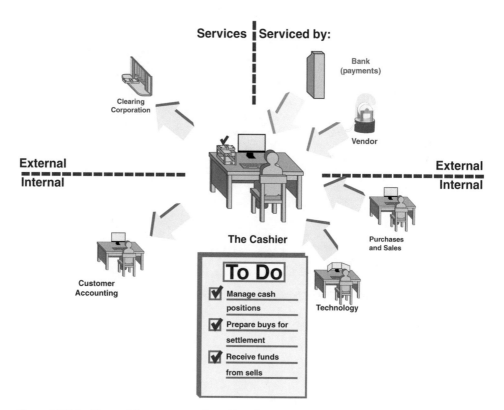

Figure 4.3.3.3 The **cashier** manages cash positions for customers and the firm.

Position Accounting and Risk Management

For firms that position securities as a part of their normal operations, accounting for the positions created is necessary both to manage the firm's capital and to control the risks that positions create. Position accounting supports the treasury function and position trading described previously (see Figure 4.3.3.4).

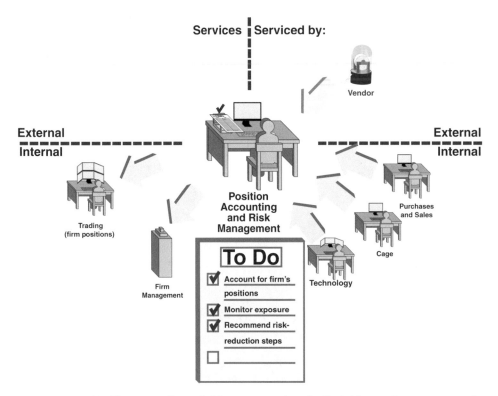

Figure 4.3.3.4 **Position accounting and risk management** monitor the holdings and assess exposure to losses in positions controlled by the firm.

TECHNOLOGY

Sell-side firms have sophisticated needs for technology (systems, data, and networks). Technology requirements can come from three sources: an in-house technology staff can create needed services; needs can be outsourced either to correspondents (described previously) that are registered as broker/dealers or vendors that operate the technology for the firm; or the technology can be purchased or leased and operated internally.[12] We describe technology in more detail in Book 3.

---

12 As with the buy side, sell-side technology is not a part of the front office, the middle office, or the backoffice. Technology supports the entire firm.

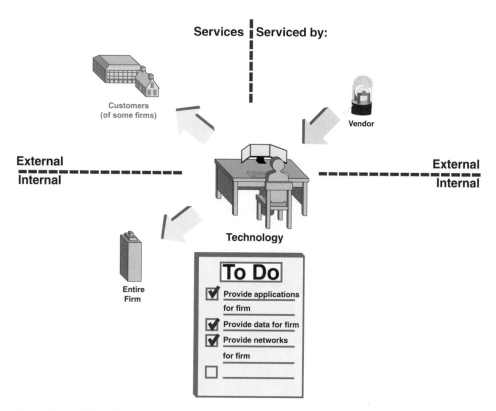

Figure 4.3.4 **Sell-side technology** constructs and/or purchases systems, data, and networks that are required for the business activities for all functions within the firm.

OTHER FUNCTIONS

A number of specialty functions such as **stock loan and borrow** are required by some broker/dealers but are not required by all. We explore some of these functions in Book 2. Some functions such as **reorganization**, or "reorg," are necessary and indirectly related but not directly involved in trading and are not considered in these books.

There are also countless other activities required to manage the day-to-day business of a broker/dealer (just like any other economic other entity), such as human resources, purchasing of needed services, accounts payable and receivable, property management, and the like. These services are important but are not unique to the trading markets and are not investigated here.

Exchanges and Other Marketplaces 4

Exchanges and other marketplaces facilitate trading and may perform other services as well. Trading venues all perform the functions required to execute a trade. For example, markets manage trading, enforce their regulations, manage members and listings, and collect and sell the data created in the market. Figure 4.4 shows the functions required for exchanges and other trading venues.

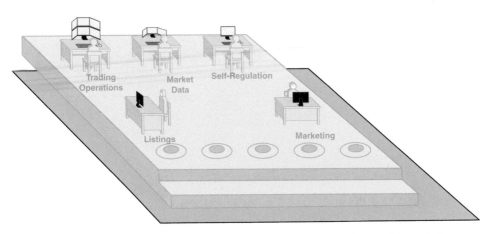

Figure 4.4   **_Exchanges and other marketplaces_** match buy and sell orders from participants in the trading markets.

TRADING OPERATIONS

The trading operations department manages the trading activities, whether on the floors, among linked dealers, or in electronic marketplaces (see Figure 4.4.1). Personnel responsible for overseeing trading must handle the processes at the start of each trading session, provide special information required by those permitted to trade, monitor the ongoing trading process for possible problems, correct any problems that occur, manage the end-of-trading-session processes, and handle any processes required following the close of trading.

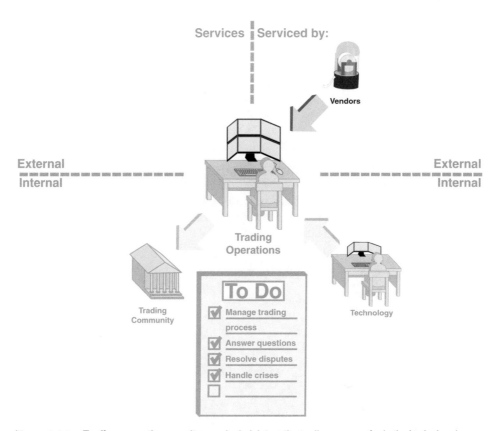

Figure 4.4.1   ***Trading operations*** monitors and administers the trading process for both physical and electronic markets.

The trading operations personnel ensure that the rules of the exchange are enforced and adjudicate disputes that arise among traders who directly participate with the trading venue. Personnel responsible for managing compliance with the rules of the venue may be employees of the exchange, and/or they may be actual traders with the extra responsibility to monitor trading and settle disputes.

SELF-REGULATION

From the beginning of trading, marketplaces have understood that the competition among traders could result in problems, and when the problems become intense, the market itself can be threatened. Therefore, most markets have rules that serve the joint purpose of encouraging more trading and also protecting the market in the event of a problem. More recently, national regulators have begun to actively monitor trading to ensure that investors and traders who are not professionals or who do not participate directly in the markets are protected (see Figure 4.4.2).

Much of the regulation of the operation of markets is accomplished by what is known as "self-regulation." Self-regulation implies that the regulations of the market itself are used to manage trading. Self-regulation is often carried on under the oversight of national regulators, and often regulations must be approved after a governmental review, sometimes including public comment.

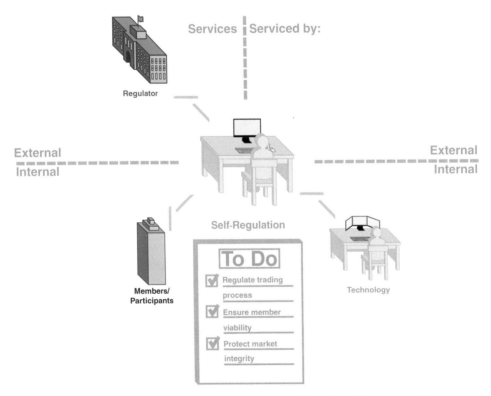

Figure 4.4.2   **Self-regulation** monitors activities and participant financial stability to ensure fairness and the protection of participants within the market.

A department (or departments) within the market center is responsible for managing all areas of regulation affecting the market. Usually, a special group monitors trading activities using sophisticated tools that are able to examine trade-by-trade activity and search for questionable patterns. The market may be responsible for making sure that member firms have adequate capital and observe settlement requirements. Rules may define the minimum requirements for companies listed on an exchange. (Listing is described in the next section.)

Derivatives exchanges monitor trading, membership, and settlement as well, but derivatives rules are different from those for equities. Other departments work with customers, trading operations, and the marketing group to craft rules and pricing that encourages the use of the market. Most incentives to trade—both pricing for services (such as trading fees) and changes in trading mechanics to attract more trading—are implemented by creating new rules. Even changes that result from new technology applications are enabled by changes in the rules.

LISTINGS

The *listings department* actively solicits companies to list on the exchange (see Figure 4.4.3). Listing involves meeting certain criteria that generally involve measures such as the number of shareholders, amount of active trading, and minimum requirements for public disclosure of financial results.

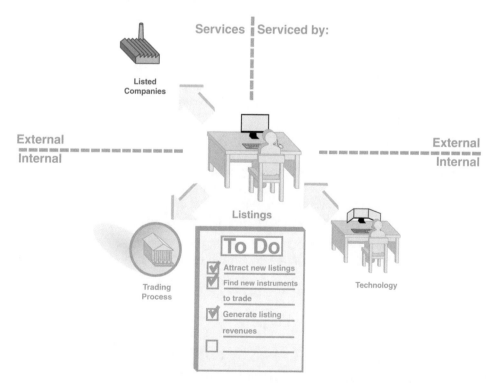

Figure 4.4.3 *Listings* supports and monitors firms that have instruments traded on the market.

Exchanges compete actively for listings. Companies want to be listed on prestigious exchanges where their securities will be actively traded. When a company first issues securities to the public through an **initial public offering** (IPO), it usually seeks to find the most attractive marketplace where its securities can be listed. Listing requirements can include minimums for market capitalization, shares outstanding, and number of shareholders.

Historically, companies would have only one exchange listing, and once a company elected to list on an exchange, it would stay there for a long while. More recently, companies that have global operations list in more than one country. Moreover, exchanges actively compete to take listings away from other markets.

Derivatives exchanges do not have listed companies. Instead, they create contracts that are traded in their market and have departments that engage in research and development for new contracts.

Options exchanges typically have many contracts on securities that are publically traded. Because the securities that underlie the contracts are fungible instruments, the same contract may be traded on multiple exchanges. Many competing options exchanges trade the same contracts.

An exception can be options on indexes. Because the company that creates the index usually copyrights that index, the index is often licensed to a single options exchange that buys exclusive rights to trade options based on the index. Because, except for indexes, options exchanges trade identical contracts, competition among options markets is based on **trading mechanics** and the cost of trading.

By contrast, futures exchanges copyright their contracts, and although markets sometimes have contracts on the same commodity or instrument, the contracts created by different exchanges usually have different details. This means that competition among futures exchanges involves contract terms as well as mechanics and fees.

MARKET DATA

The sale of the data produced from trading is an important source of revenues for exchanges. Not only is the revenue from the data important, but also market data is a kind of advertising that draws traders to the market and provides the input needed for traders to price new orders (see Figure 4.4.4).

Two primary data sets comprise market data. Quotes are potential trades that may happen if someone is interested in the price and quantity of instruments

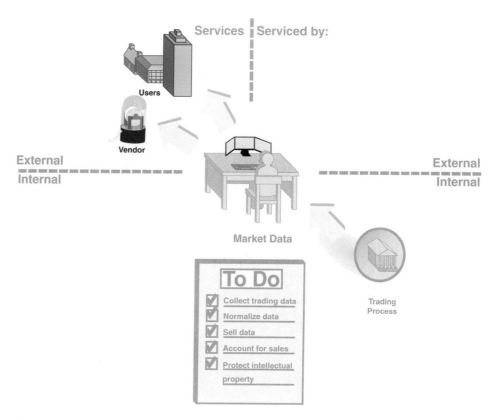

Figure 4.4.4   ***Market data*** captures, sells, and distributes information about trading and other activities within the market.

being offered for sale. Last sale information is a record of those transactions that have already occurred. Both quotes and last sale data have two components: the price of the quote or transaction, and the number or quantity of the instrument that is available for sale (quote) or that was sold (last sale).

With the advent of automated trading and widespread interconnectivity, exchanges are beginning to add a number of specialty products, including historical price information and very fast access to the market for traders. The business of market data is addressed in more detail in Book 3.

MARKETING

Exchanges have always promoted themselves and their trading capabilities to encourage potential traders to trade on the exchange (see Figure 4.4.5). Those exchanges that have become publically traded companies now focus very intently on marketing their services. Marketing includes developing pricing strategies to attract users, developing new products, promoting products, and selling services directly.

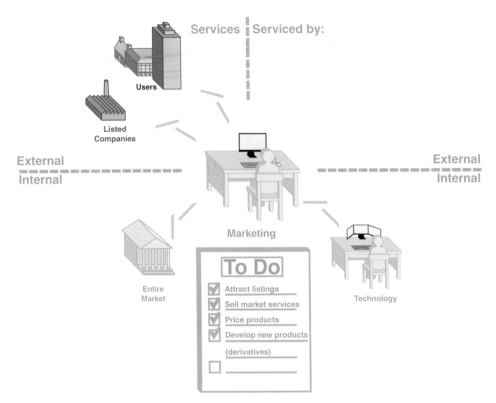

Figure 4.4.5   **Marketing** promotes the services of the firm to participants and others who use or are interested in the services of the market.

THE CHICAGO BOARD OPTIONS EXCHANGE

The marketing departments of exchanges in general and of derivatives exchanges in particular are responsible for constructing new products. Usually, this process entails developing new contracts. Perhaps the all-time success was the creation of the Chicago Board Options Exchange (CBOE) by the Chicago Board of Trade (CBOT) in 1973. The CBOT took an infrequently traded, bespoke financial product—puts and calls—and applied the standardized contract terms and features of the futures markets to puts and calls.

The result was the creation of a highly successful new trading market. Substantially every large national market now has a traded-options exchange, and many markets have competing trading venues for options. Other very successful products include the currency futures markets created by the Chicago Mercantile Exchange, which began futures trading on financial instruments, and exchange-traded funds created by the American Stock Exchange.

TECHNOLOGY

Markets are highly dependent on technology, particularly as trading is increasingly automated. Even floor-based markets require a complex technology infrastructure to move orders to the places where trades occur and then route notification of executions back to the participants. Some markets are in the business of providing technology services to both customers and other markets.

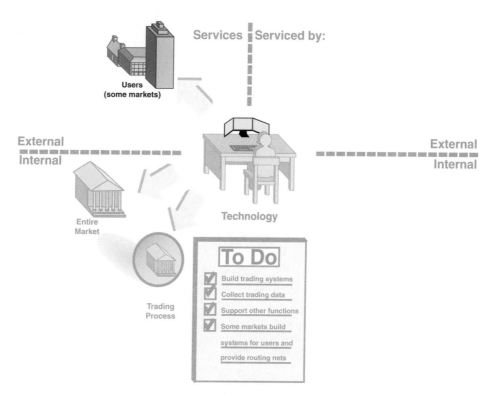

Figure 4.4.6 **Market technology** builds or acquires the systems, data, and networks required by the activities of the trading venues.

A number of functions are required in support of the trading markets. In many markets, these functions require the entity be registered as a special-purpose organization such as a commercial bank, clearing corporation, or depository (all described in Part 1 on entities). Depositories and clearing corporations are organized in many different ways in different national markets, and there is great flux in Europe at the time of this writing. Here, we describe the functions required whatever the organizational form (see Figure 4.5).

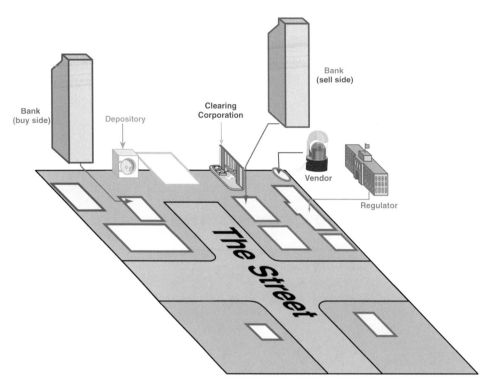

Figure 4.5 **Support** refers to the entities and functions required required to facilitate capital raising and to monitor and support trading in the primary and secondary markets.

CLEARING

When a trade is done on an exchange, with a dealer, or on an alternative trading venue, the parties must exchange money for the instrument involved in the trade. The processes that occur from the moment the trade is consummated to the moment that the instruments are exchanged for payment we define as **clearing and settlement**. Although the terms are subject to different interpretations, we define "clearing" as the process from the point of the trade until the exchange of money for value (see Figure 4.5.1).

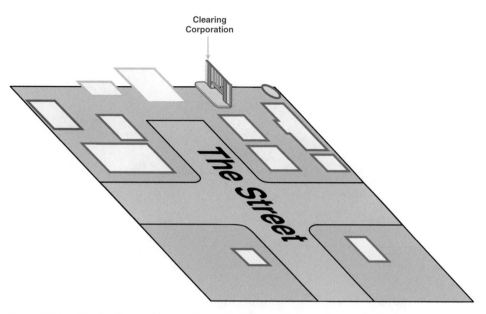

Figure 4.5.1   **Clearing** fixes problems and ensures settlement for secondary-market trades.

The purpose of clearing is twofold. First, any problems that occur in the trading process are resolved during the clearing process. Second, the clearing process provides a guarantee to both parties to the trade that settlement will occur.

SETTLEMENT

We define **settlement** as the exchange of money for the instruments. The settlement of transactions involves the buyer presenting money and the seller providing the instruments (see Figure 4.5.2). In most marketplaces, the form of the payment, condition of the instruments, and location for the exchange are carefully defined. The funds must be in acceptable form, meaning immediate or next-day value. Securities are most often delivered electronically, but if physical delivery is required, the instruments must be assigned in such a way as to satisfy the transfer requirements of the market.

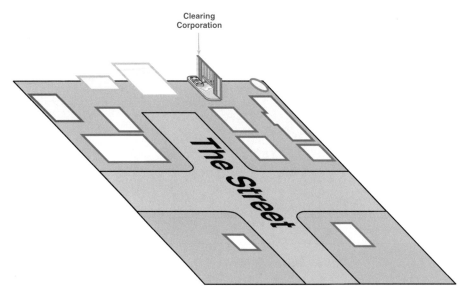

Figure 4.5.2 **Settlement** is the exchange of ownership for money for secondary-market trades.

BANKS

Many banks have investment banking and other brokerage subsidiaries. However, commercial banks play important roles in the trading markets, as was noted in Part 1 on entities (see Figure 4.5.3).

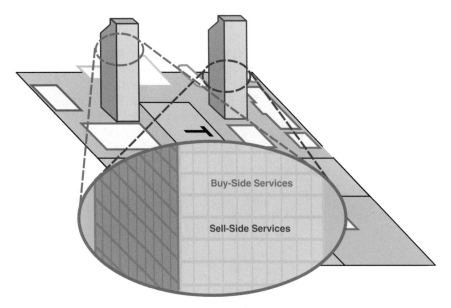

Figure 4.5.3 **Banks** provide financing, payments services, and warehouse holdings for both the buy and the sell sides.

Buy Side

Banks provide important functions for investing institutions both by processing funds transfers during trading and as custodian for the assets of institutional investors (see Figure 4.5.3.1). As custodian for the buy side, the bank must work with the market and the buy-side customers to affirm that the buy-side customers **know** the trades completed in the market and the reported details are correct. This permits the trade to be ready for settlement. The bank supporting the seller must prepare to deliver securities on settlement, and the bank working on behalf of the buyer must prepare securities for delivery.

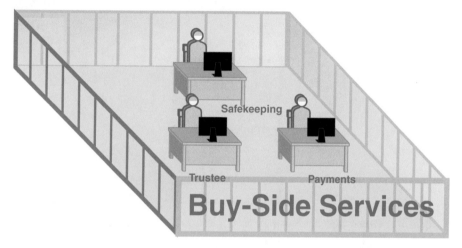

Figure 4.5.3.1 **Banks** provide payments, custody, and trustee services for the buy side.

PAYMENTS

Commercial banks have access to international and domestic funds transfer mechanisms and therefore are important for trading (see Figure 4.5.3.1.1). The buyer of traded instruments must instruct his or her bank to make payments to the seller at the location required for settlement. The buyer's bank debits the buyer's account and transfers the funds to a settlement account at the clearing corporation in most cases.

Likewise, the seller's bank must receive the funds delivered at settlement and credit the seller's account to reflect the change. Support for trading represents an important line of business for banks, and large money-center banks have whole departments set up to facilitate trading.

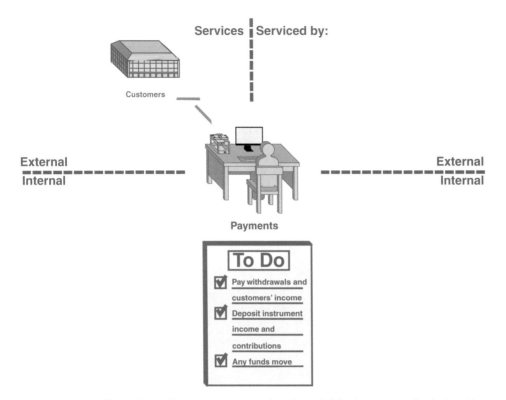

Figure 4.5.3.1.1   **Payments** provide cash management, deposits, and obligation payments for the buy side.

In addition to trading, banks pay interest and dividends to investors. As agents for companies that issue securities, banks make these payments in accordance with the terms of the instruments. This means they not only have to issue the payments as checks or drafts, but also must have access to and maintain the names and addresses of the **beneficial owners** of the securities or their agents.

SAFEKEEPING

Banks have traditionally provided storage for valuables including securities. Prior to the creation and widespread use of the central depositories described earlier, banks were the place where securities were held and where settlement occurred (see Figure 4.5.3.1.2). Now, banks are often direct participants in the depositories and handle electronic securities movement on behalf of broker/dealer and institutional investor clients.

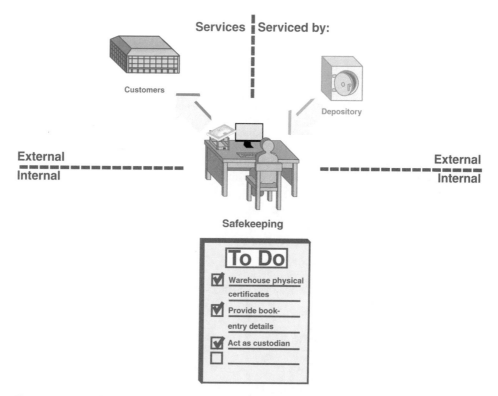

Figure 4.5.3.1.2 **Safekeeping** manages instrument holdings, acts as a custodian, and provides access to depositories for the buy side.

Where there is a depository, banks manage records of holdings of their customers, largely institutional investors and broker/dealers. The bank has positions for all its customers in the bank's account at the depository. When a security is purchased or sold, positions in the depository switch from the seller's bank to the buyer's bank. In turn, the bank maps its total holdings to the actual ownership by its customers.

Most securities are now **immobilized** in depositories or are dematerialized, as explained in Book 2. Some banks may still manage vestige certificates. Moreover, banks acting in the role of custodian still manage the bookkeeping records for their individual and institutional customers. Positions held at a bank for an owner may be used as a basis of loans, and regulatory authorities recognize instruments deposited with banks as legitimate repositories for the portfolios of mutual funds and other pooled investments. Custodians instruct depositories to initiate changes in ownership; to separate or segregate securities for special purposes, such as collateral for a loan; and to collect payments for customers from interest and dividends.

TRUSTEE

As we have noted, a trustee is a special function performed by banks, and in some cases lawyers or solicitors. Banks are the exclusive providers of several specific trustee functions. Banks are trustees for some corporate securities, ensuring the investors in the securities that the covenants in the instrument agreement are maintained. Banks maintain positions in securities that are used for collateral either for loans or trading instruments (see Figure 4.5.3.1.3).

For example, options may be written against positions in underlying securities positions held in a bank. In some national markets, traded instruments known as **depository receipts** are based on securities held in trust by banks in the same or other national markets, and those trust positions serve as the basis for trading. For example, a German electronics company might have an **American Depository Receipt** (ADR) traded in the United States. For this to occur, shares of the company are held in trust at a bank to back the ADR.

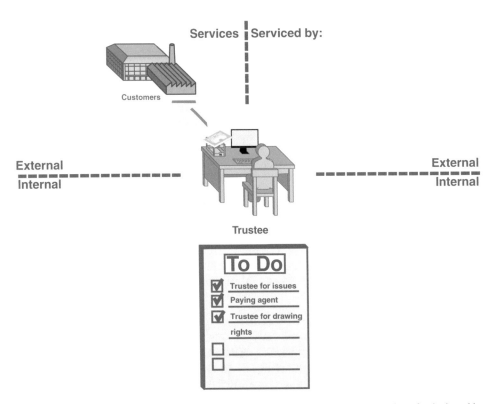

Figure 4.5.3.1.3   **Trustees** provide fiduciary services to instrument issuers and some products for the buy side.

Sell Side

Banks perform tasks for the sell side that are similar to those offered to the buy side as well as others that are different (see Figure 4.5.3.2). Banks also provide safekeeping services for sell-side firms, serving as the intermediary between the broker/dealer and the depository, and banks handle funds transfers. Banks provide an important financing role offering short-term credit to finance sell-side positions and facilitate **securities lending**.[13]

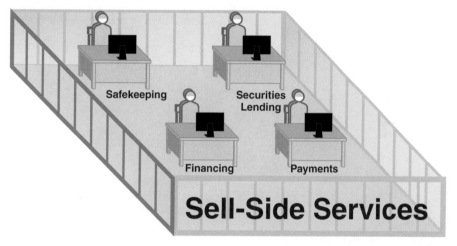

Figure 4.5.3.2 **Banks** provide financing, payments, securities lending, and safekeeping for the sell side.

PAYMENTS

As is true for the buy side, banks are required by the sell side to make the payments required for trading (see Figure 4.5.3.2.1). Banks move money as instructed by their sell-side customers for a variety of purposes. Because the margins in trading as both agent and dealer are so thin, sell-side firms have become very adept at managing their cash positions, and their banks facilitate their cash management.

---

13 Broker/dealers can also lend securities, but in their role in trading and dealing most often borrow securities. We did not show securities lending as a separate function for the sell side.

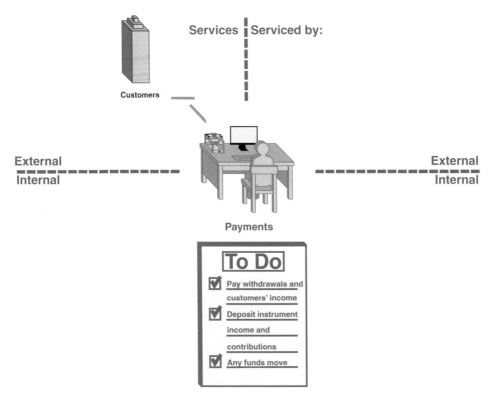

Services | Serviced by:

Customers

External — Internal

External — Internal

Payments

To Do
- ☑ Pay withdrawals and customers' income
- ☑ Deposit instrument income and contributions
- ☑ Any funds move

Figure 4.5.3.2.1 **Payments** handles cash management, deposits, payments, and other cash transactions for the sell side.

FINANCING MARKET OPERATIONS

One of the most important functions that a bank performs is to lend funds to broker/dealers to support their trading positions, and allow the firms to maintain sufficient capital as required by counterparties and/or regulators (see Figure 4.5.3.2.1).

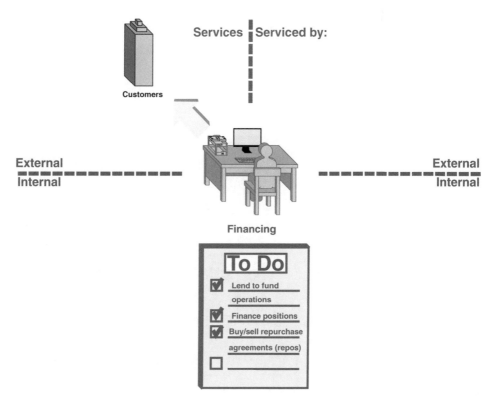

Figure 4.5.3.2.2   *Financing* supports internal capital, enabling larger trading positions and more secure post-trade positions for the sell side.

SECURITIES LENDING

Although most banking activity involves lending money or capital to broker/dealers, banks may also be involved in the process of securities lending (see Figure 4.5.3.2.3). Securities lending occurs for a variety of reasons. If a customer fails to provide securities required for settlement, the broker/dealer acting as agent may have to borrow securities to make delivery. If the broker/dealer or a customer **sells short**, the broker/dealer must borrow securities to enable the transaction. In each of these situations, the bank acting as custodian may furnish securities to be loaned, provided the owner of the position grants the bank permission.

Finally, the bank may manage securities pledged for a stock loan that are usually held in a segregated account at a depository on behalf of its trading-markets

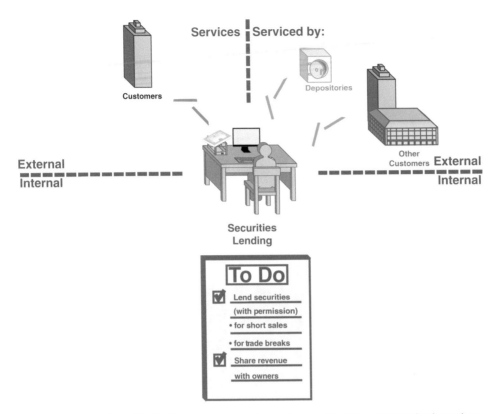

Figure 4.5.3.2.3   *Securities lending* lends instruments (mostly securities) from accounts that have given permission to other accounts for short sales and to cover fails to deliver for the sell side.

customers. As in other types of loans, securities loaned generate interest revenues for the owner of the position and fees for the bank.

SAFEKEEPING

As with the buy side, banks often maintain securities positions directly where there is no depository, and banks provide access to depositories where they exist. Banks maintain the records of holdings in either situation for their sell-side customers (see Figure 4.5.3.2.4).

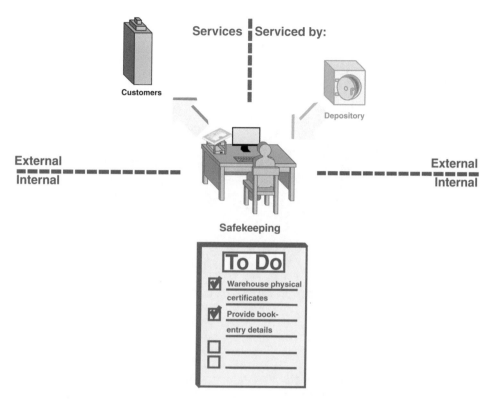

Figure 4.5.3.2.4 *Safekeeping* serves as a warehouse for instrument holdings and provides access to depositories for the sell side.

VENDORS

We use the term "vendor" to mean organizations that provide technology and other support that does not involve being registered as a financial entity of the types described in Part 1. Much of this support involves technology. Functions within vendor organizations include content creation and acquisition; service development, maintenance, and support; technical infrastructure development and maintenance; sales and customer support; and the accounting, administration, invoicing, and ***intellectual property*** protection required to provide services to customers (see Figure 4.5.4).

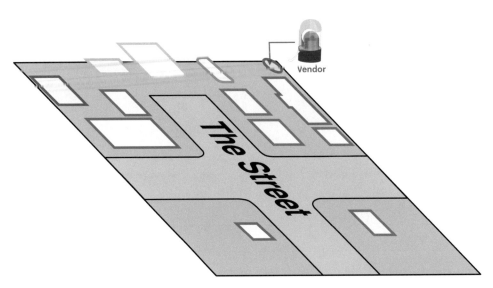

Figure 4.5.4   **Vendors** provide systems, data, and networks to participants on the Street.

REGULATORS

Regulators, whether an outgrowth of national governments or self-regulation, must oversee the markets and some or all of the entities operating in the markets (see Figure 4.5.5). Typically there are functions within each regulator that are focused on each different type of regulated entity, a regulator for the market itself, an enforcement division charged with prosecuting infractions of rules, and a body charged with creating new rules and interpreting existing rules for new or unclear situations.

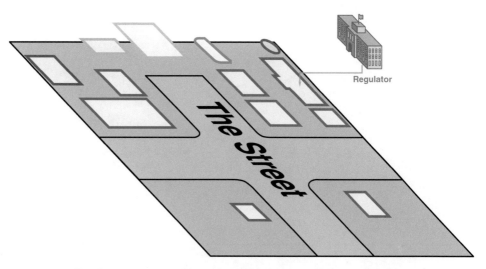

Figure 4.5.5 **Regulators** oversee activities and participants to ensure fairness, efficiency, and financial stability in the trading markets.

Education 6

Before ending this part, we briefly discuss the types of education required for different functions with the caveat that generalizations about education and background are subject to many exceptions and counterexamples. One generalized statement can be made without qualification, however. Over time, all jobs in the trading markets require increasing levels of education. Forty years ago, individuals with only a high school education filled many if not most jobs in the backoffice.

Now a majority of those in the industry probably have at least some college although many people earn degrees while working. Now most front-office functions require at least a degree and many, such as portfolio management, investment banking, investment research, and some types of trading, are dominated by MBAs. Law degrees are common in certain functions, and a number of PhDs can be found in some of the more esoteric jobs. For many functions in the front office, just having an MBA may not be enough. Many front-office functions demand top-ranked students from prestigious schools.

Forty years ago, few firms had technology departments, and those departments that did exist were staffed by people without degrees who had learned to program or gained communications skills in trade schools and the military. Now most firms have complex technology organizations staffed by engineers and technicians with degrees in science and engineering, many with advanced degrees. It is reasonable to expect this trend to continue as the business becomes more complex.

Many of the most prestigious investment-banking firms prefer to recruit only at the most prestigious business schools. Many universities and colleges now have specialties in the trading markets. Indeed, many schools have mock-trading rooms where students can learn the business in a pitch-perfect simulated environment. Universities sponsor seminars where industry professionals return to tell students about life in the real world. Firms also sponsor internships that permit students to get a taste for work in the markets before they leave school.

Most law schools have specialties aimed at securities law and regulation. Graduates work for industry firms, law firms with securities law practices, and regulators. There is active movement of lawyers among these three groups as specialists in securities law build their careers.

Some consulting and accounting firms also have practices devoted to the trading markets. As with law firms, industry professionals often move back and forth between line jobs in the industry and supporting entities as they develop their skills.

In the sections that follow, we do not make distinctions among the buy side, sell side, and supporting functions for the most part. Similar skills are required for each, and many people move back and forth among the industry groups.

EDUCATION

Portfolio managers most often come from business schools, and particularly graduate programs. Those managers that engage in quantitative investing may have engineering or scientific degrees if modeling is an important part of their investment style. Even though prospective managers may have advanced degrees, most firms put them into training and apprentice programs before they are permitted to make investment decisions on their own.

Buy-side traders often come from jobs on the sell side. Sell-side firms often have strong training programs and employees gain valuable experience that helps in the role of buy-side trader. Many traders have MBAs, but not all.

DEALERS FROM THE EAST END

Up until the 1980s, many senior dealers in the City of London were "cockneys" from London's East End. The theory was that education hampered a person's ability to make fast decisions. We were once entertained in the late 1970s by a floor trader on one of the Chicago futures exchanges who described with glee how professors would come to the pits with family money and trading theories only to be wiped out and return to the classroom. The disdain for education has passed.

Most trading operations actively seek academics to help in developing trading strategies; however, the late Fischer Black, co-creator of the Black/Scholes model, famously stated: "Markets look a lot less efficient from the banks of the Hudson than from the banks of the Charles."* (Black had moved to Goldman Sachs in New York from an academic post at the Massachusetts Institute of Technology in Boston.)

---

*Peter Bernstein. *Against the Gods: The Remarkable Story of Risk* (New York: John Wiley & Sons, Inc., 1996).

Historically, traders were successful because of personal traits more than education. However, almost all traders now have degrees, and many have advanced degrees. Sales and trading are more a function of interpersonal skills (sales) and ability to perform under intense pressure (trading) than knowledge that can be easily taught. A notable exception is quantitative trading employing models where degrees in computer science and mathematics are critical.

Research analysts often have advanced degrees, many in finance or accounting. They need to have good skills in financial analysis and the ability to write and communicate with portfolio managers, sales personnel, and customers.

As we noted previously, education is extremely important for investment bankers. Investment-banking departments usually have a mix of lawyers and people with advanced degrees in finance. Jobs in investment banking are both extremely prestigious and extremely well paid. Competition for the jobs is intense, and successful candidates are usually top students who come from the best business and law schools.

Account managers and sales personnel need interpersonal skills more than formal education. An exception to this is in trust accounts where tax lawyers often serve in the account management department because of the tax implications of trust and estate accounts.

EDUCATIONAL REQUIREMENTS

The diversity of functions in the middle and backoffice make generalizations about educational requirements difficult, and there are too many different functions to permit us to cover them all. Most middle-office and backoffice professionals have degrees although many people earn undergraduate and graduate degrees while working and taking courses at night. In fact, many financial centers have universities and colleges or university extension centers located near the financial district to facilitate night courses.

A number of job specialties have evolved quickly, and formal university training has not yet caught up. As a result, professional training within firms, training sponsored by vendors, and training offered through trade associations have evolved to fill the void. As an example, although systems and communications are usually offered in technical universities, data management as it relates to the trading markets is not yet a common university discipline even though it is becoming an important part of the support for trading markets. As a result, most data management professionals have degrees in other disciplines such as technology. They learn the data management business on the job and through professional training.

RELATED INFORMATION IN OTHER BOOKS

In this part, we define functions, describing broadly what is required with each function. In Book 2 we show how functions interact in some of the most important processes in the financial markets. In Book 3 we show the applications, information, and networks used by various functions and the information they produce. Finally, we employ the functions in Book 4 to explain how tasks, applications, data, and networks interact in a hypothetical trade that we title "Playing the Game."

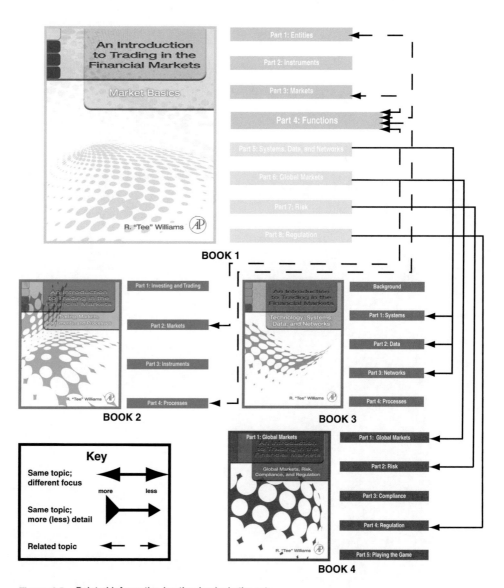

Figure 4.6   Related information in other books in the set.

Technology— Systems, Data, and Networks

Part 5

Technology has been one of the primary forces shaping trading markets from their inception (see Figure 5). As noted in "History" at the front of this book, the absence of technology in early markets meant that a principal (or his or her agent) who wanted to discover prices or to transmit an order had to be physically present at an exchange, coffeehouse, or tavern to find the market price and to interact with other traders. Now technology underlies the trading process, reducing the need to be physically present at a market.

Technology falls into three major categories: **systems, data,** and **networks**. Although we discuss the general categories, the number and diversity of specific technologies within the industry are vast. We discuss technology in much more detail in Book 3.

Figure 5   *Technology*: systems, data, and networks together form the infrastructure needed by entities on the Street to function in the trading process.

SYSTEMS

Securities in the markets can be thought of as relating primarily to customers and/or accounts, instruments, and processes. In general, the purpose of systems is to report on positions or the transactions' status to those interested in the trading. Interested parties include customers, also known as beneficial owners; **regulators**; and firms' **shareholders** or **partners** that operate in the markets. Until recently, the output of systems was printed reports. Now information is presented in real-time displays often connected to the systems through the Internet (see Figure 5.1).

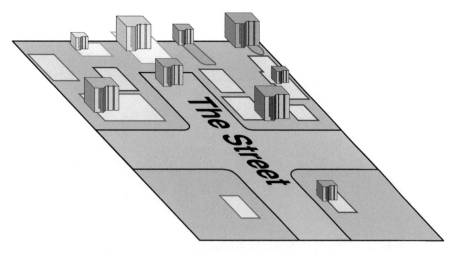

Figure 5.1 ***Systems*** in the trading markets facilitate the steps in the trading process and the functions that are performed by entities on the Street.

The systems used in the trading markets must process data that changes from moment to moment. This type of system places unique demands on the system design, as it must be able to process huge flows of information and continually react instantaneously to asynchronous events as they occur. Each entity, and each function within each entity requires specialized systems that employ designs that reflect both the function being performed and the approach and style of the entity.

In general, there are systems within each of the entities on the Street that perform their specific tasks in the trading process as well as many other tasks. A remarkable amount of commonality exists among tasks for different types of firms. For example, substantially all the entities require the master files described in the next section. Systems that maintain these files perform similar functions even when the nature of the entities is different.

A dedicated staff within each organization generally maintains the systems, and as systems have become more complicated, it is common for the systems department to specialize by function within the firm. Systems departments often report to a single ***Chief Technology Officer*** who has responsibility for the entire organization's systems. Large global organizations sometimes separate the technology function by region, whereas others focus by major department.

DATA

Data in the trading markets generally is produced by and may support the various systems described in the preceding section. Data has historically been maintained within each system that used the data, but this resulted in duplicate data and the strong possibility that data elements are not consistent across all systems. Now, increasingly, data is maintained in ***data warehouses*** where data is shared by multiple systems and is managed independently of the systems that use it.

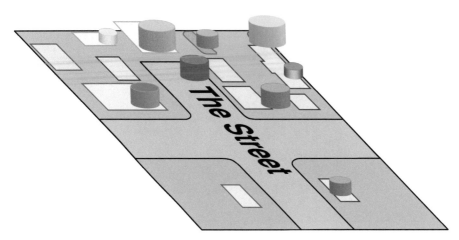

Figure 5.2 **Data** in the trading markets provides the information necessary to support the steps in the trading process and to perform the functions of entities on the Street.

Data in the trading markets come from two sources: Data about the markets generally comes from outside financial firms, often provided by market- and reference-data vendors. The other source is information produced within the firms: (1) data about the markets generally comes from exchanges and other data creators through market- and reference-data vendors and (2) the other source is information produced within firms (see Figure 5.2).

External Data

Data about the trading markets, to a greater extent than most other commercial organizations, occurs in a spectrum that ranges from static data that changes infrequently to real-time data that changes instantaneously and continuously when the markets are open. Data that is static generally relates to accounts, positions, and historical prices. Data that is dynamic includes quotes, prices, and news that are broadcast instantaneously as they occur in the economy and markets. Market data (quotes, last sale prices, and other information generated in the market) is sold by exchanges usually through vendors. As trading becomes more automated, market data is often subject to execution if it comes directly from a marketplace. We refer to this information as **actionable market data** because it can be acted upon. (Data that is not actionable is passive and must result in actions that are sent to the markets through other channels.)

Beyond prices and quotes, information that affects trading includes financial news and commentary on the markets. In addition research information that analyzes companies and makes investment recommendations is important to the trading process.

External data that changes only infrequently includes details related to securities and information on major market participants such as corporate financial data. Collectively, this information is often referred to as **reference data.** Reference data provides details about securities such as the structure of bonds (known as **terms and conditions**) or changes to stocks that have the effect of changing the quantity or value of holdings. Capital changes describe events that alter the value or quantity of holdings in securities, such as stock splits or bond calls.

Counterparty data describes the details of all firms a broker/dealer or investing institutions must deal with as a result of events in the trading markets. This can include addresses and contact information for branches of the firm, as well as bank account data and **delivery instructions** for instruments that are purchased or sold.

Data within Firms

Data created within firms generally relates to customers, accounts, products, and holdings. This breaks down into information about each instrument a firm holds that is kept in a file known as a **security master file**. Information about specific holdings is mapped to each account within the firm in a **holdings file**.

Information that is related to customers includes general information such as names, addresses, banking details, investment goals and constraints, and other data specific to the individual or institution. This general data is maintained in a **customer master file**. For some customer types, such as trusts and investment counsel accounts, holdings are recorded based on individual purchases of securities at specific prices. These details are known as **tax lots**. In other cases, securities holdings are mapped to products such as mutual funds, and customers own shares or units of the product.

In addition to securities holdings, customer accounts also have to record cash positions that may be held in **bank accounts**, **money-market securities**, or **money-market accounts**.

Data Management

Different types of data are required to manage each step in the trading process. For all types of firms involved at each step in the process, external information must be found, contracted for, collected, and perhaps stored and made available in a format required by internal systems. Internal data must be collected, verified, stored, and perhaps packaged for sale. Both internal and external data that is purchased or sold demands business processes to account for either usage or revenue. All these activities generally happen under great time pressure.

Because data has become more complex and varied, data managers specialize, as do systems managers. Data is also becoming an area with several specialties. In many larger firms, the role of a **Chief Data Officer** is beginning to emerge.

NETWORKS

Networks have substantially replaced physical distribution of magnetic tapes and printed reports as a means of moving both data and information throughout the trading markets (see Figure 5.3). Since the mid-1990s, the public Internet has become increasingly important as a communications medium. Networks tend to be specialized by function. A special-purpose network supports almost every activity in the trading markets that results in interaction among different entities. Of equal importance, large global firms have highly sophisticated internal networks for distributing information among their departments and branches.

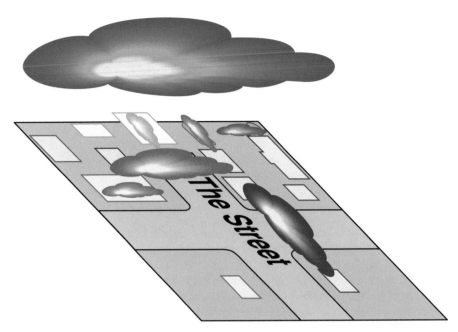

Figure 5.3   Data *networks* within the trading markets connect the entities and integrate activities within each entity.

Trading markets employ three major categories of networks. The first category is the market data network provided by data vendors such as Bloomberg, Interactive Data, and Thomson Reuters. The second category is the enterprise distribution infrastructure. This category represents specialized local-area and wide-area distribution networks that permit information to move throughout global financial organizations. The third category provides dedicated order routing among firms and between firms and marketplaces. Other specialty networks provide a variety of services. For example, the Society for Worldwide Interbank Society for Worldwide Interbank Financial Telecommunication (**SWIFT**) permits banks to move money that is critical for trade settlement.

Order routing networks have been greatly enhanced by the development of specialized standard information protocols such as the ***Financial Information eXchange (FIX)*** beginning in the 1990s. Indeed, the development of standards for transmitting all manner of information that supports the markets has been of great benefit to the trading markets. Among these standards are XBRML for business reports, NewsML for news, FPML for OTC derivatives, RIXML for research, and others. The existence of standards reduces the need for specific programming for new information sources. It also has the benefit of simplifying the task of changing vendors, which has been extremely difficult historically.

As with systems and data, networks and communications have become highly specialized activities in most firms. Within this general area are the specialties of ***capacity planning***, ***bandwidth acquisition***, and ***network design***. Often the process is to choose among commercial offerings with differing capabilities rather than designing bespoke networks. The ***Chief Communications Officer*** often heads enterprise-wide communications activities.

RELATED INFORMATION IN OTHER BOOKS

In this part, we very briefly described the three key components of technology in the trading markets: systems, data, and networks. In Book 3, we examine the most important technology used to support the trading markets (see Figure 5.4).

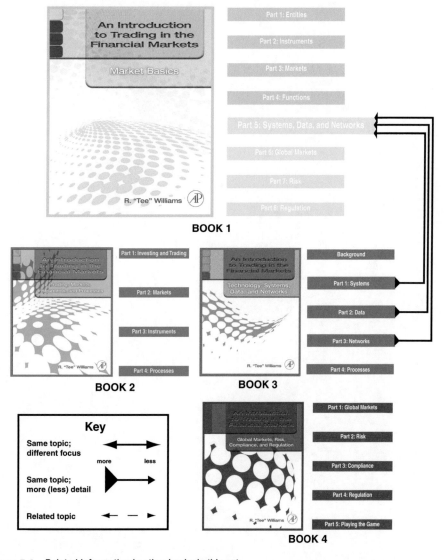

Figure 5.4   Related information in other books in this set.

Global Markets

Part 6

Since the 1960s, there have been three major international financial regions in the world: Asia, Europe, and North America. Other regions in Africa, Oceania, and South America have operated as important satellites.

Within the regions, cities have emerged in the role of the dominant financial centers, and most of the rest of the world's trading markets have revolved around those centers. The tendency of financial centers to coalesce around a single city has been helped by two trends. First, technology made trading at a distance possible. Second, economics caused global financial firms to choose a structure where all trading in a region is focused in one dominant city, and smaller satellite cities primarily have sales offices with limited trading for the local market.

Tokyo was the major financial center in Asia for most of the past 40 years; however, as other financial centers began to liberalize their policies, the Japanese retained the restrictive financial regulation created in the aftermath of World War II. This more restrictive environment caused Hong Kong and Singapore to become coequal centers. Many international organizations chose Hong Kong or Singapore because of their relatively free environments, which made those cities preferable to Tokyo. In the rest of Asia, Jakarta, Manila, Seoul, and Sydney are important regional markets, and smaller centers are growing rapidly in Bangkok, Kuala Lumpur, Mumbai, and Shanghai. China is committed to making Shanghai a global center.

In Europe, London was a primary financial center for more than two centuries, but other European centers became rivals prior to Big Bang in 1986. More liberal policies following Big Bang permitted London to resume its dominance. However, Eurex has made Germany a critical market in futures. Amsterdam, Frankfurt, Paris, and Milan are important centers in Europe, while Copenhagen, Helsinki, Oslo, and Stockholm represent a coordinated regional submarket known as the "Scandinavian markets."

For North America, New York has been the dominant market in the Americas for equities and fixed income. Other important trading centers in the Americas include Boston, Chicago, and Philadelphia in the United States, while Mexico City, Montreal, São Paulo, and Toronto are important non-U.S. regional centers. Dominant futures and options markets are found in Chicago, but there are also important derivatives markets in Montreal, São Paulo, and New York.

In Africa, Cairo and Johannesburg are important markets. Dubai and Tel Aviv are emerging as important centers in the Middle East. In addition to the centers of trading, Basel, Boston, Edinburgh, Geneva, and Zurich have large concentrations of investment management activities.

Although it is possible to trade linkages across national borders, most firms trade within their time zone(s). When firms, even global firms, trade in remote time zones, they either use local intermediaries or ship orders to their own branches in the time zone where the trade is to occur.

An important trend has emerged in the global markets (see Figure 6.0). Both broker/dealers and exchanges have begun to acquire or invest in trading venues in other global markets. So far, these subsidiaries operate largely independently, often because of differences in national regulation. Coordinated technology and other support services are the primary benefits of these consolidations. It will be fascinating to monitor these consolidations to determine if coordinated trading in multiple markets develops over time.

One interesting observation is that when exchanges or other trading venues merge there is generally not a significant reduction in the number of trading venues. Sell-side firms in particular seem to immediately invest in existing smaller competitive venues, or they sponsor new venues. We address this trend in more detail in Book 2, *An Introduction to Trading in the Financial Markets: Trading, Markets, Instruments, and Processes*.

This part provides a general overview of the global trading markets.

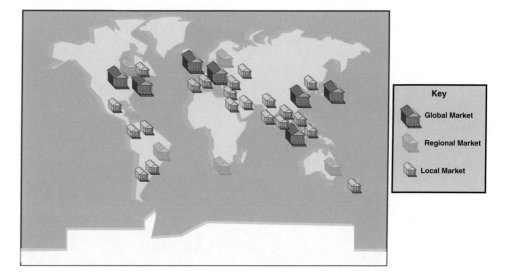

Figure 6.0 The *global market* is composed of global, regional, and local markets operating both independently and in concert to facilitate trading among market participants in all nations.

Because Parts 6, 7, and 8 are brief, the conclusion and references to other books for all three follow this book's Part 8.

Risk Management

Part **7**

Risk management may well be one of the more confusing topics commonly discussed in the trading markets. Confusion arises because there are so many different definitions of what is meant by the term "risk." A senior executive at a major investment bank described an attempt by his firm to come to grips with the firm's exposure to different types of risk in the aftermath of a very large loss as a result of trading in a security. The size of the loss caused the firm to reevaluate its exposure to the markets and to attempt to categorize the types of risk to which the firm was subject.

Apparently, the total number of different types of risk exceeded 20. The person describing the activity suggested that each different type of risk identified was both understandable and unique, although there was overlap at the fringes of each category. We do not have access to the list of all the identified types of risk, but the story illustrates how complex and diverse the notion of risk is. Moreover, the story suggests that any discussion of risk requires that the parties to the discussion clearly identify which types of risk are being discussed to avoid confusion.

Several important categories of risk include the following:

Market risk   The chance that an investment or a position in an instrument can sustain a negative impact as a result of changes in the overall market.

Counterparty risk   The possibility of losses resulting from problems created by another market participant. Counterparty risk becomes a particular problem for the markets if an active market participant becomes insolvent while a number of trades to which it is a party have not settled. This situation happens frequently when major regional or global financial problems occur.

Credit-default risk   The exposure caused by a debtor defaulting on a loan, or at least failing to fulfill all the obligations.

Instrument risk   The losses resulting from adverse performance from a specific instrument.

Economic risk   The negative impact on a position or portfolio resulting from changes in the economy where a security or an investor resides.

Regulatory risk   The potential for regulatory changes to adversely affect either an investment or an investor.

Managing risk involves assessing potential exposure and developing either ways to avoid the exposure or to protect against the exposure if it cannot be avoided. A number of vendors provide a variety of software products and services designed to measure and/or quantify some or all the risks listed here. Moreover, a number of special-purpose financial products such as credit default swaps and portfolio insurance schemes are sold to help ameliorate or transfer risk.

Most financial institutions have individuals or committees charged with managing a firm's exposure to the markets and to monitor risk. Most significant financial disasters ultimately are traced to a failure to monitor, assess, or understand some facet of risk.

This section is brief and is only intended to provide an introductory description of risk. Book 4 includes a detailed description of risk and the related topic of compliance.

Regulation

Regulation is highly dependent on national law and custom; however, most regulation in the financial markets has evolved from self-regulation. Self-regulation has developed within markets as members and participants were forced to enact rules and procedures to govern activities. In many cases, countries have developed national regulation to correct problems that have occurred as a result of financial panics and crises, to promote the national economy, and to protect citizens and organizations that invest within the country. In countries in which there are strong political subdivisions such as the interstate divisions in the United States and provinces in Canada, there is also regulation on the state/province level.

General regulation categories include regulation and governance of entities such as banks, broker/dealers, and investment institutions; protection of investors in a market; control of market structure; and control and protection of national markets.

Some of the issues of concern to regulators include the following:

Investor protection   Ensuring that investors participating in the market are adequately informed to make reasonable decisions. Further, that all market professionals give adequate care to protect the interests of investors.

Transparency   Demanding that quotes and transactions prices are publicly reported.

Best execution   Requiring that intermediaries seek the best possible price and lowest possible transaction cost for protected customers on each transaction.

Competitive parity   Creating rules that provide competitive organizations with a regulatory environment where each is subject to the same requirements and regulatory burdens when performing the same activities.

Conflict of interest   Eliminating or discouraging incentives that cause market professionals (such as broker/dealers) to place their own interests ahead of their customers, particularly when those customers are less sophisticated. Further, where conflicts of interest are impossible to avoid that harsh penalties accompany any attempt to harm the interests of the unsophisticated.

National market defense/protection   Protecting both local investors and institutions from foreign entities that might damage what is perceived to be in the national interest.

Two fundamental approaches to regulation are prevalent in the world today. The first, typified by the European Union and much of the British Commonwealth countries, can be categorized as regulation based on principles. The idea of this type of regulation is that general principles related to a number of important issues are laid down and regulations are crafted to accomplish those principles. Courts and arbitrators then interpret the applicability of the principles to specific events.

By contrast, regulation in the United States is based on rules that result from the correction of wrongdoing. Other countries throughout the world tend to fall more or less into one category or the other based on culture and the influence of other countries.

RELATED INFORMATION IN OTHER BOOKS

Parts 6, 7, and 8 present a cursory explanation of how global markets, risk, and regulation are factors in the trading markets (see Figure 8.0). These topics are major sections in Book 4. Compliance was also introduced in Part 4, "Functions (Activities)," of this book.

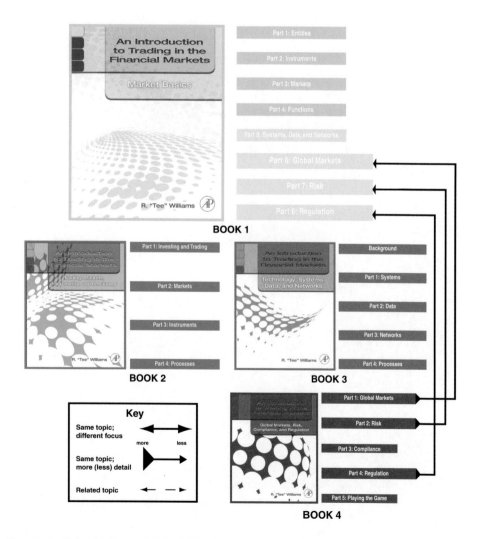

Figure 8.0   Related information in other books in the set.

This book presented a description of the trading markets. Our goal here was to introduce the entities, instruments, markets, and functions and then to give a brief overview of technology, regulations, risk management, and global marketplaces. A basic book is able to provide you with only a general impression of trading and

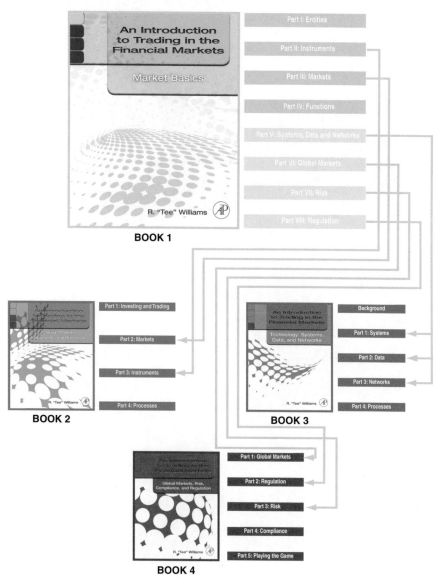

Figure C.0   The *relationship of topics* among the books in this set.

247

a summary of the markets' structure. Except for entities and functions, which are only described here, the three accompanying books investigate each of the parts of this book in more detail.

BOOK 2: *AN INTRODUCTION TO TRADING IN THE FINANCIAL MARKETS: TRADING, MARKETS, INSTRUMENTS, AND PROCESSES*

Book 2 begins with a description of the trading process from the perspective of investors and traders using the markets as well as the different structures, formats, and mechanics found in alternative types of markets. Next the book provides a more detailed look at securities and instruments, focusing on the features that different instruments can include, the measures used to evaluate and compare instruments, the participants that invest in and trade instruments, and the market characteristics in which each instrument trades. Finally, it looks at some of the important processes that enable the trading markets, with a focus on how the functions presented in Book 1 facilitates completion of the processes (see Figure C.1). The trading and primary markets are the dominant processes considered, but other types of important processes are investigated as well.

Figure C.1   Book 2: *An Introduction to Trading in the Financial Markets: Trading, Markets, Instruments, and Processes*

BOOK 3: *AN INTRODUCTION TO TRADING IN THE FINANCIAL MARKETS: TECHNOLOGY—SYSTEMS, DATA, AND NETWORKS*

Book 3 focuses on the technologies that serve as infrastructure for the trading markets. In it computer and web applications are grouped under the general term "systems." Here some of the most important types of systems and computer applications are considered both within individual entities and among entities. Next we look at the different types of information consumed and generated in the markets and transported throughout the industry. Finally the book considers supporting and connecting systems and applications that are communications networks, which move data and eliminate most of the physical transfer of paper. (See Figure C.2.) Book 3 does not attempt to define technology and how it is created nor the equipment and programming that comprise the technology. Rather it describes how the business processes that are examined in this set are supported by technology.

Figure C.2   Book 3: *An Introduction to Trading in the Financial Markets: Technology—Systems, Data, and Networks*

BOOK 4: *AN INTRODUCTION TO TRADING IN THE FINANCIAL MARKETS: GLOBAL MARKETS, RISK, COMPLIANCE, AND REGULATION*

The final book of the set begins with a description of the important global trading markets and how the entities in the markets interact across national borders. Book 4 then introduces the concepts of risk, compliance, and regulation (see Figure C.3). The goal is not to examine every regulation or to provide a "how-to" of risk management. The objective is to show how risk, compliance, and regulation facilitate markets and ensure their smooth operation. Finally, the book ends with a description called "playing the game." It is meant to show how a complex global (hypothetical) trade occurs from inception of the idea to settlement. An effort is made to explain how each of the intervening steps occurs, with entities performing functions, employing the market's processes using technology while evaluating the risk, ensuring compliance, and abiding by regulations.

Figure C.3   Book 4: *An Introduction to Trading in the Financial Markets: Global Markets, Risk, Compliance, and Regulation*

Acceptable funds   The form of payment that will satisfy a clearing corporation for settlement. Increasingly, same-day funds are demanded for most settlements. Historically, next-day funds were acceptable, but the movement to reduce the length of time in the settlement cycle has required shorter payment.

Accommodations   A transaction or other activity that is incidental to the primary activity. For example, when an instrument is bought or sold in another country, a foreign exchange transaction must take place at the same time as the instrument trade. The FX transaction is known as an accommodation trade.

Account management   The function within the buy side where a customer is represented by an individual who is responsible for customer support. On the sell side, this role is generally the responsibility of the salesperson.

Actionable prices or Actionable market data or Actionable quotes   Information from a market center (or centers) that can be converted to an order ready for transmission through simple actions such as a mouse click or a drag-and-drop operation. "Actionable market data" implies an electronic linkage between the trader and market or trading venue. Actionable market data is typically available only to those authorized by a firm or the market center to enter orders. (See also "Executable prices.")

Agency broker   A firm that deals with institutional customers only as a broker or agent. The term is redundant but widely used.

Agency market   A market where trading is accomplished by matching orders from principals (either individuals or investing institutions) without the intervention of dealers or market makers unless no trade is possible without the services of a dealer. (See also "Dealer market.")

Agent   A legal term for a broker who acts on behalf of a customer in finding a buyer or seller for the customer's order. Agents receive commissions for work and generally have a fiduciary responsibility to act in the best interest of the customer. (See also "Broker.")

Alternative trading system (ATS) or Alternative trading facilities   The general term for all new or nontraditional trading venues. Most of these facilities are organized as brokers. The U.S. SEC permits experimentation in new forms of trading systems but requires the proprietors of each system to elect whether to be classified as a broker (ECN) or an exchange (SRO) for regulatory purposes. In Europe, the corresponding broker trading system is known as a multilateral trading facility (MTF). (See also "Electronic communications network" and "Multilateral trading facilities.")

American Depository Receipt (ADR)   ADRs are traded on various U.S. stock markets. They represent ownership in a foreign corporation. The foreign shares are deposited with a custodian in the country of origin; then certificates are created by U.S. banks to enable trading on U.S. exchanges.

American-style options   An option contract that can be exercised at any time during its life. (See also "European-style options.")

Ask (See "Offer.")

Asset allocation The process of dividing the investment funds in a portfolio among a series of specific asset types (e.g., stocks and bonds) based on the overall prospects and assumed average risk for each asset. Beyond overall asset types, asset allocation may be extended to specific categories of assets (e.g., corporate and government bonds) as well as specific industries.

Assets-under-management A common means of size comparison among specific investment funds or whole investment companies. Assets-under-management is also a common unit of measure used to determine the compensation an investment manager receives.

Average price When an order results in multiple executions to complete the entire order, accounts that participate in the order receive a single price for the entire order that is computed by multiplying the shares in each execution times the price for the execution and dividing by the total number of shares in the order. When an order takes longer than one trading session to complete, there is often an average price for each session.

Backoffice The several departments of a securities firm concerned with the operations aspects of trading, such as comparing; confirming; settling trades; providing credit (margin); and creating and distributing dividends, proxies, and statements.

Bandwidth acquisition The process of acquiring a communications circuit for a vendor or market participant to support a network.

Bank accounts Accounts, both time deposit and demand deposit, where funds are deposited or withdrawn particularly for settling transactions.

Beneficial owner or Beneficiary The individual who receives the financial rewards from an investment.

Best efforts An underwriting where the underwriter does not guarantee the price for the transaction. In effect, the underwriter sells instruments owned by the issuing company, and the company receives whatever price the underwriter is able to get.

Best execution The concept of trading an order to get the optimum combination of execution price and transaction cost to meet the demands of the funds being managed. The concept implies that professional managers should seek to achieve best execution on all trades for their customers.

Bid The price at which a market maker will buy a security. In the marketplace, this is the "demand" price, as contrasted to the "supply" price. (See also "Offer" and "Quote.")

Big Bang The term for the major market changes in the United Kingdom on October 27, 1986. Many of the changes paralleled the changes in the United States on May Day (May 1, 1975). For the most part the changes created a new, more competitive market. The term "Big Bang" was subsequently applied in other markets where dramatic market structure changes occurred.

Block An order too large for a dealer to buy or sell from its inventory. The size of a "block" can be very different depending on the liquidity of the security. For reporting purposes, the NYSE defines a block as any trade of more than 10,000 shares. For liquid securities, a block is typically 100,000 shares or more. Blocks are typically allocated among several customer accounts after the trade is completed.

Bond   A securitized debt instrument, usually packaged into instruments that have a face amount of $1,000.

Bond call   Some bonds are permitted to pay off early. The provision that makes this possible is known as a call feature. The issuing company includes the provision to call the bond in the original bond indenture. If the company chooses, the bond is called, and the company pays off the bond before maturity.

Bourse (Beurs, Börse, Bolsa)   The general European term for a stock exchange. Named for a family that owned a bar in Bruges in the sixteenth century where the first trading in instruments began.

Broker   (See "Agent.")

Broker's broker   (See "Correspondent" and "Interdealer broker.")

Broker/Dealer   An overarching term used to describe multi-function companies that provide a variety of services in financial markets, including acting as brokers and as dealers. "Brokers" act as middlemen, arranging sales between parties and receiving a commission for this work. "Dealers" buy and sell stock out of their own inventory. Rather than charging a commission, dealers, sometimes called "market makers," make money on the "spread," or difference between their buying price and selling price.

Bull market   A market slang term that describes a market where securities are rising in value aggressively.

Buy list   The name for an "approved" list of investments that some institutional investors create to provide guidance to the firm's portfolio managers. These lists are often created by an investment committee composed of senior portfolio managers and research analysts. In addition to suggesting which instruments should be bought, a buy list also contains instruments that should be sold because of perceived inferior performance and others that should not be owned because of strategic and philosophical conflicts.

Buy order   An order to purchase securities.

Buy side   The institutions and individuals that buy brokerage services from the securities industry. Institutions include professional money managers, insurance firms, state and local governments, and so on.

Buy-side trader   A trader working for an institutional investor charged with managing decisions to trade generated by portfolio managers, and deciding how to structure the order(s) required to complete the desired trade, which broker/dealer(s) to use, and what instructions to use to manage the trade. Buy-side traders are often charged with ensuring best execution and repaying broker/dealers for soft-dollar obligations. (See also "Portfolio manager.")

Cage   An antiquated term for the backoffice department that is responsible for tracking securities holdings. The term derives from a room that was reinforced to protect security holdings in the time when many certificates were barrier instruments and subject to theft.

Call option   An option contract in which the owner of the contract has purchased the right to sell a fixed amount security at a predetermined price up until a set date when the contract expires without value if nothing has been done.

Capacity planning   The process of anticipating the growth or change in message volumes and projecting system and network capacity to accommodate the anticipated change. This has become extremely important because automated trading has caused an explosion in message traffic.

Capital   For our purposes, the total financial wealth directly invested in an entity. Capital usually includes both the equity invested and the liabilities that are able to fund operations. Raising capital is the purpose of investment banking. (See also "Net capital.")

Capital changes   Activities undertaken by a company that can result in changes in the structure of the company. These changes include stock dividends, stock splits, cash dividends, mergers, and other events that can affect the book value of securities and/or market price of a security.

Capital commitment   A buy-side firm's willingness or ability to use its invested wealth to help a customer complete a trade or to employ that wealth for profit in the markets.

Capital markets division   A set of functions within a sell-side entity engaged in activities related to both trading and investment banking for institutional customers and the firm's direct investment.

Carries customer accounts   A service provided by correspondents and FCMs for introducing firms in which customer accounts that are "introduced" by the introducing firm are actually carried on the books of the FCM or correspondent. Customers receive statements that show the FCM or correspondent on the masthead of the statement with a notation that the customer is also a customer of the introducing firm. This practice makes the customer the financial responsibility of the correspondent or the FCM.

Cash delivery   A feature of futures contracts where the actual delivery required by the contract is cash as opposed to the subject of the contract. This provision makes the contract a pure hedging instrument and not a commercial contract.

Cash market   A market in which a physical commodity, security, or instrument is traded. (See also "Derivatives market.")

Cashier   A department in a securities firm responsible for receiving and delivering cash. (See also "Cage.")

Certificate   A paper document that is evidence of ownership of securities. In countries that use English Common Law, an owner of property including securities is entitled to a document proving evidence. Although certificates are expensive to manage and process, completely doing away with them has proven difficult.

Chief Communications Officer   The position in a financial firm or vendor organization for an individual who is given the responsibility to plan for and manage the networks and internal distribution for the firm.

Chief Data Officer   The position in a financial firm or vendor organization for an individual who is given the responsibility to plan for and manage the data content for the firm.

Chief Technology Officer   The position in a financial firm or vendor organization for an individual who is given the responsibility to plan for and manage the processing systems of the firm.

Clearing and settlement   The imprecise term for the post-trade processes that end with the settlement of the trade by exchanging funds for transferrable ownership. We separate the term into its components. (See also "Clearing" and "Settlement.")

Clearing corporation   An organization historically affiliated with an exchange or market center that serves to manage the process between execution and settlement. Many clearing corporations take the position of the counterparty to every trade to permit trades to be netted, reducing the number of deliveries required at settlement.

Clearing or Clearance   The process of assuring that details (price, quantity, symbol, counterparty, etc.) of trades are "good" (accurate and agreed between the parties) prior to settlement. May also involve a method for insuring parties against the failure of a counterparty.

Clerk   A nonregistered employee of a broker/dealer either on an exchange floor or in a trading room that helps in the trading process. Clerks are not involved in the actual trading decision.

Closing price   Typically, the price defined by an exchange as the price that will be used for the valuation of accounts, the determination of margin calls, and so on. The exact definition and calculation of the closing price varies from exchange to exchange.

Comingled funds   Internal investment funds within an institutional investor that puts funds from many individual accounts into a single investment fund, or more commonly, a set of investment funds with different investment objectives. This practice makes managing customer investments more efficient.

Commission   A fee paid to an agent as compensation for assisting a principal to execute a trade in the market. (See also "Agent" and "Principal.")

Commodities   Goods such as agricultural products and natural resources that are traded as both cash assets and futures or forward contracts.

Common shares or Common stock   Equity securities. (See also "Ordinary Shares," "Shares," or "Stocks.")

Compliance   The departmental function within both buy-side and sell-side firms that assures trade compliance with both statutory regulations and constraints from customers and/or charters.

Compounding   The financial effect of the fact that interest (or other income) paid on an investment can be reinvested to earn additional income.

Confirmation   The notification from a broker/dealer to a customer specifying that an order has been executed with details of the trade, such as symbol, size, price, and so on.

Contract (legal)   A legal instrument that binds one party to perform a specified act or service for the other party in exchange for an agreed fee.

Contracts (financial)   Financial instruments that are based on contracts between the writer and purchaser in which the writer undertakes an obligation to the purchaser in exchange for a fee. These are different from securities that convey ownership of a financial good.

Controlling interest   The ownership interest required to exert effective control of an economic entity. In private companies, controlling interest usually involves one share over 50% of the total shares. In publically traded companies, ownership can often be represented by much less than 50% of the outstanding shares because many shareholders are passive and do not vote on matters of control for their investments.

Corporate finance   Another term sometimes used for investment banking or for functions within investment banking such as financial consulting.

Corporate trust   A series of services provided by banks to companies that issue securities. This line of business, typically offered by banks, generally requires trust powers. Examples of corporate trust services are paying agent and registrar. (See also "Trust powers.")

Correspondent or Correspondent broker/dealer or Correspondent firm   A term used in both banking and brokerage to mean a firm that acts on behalf of another (often smaller or remote) firm. Actually, the term "correspondent" can be used to mean both parties in the relationship. A correspondent broker may clear on behalf of the other firm or could execute trades or handle transactions that require a local presence for another firm that is in a remote location. A correspondent bank might perform funds transfer activities in its home market for other banks that are not members of the local clearing association.

Cost of capital   The concept that capital for an entity has a cost for the shareholders or owners of the company. Conventional views of cost of capital suggested that new equity was very expensive because it diluted the ownership of the existing shareholders. Debt was cheaper because it permitted new investment but would eventually be paid off, leaving the existing shareholders with undiluted positions. In 1958 professors Franco Modigliani and Merton Miller of Carnegie Mellon wrote a paper suggesting this view was false. Whatever the views on this debate, the cost of capital is an important consideration in raising new capital for a commercial entity.

Counterparty   The other side(s) of a trade. For the buyer, the counterparty is the seller.

Coupon or Coupon rate   The rate of interest paid on a fixed income or fixed interest instrument expressed as a percentage.

Currencies   Deposits in banks around the world that are exchanged for corresponding deposits in other countries to facilitate international trade and investment. Trading in currencies is also known as Foreign Exchange, or ForEx. ForEx is the largest trading market in the world.

Custodian bank   Institutional investors that are not affiliated with a banking institution have a custodian who is responsible for managing the holdings of the manager and, in particular, assets held in depositories. Custodians provide reports on holdings and assist in the settlement process following trades. Global custodians provide consolidation for positions held in more than one country.

Custody or Custodian   A service offered by banks to institutional investors such as mutual funds and pension funds. Custodians perform both accounting and settlement services for the funds and are responsible for holding assets in countries that do not have a central depository.

Customer accounting or Customer-side accounting   The accounting for customer holdings as well as transactions that affect customer holdings on both the buy and sell side. Broker/dealer accounting for customer holdings and accounts. Broker/dealers use this term to distinguish all accounting required to support customers. (See also "Street-side accounting.")

Customer activities or Customer-side activities   All operations of a buy-side or sell-side firm oriented to support of customers and their accounts. (See also "Street-side activities.")

Data   One of three major categories of technology supporting the financial markets.

Data warehouse   The concept of a single repository for all data used by an entity. (Data management is described in more detail in Book 3.)

Day trader   Strictly speaking, a trader who takes long or short positions during the trading day to take advantage of price fluctuations and then liquidates all positions by the end of the trading day so that the trader's position is "flat."

Dealer   A principal making money by trading for his own account. In the United States, dealers are regulated as broker/dealers under the Securities Acts and therefore can be members of exchanges or the NASD. Dealers generally have special access to capital and unique margin requirements.

Dealer market   A market where all orders are traded against a dealer's inventory. The dealer is the principal on the other side of every trade. (See also "Agency market.")

Debt instrument   A fixed-income instrument that is a securitized loan. (See also "Bond", "Fixed income," "Fixed interest," or "Money market.")

Deliver   To present transferable proof of ownership in satisfaction of settlement. Most often delivery is made in the form of transfer instructions that shift official records of ownership from a seller to the purchaser in a trade.

Delivery instructions   Instructions on how instruments or payment should be sent to counterparties to ensure efficient receipt for the settlement of transactions. Each counterparty has unique delivery instructions, and individual departments and offices may have different instructions from other offices within the same firm. Delivery instructions are becoming reference data to simplify the amount of collection and maintenance required for settlement.

Delivery month   The month when delivery is required for a futures contract and when the contract expires.

Demand-deposit accounts   Bank accounts in which funds are available "on demand." Historically, checking (chequing) accounts were demand deposits, but increasingly payments are made using electronic transfers. (See also "Time-deposit accounts.")

Dematerialization   The attribute of financial assets that does not require or permit a physical certificate to prove ownership of a financial instrument.

Depository   An organization that is charged with holding most or all securities within a market centrally so that deliveries of securities can be made electronically rather than physically.

Depository receipts   Securities held in trust by a bank as collateral for instruments issued that trade independently, but closely aligned to the instrument that is the basis for the receipt. Originally created in the United States as a means to permit trading in the securities of other countries; many countries now have local depository receipts. (See also "American Depository Receipt.")

Derivatives market   A market that trades an instrument—usually a contract—that derives its value from its relationship to an underlying commodity or security. Typical derivatives include futures and options. (See also "Cash market.")

Derivatives   Instruments (generally contracts) that are traded and derive their value based on the value of an underlying instrument, usually a security. Generally, the derivative contract obligates the writer of the contract to perform a service for the purchaser of the contract (e.g., futures and options).

Direct costs   For investing institutions, direct costs are typically paid by the customer; indirect costs are paid by the firm. Therefore, commissions and spreads on securities transactions are direct costs and are paid by the customer. Indirect costs such as facilities and staffing are indirect costs paid by the firm from its revenues. Some costs fall in between. For example, research and some other information clearly benefit the customer and may be paid by the customer depending on regulations in the local market. (See also "Indirect costs" and "Soft dollars.")

Direct market access   This access provides a buy-side trader with electronic access to the marketplace, so that an order submitted goes directly to the point of execution, either on the floor or in an electronic matching system. Thus, direct market access bypasses brokers as human intermediaries.

Direct sales   For retail customers, particularly of the sell side, sales using account executives, financial consultants, or registered representatives who sell financial services directly to the customer. In contrast, indirect sales employs web sites and the Internet. (See also "Indirect sales.")

Discount   (1) A means of providing interest on a bond or other securitized loan in which the initial amount borrowed is less than the amount owed when the bond matures. The difference between the amount borrowed and amount repaid is the "discount" and is the lender's payment for the use of the money lent. (See also "Bond," "Fixed income," and "Interest.") (2) The amount by which the price of a bond falls below its face amount. (See also "Premium.")

Discount brokerage   A category of primarily retail buy-side entities that evolved in the aftermath of the switch from fixed to competitive commissions in the 1970s and 1980s. Discount brokers offered discounted commissions (when compared to traditional broker/dealers) by depending on technology, paying customer-support personnel salaries instead of commissions, and selling order flow.

Display devices   A pricing unit for selling market data. (This is discussed in detail in Book 3.)

Distribution capacity   (1) A measure of the ability of a network to handle the volume of message traffic it is asked to handle. (2) The ability of a retail or institutional sales network to sell issues when needed, particularly for new issues.

Diversified portfolio   A portfolio containing a number of different holdings where the components are not highly correlated with each other, and it is hoped, not with the market as well.

Dividend   Income paid to the holder of an equity security.

Dumb terminal   A largely archaic term for a display device that did not have the capability to manipulate the data it displayed. This type of terminal is the founding assumption in the pricing structure used for selling market data. (This is discussed in detail in Book 3.)

Efficient market hypothesis   The concept in academic finance that says markets quickly process new information on securities, both information on the issuing company's financial condition and any information from past market prices, and therefore, it is not possible to achieve greater returns than those on a diversified portfolio by trying to select specific securities.

Electronic access   (1) Access to a marketplace or trading venue using electronic means exclusively. (2) Some exchanges have created a special class of membership for members that do not need or want physical access to the markets. For purely automated markets, all access is electronic.

Electronic access broker/dealers   Broker/dealers primarily servicing retail customers that employ web sites and the Internet as their primary service delivery channel. Many of these firms are descended from discount brokers. (See also "Discount brokerage" and "Traditional retail broker/dealers.")

Electronic communications network (ECN)   A special class of alternative trading system defined by the SEC that acts like a market center but is currently regulated as a broker/dealer.

Eleemosynary funds   Investments managed for charities and educational institutions.

Equity   An ownership share in an entity organized as a corporation. (See also "Common stock," "Common shares," "Ordinaries," "Ordinary shares," "Shares," or "Stock.")

Equity shares   (See "Equity.")

Estate   Property and investments held on behalf of a deceased person until the assets can be disposed of in accordance with the terms of the will of the deceased. Managing an estate requires trust powers.

European-style options   Options contracts that can be exercised only on a single date just before the contract expires. (See also "American-style options," "Expiration date," and "Exercise date.")

Exchange   A trading venue dedicated to trading instruments that exists in substantially all national markets. The original exchange was created in Amsterdam and was quickly copied in London. (Prior to the Amsterdam Exchange trading had occurred in taverns and coffee houses.) The U.S. regulations for exchanges are typical. Exchanges were formally defined in the Securities Exchange Act of 1934 and further refined in Regulation ATS. U.S. exchanges are regulated by the SEC. An exchange is permitted to list securities (and charge for listing), promulgate rules for trading, oversee the trading of securities, and charge fees for the sale of trading information (market data). Exchanges had to be membership corporations prior to Regulation ATS but can now be for-profit corporations. Exchanges are self-regulatory organizations (SROs). They are permitted to charge only transaction fees, not commissions. In London, exchanges are regulated by the FSA. In most other countries, the national regulator either directly or indirectly regulates exchanges.

Exchange-traded funds (ETF)   Funds (portfolios of securities) managed by an independent fund manager that are traded on exchanges and have the characteristics of equity securities. ETFs were pioneered by the American Stock Exchange (AMEX) but are widely traded on other markets as well.

Execution   Typically, the agreement between a buyer and seller on a single price and the quantity of instruments involved in a trade. The execution can occur face-to-face, as it often does on exchange floors; it can also occur over the phone or, as it does increasingly, by computer.

Execution-management systems (EMS)   Systems used by buy-side traders, often provided by broker/dealers, that specifically control the selection of trading venues and control the release of orders to those venues.

Exercise date   For European-style options, an exercise is possible on only one date when a holder must either elect to exercise or permit the option to expire valueless. American-style options may be exercised at any time.

Expiration date (U.S.) or Expiry date (U.K.)   The date on which an option contract becomes valueless.

Expiration month   The month in which an option expires. The expiration month is often referenced in naming the contract.

Expires   The process of an option becoming worthless at a predetermined date and time.

Exposure   The amount by which a portfolio or holding is affected by a risky event or circumstance.

Face amount or Face value   For instruments such as bonds, the amount repaid to the owner when a bond matures.

Fiduciary   A person or institution having a special financial responsibility to a customer or client. In general, a fiduciary is supposed to act on behalf of the client as a prudent person would act in managing his or her own affairs in a similar situation.

Fiduciary obligation   A set of required practices with which a person or firm that is a fiduciary is charged when dealing with customers.

Financial assets   All instruments and property that are owned to produce income directly. Financial assets are in contrast to other assets that are owned for personal pleasure, for shelter and sustenance, or to produce goods and services for sale.

Financial consultants   One of several names for retail sales personnel working for sell-side firms. (See also "Registered representatives" and "Wealth management.")

FIX (Financial Information eXchange)   A message protocol that is growing rapidly as a means for institutional buy and sell sides to exchange order and trade information. The protocol defines a number of message types: orders, trades, quotes, indications of interest (IOIs), and trade reports, as well as many types of administrative messages. FIX originated with Salomon Brothers and was quickly embraced by Fidelity. Many of the largest securities firms and institutional investors are active members of the FIX community. (See also www.fixprotocol.org.)

Fixed commissions   A pricing scheme for agency trades in which the rate charged is fixed by law or by an SRO. Fixed commissions are now largely gone from most markets because regulators and competitive pressure have forced competitive pricing.

Fixed income or Fixed interest securities   A financial asset, usually a security, which represents a securitized loan. Owning the security entitles the owner to an income stream in exchange for the use of money for a specified period. The income may come from a discount, which means the amount of money that is repaid at the end of the loan period is larger than the amount originally lent.

Flat   A trading term meaning having a zero balance.

Float   Income earned by financial firms on cash balances left with the firms overnight as a result of unrelated activities. When a customer leaves cash at a firm and/or if cash is on balance with the firm awaiting subsequent movement, in some cases the firm is able to use the funds to generate short-term income until the funds are demanded by their owner or the balances are required for their original purpose.

For-profit corporations   (See "Publically owned corporations.")

Front office   A term in common usage with respect to financial companies that generally refers to people who deal directly with customers or the markets. (See also "Backoffice" and "Middle office.")

Full-service firms   Firms that have both brokers and dealers for both institutional and retail customers. Full-service firms are most often investment banks as well.

Funds-transfer mechanisms   Both the technological facilities and regulatory authority that permit commercial banks (for the most part) to move money among themselves to satisfy the requirements of both commercial and financial customers.

Funds-under-management   (1) A measure of the size or quantity of the assets an institution is charged with investing either for itself or for clients. Assets-under-management is the measure most commonly used for comparing the size of different investment organizations. (2) A measure used to price services in the financial markets. Investing organizations and those sell-side firms that choose not to price based on commissions (commonly known as wealth management) charge a small percentage of assets-under-management to price their services. In principle, this pricing mechanism provides the manager with the incentive to increase the value of the assets managed. (See also "Wealth management.")

Fungible   The property of two or more items being completely interchangeable. Because securities are fungible, it is sufficient that someone who owns a security receive a share of the security on demand. It is not necessary that the share be exactly the same one originally purchased.

Futures   A derivative contract that promises delivery of a commodity or financial asset at a fixed future point for an established price.

Futures commission merchant (FCM)   A firm that provides a full range of brokerage and clearing services and specializes in the futures business. Many FCMs clear for futures introducing firms, making them functionally similar to correspondents.

Future value   The value of a future cash flow assuming that time has "value." If a sum today is invested presumably it will be worth more in the future. Conversely, a fixed sum in the future is worth less today because there will not be a benefit from investment before it is received.

Go public   The slang term for a company's first public offering of equity securities. It means the company (previously privately owned) is now publically owned. (See also "Initial public offering.")

Good delivery   A definition of what, and in particular what form of, asset delivery is acceptable in a market. A seller makes "good delivery" by presenting assets in the prescribed form at the prescribed location at the prescribed time for settlement. Good delivery varies from market to market (both geographic and instrument markets), but there is a long-term trend to uniformity across regions and shorter time frames for all instruments.

Hedge fund   A generalized term for a fund that is available for investment only by sophisticated investors, according to SEC rules in the United States. These funds are permitted to engage in strategies that are not available to other types of funds, such as mutual funds. Such strategies can include short selling and highly leveraged positions.

Hedge or Hedged   A position in which the risk of holding the assets in the position is reduced or eliminated by simultaneously holding another asset designed to insure against the risk.

High street   A British term for the main street of a town; most commonly used to refer to an office of a financial institution (or other entity) that is located in the downtown area.

Holder   An individual or entity that has possession of a financial asset. (1) When assets, particularly securities, were bearer instruments, having physical possession of a certificate was necessary to receive income payments and/or to be repaid when a fixed-income instrument matured. Because more instruments are now registered, certificates do not matter and may not exist. (2) A word used in conjunction with an asset type to indicate ownership. Examples include "stockholder," "bond holder," and "option holder." Probably derived from the notion of bearer instruments, as described in (1).

Holding companies   Companies that own different subsidiaries registered in different ways. In markets where different financial functions are separated by law, holding companies sometimes provide a way for companies registered for different functions to be jointly owned by a single entity.

Immediacy   The financial service provided by a dealer in which the dealer is willing to execute a transaction (buy or sell) in the affected securities whenever a prospective trader wishes. The quid pro quo is the dealer establishes the price for the transaction and the maximum number of shares the trader can expect.

Immobilization   A technique used in countries where securities ownership requires a physical certificate to reduce settlement costs. By holding a certificate with substantially all units of the security in a single certificate at a depository actual individual ownership can be managed by bookkeeping entry against the single global holding.

Income stream   A series of payments, usually at set intervals, when an investment returns income to a holder of a financial asset.

Index   A calculated measure of the market performance of a group of securities. An index can be for an entire market or a portion of a market. Different types of indexes have different calculation methodologies that affect the characteristics of the index. The two major calculation methodologies are price weighted (such as the Dow Jones Industrial Average) and market weighted (such as the S&P 500). Indexes are typically licensed by the creator and are calculated by the vendors.

Index funds   An investment technique based on Modern Portfolio Theory that attempts to emulate the returns on the market by holding a portfolio that replicates the market by investing in shares that track a broad-based market index.

Indication of interest (IOI)   An indication is a message between market participants to convey that the initiating party has a position of "significant size" that is available to be traded under the right conditions. It asks whether the receiving party has any interest. Under the rules of decorum for this interaction, the initiating party is not supposed to send an IOI unless there really is a potential order. The receiving party is not supposed to take actions that would disadvantage the initiator.

Indirect costs   For an investing institution, all costs that are not directly the result of providing investment services to a customer are indirect and must be paid by the company out of the company's revenues. Direct costs are paid by customers. Although many elements are clear (commissions are direct costs, and facilities and staff are indirect), some costs are subject to interpretation. Generally, sell-side research costs are considered to be direct, but some other costs such as information services and research from third parties may be paid for by soft dollars and thus may be treated as if they were direct. (See also "Soft dollars.")

Indirect sales   Retail sales that do not involve registered sales personnel. Initially, telephone call centers were used by discount firms, but now the Internet is the primary indirect sales channel. (See also "Discount brokerage.")

Individual investor   An individual managing money for his or her own benefit or that of his or her family. (See also "Retail investor.")

Initial public offering (IPO)   A new issuance of securities. Although the term seems to imply the first issue by a private company going public, the term is also applied to companies that are already public making further issues of either debt or equities. (See also "Go public" and "Underwriting.")

Institutional broker/dealers   Broker/dealers that focus on institutional customers.

Institutional investor   A collective label for professional money managers. The term includes bank trust departments, hedge funds, investment advisors, insurance companies, mutual fund managers, and pension managers.

Institutional sales   The function within a broker/dealer (sell-side firm) that is responsible for the customer relationship. Institutional sales is responsible for managing the customer, providing service, delivering soft-dollar services, and encouraging the customer to use the broker/dealer's products. In some firms this function may be combined with the sales trader. (See also "Position trader" and "Sales trader.")

Institutional services   Any services particularly directed to institutional investors. Although primarily applied to services from the sell side, many vendors also target institutional investors as an attractive market segment.

Instruments   The general term for financial assets that do not involve holding physical goods.

Insurance   The general term for financial services that provide protection from loss of life or property. Insurance usually involves polling known risk such as death, weather damage, fire, or transit losses among a group where each participant makes a payment into the pool that is paid to any member that suffers a loss from the insured event.

Insurance premium   The payment(s) to an insurance company for the financial protection of the insurance policy. Payments can be "lump sum" (meaning a single one-time payment), annual, quarterly, or monthly. (See also "Insurance.")

Intellectual property   A property right that provides an ownership interest in any value that is derived as the product of an activity or service. Intellectual property often permits the owner to lease or license the product, such as data, and charge for its usage.

Interdealer broker (IDB)   A broker whose customers are dealers. Prominent especially in foreign exchange and fixed income dealing. (See also "Broker's broker" and "Voice broker.")

Interest   The payments received from a loan or from owning a fixed income instrument.

Interest Rate   The stated amount of income on a loan or fixed income instrument usually stated as a percentage of the total amount of the loan or instrument.

Intermediaries   The persons or firms that act as middlemen in arranging a transaction, or sponsor a customer to participate in a restricted financial service. Brokers and dealers perform this function.

Introducing broker or Introducing firm   A broker that is not a member of an exchange or clearing corporation. An introducing firm has a customer relationship, but its clearing firm provides execution services and/or clears trades.

Inventory   The securities that a dealer or market maker maintains to provide liquidity to a market.

Investment bank   A financial institution that engages in the process of investment banking. The activity may be a stand-alone service, as in the case of Merrill Lynch or Nomura, or it could be a part of a commercial banking operation, as in the case of HSBC, Citibank, or Deutsche Bank.

Investment banking   The group of activities generally involved in helping governments and corporations raise capital. (See also "Primary market" and "Underwriting.")

Investment counselor   A firm that manages individuals' investment accounts as separate portfolios rather than pooling funds from multiple individuals.

Investment management   A general term for the activity of professionally managing the assets of individuals and other organizations.

Investment style   The theory of portfolio management and/or stock selection employed by a portfolio manager to manage the funds entrusted to him or her. Most large investment management complexes employ many different investment styles for different funds entrusted to the complex. In general, investment style determines many of the trading strategies and choices of intermediaries used by a fund.

Know   A slang term that implies accepting responsibility for a transaction. A broker/dealer that "knows" a trade is stating that the details as reported conform to the broker/dealer's records for the transaction, and the broker/dealer accepts responsibility for fulfilling its obligations for settlement.

Last sale   The price of the last trade for a security.

Latency   The natural delays that occur in distribution systems when physical distances and computer processes slow the delivery of data. Although the delays are usually short in human terms, as more trading involves computers and models, traders and trading firms are seeking to minimize latency. Most traders accept latency as the unavoidable result of physics but are strongly opposed to "queuing."

Lead underwriter   In an underwriting (the primary market), the lead underwriter manages the syndicate and directs the underwriting process. The lead underwriter is most often the firm that has an established relationship with the issuing company. On some very large underwritings, the issue may actually have co-lead underwriters who share the responsibility.

League tables   Published results ranking investment banking business firms in terms of the business they generate over a time period. This is the term used for football (soccer) rankings and suggests the level of competition among underwriters. Similar rankings are published for a number of other activities of firms in the trading markets, such as the largest investment companies and the most respected research analysts.

Leverage   The act of employing debt to enhance the capacity of investors and traders to acquire securities. By borrowing money to finance positions, companies are able to increase their return for every unit of their own capital that is invested. However, with leverage comes much greater risk. If the price (total value) of a leveraged position moves against the position holder, the holder not only loses money on the position but must also repay the loan.

Life insurance   An insurance product that pays a beneficiary in the event of the death of the insured.

Liquidate   Convert something into funds. To end an investment.

Liquidate the position   To convert an instrument position into cash most often by selling it in the trading markets.

Liquidity or Liquid   Liquidity consists of executable buy and sell orders. A liquidity pool is a place (either physical, such as an exchange floor, or virtual, such as a computerized system) where executable orders come together for trading. A liquid marketplace is a set of liquidity pools that collectively provide the ability to trade reasonably sized orders at reasonable hours under all market conditions without significantly affecting the market price.

Listings department   A function or division within a trading entity that is responsible for finding new listings for the market and/or to serve as liaison with existing listed companies.

Load funds   Mutual funds sold through broker/dealers. Such funds carry a commission on top of the management fees for the fund manager and are thus "loaded" with additional costs. (See also "No-load funds.")

Long or Long position   A general trading term for a trader with a positive security position. "Long" is also used in clearing to mean the firm or individual that is obligated to deliver securities (the seller or the seller's agent.) (See also "Short or Short position.")

Margin calls   Margin calls are issued by exchanges requiring traders with open positions to post cash or securities to cover negative price movements, making the open position worth less than the value at the time the original trade was initiated. (Margin is described in more detail in Book 2.)

Market   A generic term used in several different ways: (1) Each issue has a market of those interested in trading that security. (2) A specific exchange or trading center is termed "a market." (3) All buying and selling interests as they come together to trade are referred to as "the market."

Market data   A collective term for quotes, last sales, volume statistics, and other information used by the market to evaluate trading opportunities. Market data is generally distributed by a number of firms such as Bloomberg, Thomson Reuters, and Interactive Data. Market data is sometimes imprecisely referred to as "quotes," as in "quote vendors" or as the "tape."

Market maker or Market making   A special class of dealer with the obligation to provide liquidity by making continuous two-sided markets (both bid and ask).

Market price   The price that exists in the market at a given instant in time. It can mean a last sale price, but if quotes exist in the market, then the bid or offer price in the quote is a better predictor of the market price than the price of the last transaction. Quoted prices incorporate new information that may have come into the market.

Market risk   The risk to a position or a portfolio. Market risk occurs because most securities positions are to some extent covariant with the market. Thus, when the market as a whole moves up or down, portfolios and positions tend to move as well.

Marketplace   The generic term for exchanges, dealer markets, and other trading centers.

Mature or Maturity   The process that occurs when a bond reaches the end of its term and the face value is repaid to the lender.

Membership corporations   Corporate forms in which the participants in the organization are the owners. This form of corporate structure was common for exchanges prior to the movement by exchanges to become for-profit or public corporations. Membership corporations are generally run purely to service the members and not for profit. (See also "Mutualized.")

Merchant banks   The British term for a bank that takes long-term equity positions in corporations providing both financing and management expertise. The assumption is that the position will be liquidated in time at a profit. This usually involves more direct involvement in the company that is the target of the investment than would be expected from a typical portfolio investment. Merchant banks are related to private equity firms, but the merchant bank may not be attempting to restructure or sell off parts of the company in which it invests as a private equity firm might do.

Mergers and acquisitions   The activity, and sometimes the department name, within investment banking that focuses on helping companies acquire and be acquired or merge with other entities.

Middle office   The activities in a buy-side or sell-side firm that support primary lines of business and/or directly support customers.

Money manager   A generic name for an individual or company that manages investments for others. (See also "Institutional investor" or "Investment management.")

Money-market accounts   A mutual fund or unit trust that invests in highly liquid short-term securities with the intent of keeping cash balances in a form that provides demand-deposit-like liquidity but still provides interest income. Money-market accounts are frequently offered as the repository for free cash balances for investment accounts. (See also "Money-market securities.")

Money-market securities   A collective term for short-term securities often classified as 90 days to maturity or less. Sometimes longer-term issues are included when they have a short time to maturity because their price behavior begins to emulate the behavior of short-term instruments.

Multilateral trading facilities (MTF)   A trading facility defined by MiFID with the intent to encourage experimentation with new methods of trading. Thus, an MTF is similar in nature with an ECN or ATS defined by Regulation ATS in the United States. Both attempt to create two alternative types of trading venues. One is an exchange and is more highly regulated. MTFs, ECNs, and ATSs anticipate lighter regulation depending on other entities (exchanges or other regulators) for regulatory oversight.

Mutual fund   A professionally managed portfolio in which shares can be purchased representing a percentage of the fund. The values of the shares fluctuate based on the market value of the assets in the fund. Mutual funds can be open (the number of shares can fluctuate) or closed (the number of shares is fixed). Also, funds can be "load" (a broker's commission or fee is built in to the purchase price over and above the proportional value of the fund) or "no load" (there is no built-in commission). Brokers or agents usually sell load funds, whereas the management company usually sells no-load funds directly.

Mutualized   The attribute of an entity or service in which the entity/service is jointly owned by a number of participants to provide the service or function performed by the entity at cost. Exchanges and clearing corporations began as mutualized entities although a number have become for-profit. In principle, mutualized entities are suited for activities where the service or function is expensive to offer, but not highly valued by its beneficiary.

Net asset value   Mutual funds must report the value of their shares at the close of trading each day. Shares are valued by computing the aggregate value of holdings (the sum of the total number of trading units times the official price for the day) divided by the total number of trading units. The net asset value is then used to redeem outstanding shares or sell new shares. (See also "Official prices.")

Network design   The technical activity that designs the infrastructure required to move information within and among the entities in the financial markets.

Networks   One of the three major categories of technology supporting the financial markets.

No-load funds   Mutual funds sold directly by the mutual fund company without a broker. No-load funds do not have the additional "load" of the cost of the broker's commission; however, a no-load fund does have marketing costs. The marketing costs for a no-load fund do not show up explicitly when shares are purchased or redeemed. (See also "Load funds" and "Mutual funds.")

Nonfinancial companies   A category of entities that seek the services of a financial company as a customer and not as a provider of financial services. The term refers to companies that use the markets to invest funds, acquire commodities for production, hedge risks of all sorts, and raise capital. When a financial company seeks these services as a customer rather than as a provider, it falls into this category. As an example, when an investment bank seeks to raise new capital or to merge with another firm, it frequently hires a competitor for advice and/or to manage the transaction.

Nongovernmental organization (NGO)   The term for organizations that are not part of any specific governmental body that generally provide financing and aid. These organizations are often affiliated with world and regional associations of nations. In their role of financing and providing aid, NGOs issue instruments, particularly fixed income in the primary markets, and the issued instruments are traded in the secondary markets (e.g., the World Bank and European Development Bank).

Offer   The price at which a market maker or any other seller prices an instrument to be sold.

Official prices   The prices acceptable for valuing portfolio holdings in a market. In many markets, but not all, the last or closing price for the day in which holdings are valued is the official price. Other markets use the volume-weighted average price (VWAP) as the official price.

Open interest   A measure of the number of a specific derivative contract that is active or open in the market at any time. Open interest applies to both futures and options. When a new contract in the derivative is purchased or written, the open interest increases by one contract. When an open contract is exercised, delivered, expires, or if the holder of a long position in a contract acquires a short position, the open interest decreases by one.

Option   An option is a contract to purchase (call option) or sell (put option) a specified quantity of a financial asset at a specified price at a specified future date or during a specified time period. Options differ from futures in that an option is an opportunity to buy, but there is no obligation as there is with a future. If no action is taken at the end of the option period, the option expires without value. (See also "Call option," "Put option," and "Strike price.")

Option premium   (See "Premium.")

Order   An instruction to buy or sell an instrument.

Order flow   The aggregate term for all the orders, both to buy and to sell, flowing from the buy side through the sell side or to a market.

Order management systems (OMS)   Information systems and networks that enable traders to enter and transmit orders to multiple execution points through electronic linkages and to keep track of the results. Functionality includes the ability to handle various order types (e.g., market orders, limit orders, baskets).

Ordinary shares   A term for equity shares or common stock, used most frequently in the United Kingdom. (See also "Shares," "Common stock," and "Stock.")

Over-the-counter market (OTC)   A generalized term for a market in which securities are traded by telephone, instead of on the trading floor of a stock exchange. In U.S. equities, the term has been replaced by the Nasdaq Stock Market (the SRO for the old OTC equities market). We refer to Nasdaq securities rather than OTC securities. The telephone is rapidly being replaced by various Nasdaq computer systems such as SOES and SelectNet.

Packaged instruments   An aggregate term for instruments available for investment that represent participation units in an investment portfolio. (See also "Exchange-traded funds," "Mutual funds," and "Unit trusts.")

Partners   The owners of a firm organized as a partnership. In many legal systems, partners are different from shareholders in a corporation because they are personally liable for the debts of the organization. (See also "Shareholders.")

Partnership   An organizational structure in which partners jointly own the assets of the entity and share in the profits in mutually agreed percentages. A partnership is not a legal entity as a corporation is. The liabilities of a partnership flow through to the partners, and the partners are personally responsible for those liabilities. Substantially all decisions made on behalf of a partnership are made by a vote of the partners.

Payment for order flow   In the United States, many regional exchanges, ECNs, and third-market firms pay retail brokers for orders routed to them.

Pensions   Money set aside to be professionally managed on behalf of workers who will use the money for their retirement.

Personal trust   An investment account where the manager of the account must have special trust powers. The trust manager not only has to manage the funds in the account, but also may be responsible for managing the payout to the beneficiary of the trust. Trusts are commonly used to care for individuals who are not able to care for themselves because of age or incapacity. (See also "Trust" and "Trust powers.")

Portfolio   A group of securities managed for a single fund or customer.

Portfolio diversification   (See "Diversified portfolio.")

Portfolio management   The role of the individual charged with making investment decisions such as in which securities to invest and how to allocate the assets of an institutional portfolio among different classes of assets.

Portfolio manager   An individual charged with making investment decisions such as in which securities to invest and how to allocate the assets of an institutional portfolio among different classes of assets.

Position   A holding in a security. Also, all or a portion of a dealer's inventory of securities.

Position trader or Position manager   An individual within the trading operation of a broker/dealer that is responsible for managing the firm's inventory position in a specific security. This individual would typically set the firm's quote (if the firm is a market maker) and determine the quantity and price a firm would bid or offer as a participant in a block trade.

Positioning   The process of a dealer purchasing or selling an asset, usually from a customer, into the inventory of the firm.

Preferred shares   Equity securities that generally do not have voting rights but are entitled to receive dividends before common shares if the issuing company is able to pay out any income.

Premium   (1) The amount a buyer of an options contract pays to the writer of the contract. (2) The value of a bond in excess of the face amount that results from market rates on comparable bonds (the market yield) falling below the coupon rate on the bond. The sum of the face amount on the bond plus the premium causes the coupon rate to produce a yield that is equal to the market yield. (See also "Discount.") (3) (See "Insurance premium.")

Present value   Describes the current worth or value of a payment that will be received in the future under the assumption that time has "value" (i.e., that money today can be invested and will be worth more in the future).

Primary market   (1) The initial issuance of securities. Securities are underwritten in the primary market to raise capital. (See also "Secondary market" and "Underwriting.") (2) When an instrument is traded on multiple markets, the market of the original listing is sometimes designated as the primary market. The primary market may set the official trading hours for the instrument and determine other conditions for trading.

Prime broker   A broker that services hedge funds. The prime broker can consolidate trades from multiple broker/dealers, provide financing for trading, clear trades, and provide technical infrastructure for the hedge funds.

Principal   Any person who buys or sells a security for his or her own account. Also refers to an executive of a firm that actively engages in that firm's trading business.

Private equity firms   Firms, like merchant banks, that take substantial equity interests in target firms for more than investment reasons. Targets are often firms in financial difficulty. A private equity firm may seek control of a target company and either reform management or break the company into pieces to be sold off independently.

Profit and loss (P&L)   Most financial firms produce a general ledger account that balances the revenue that each revenue-producing department generates against the costs it incurs, including an allocated portion of the costs for non-revenue-producing departments. The P&L is the major input into bonuses paid to staff members.

Proof of ownership   Proof of ownership is the means for a holder of an instrument to demonstrate legal title both to receive any income the instrument produces and to be able to satisfy settlement. Settlement requires that the seller be able to provide title in a form that can be transferred to the purchaser. Historically, certificates or contract documents were proof of ownership, and endorsed certificates constituted good delivery. With computers and depositories, bookkeeping entry has replaced certificates as the record of ownership. Delivery often requires that the depository be provided with instructions to transfer ownership.

Property and casualty   Insurance against property or financial loss as a result of events such as weather, fire, or medical losses. Property and casualty insurance is pure protection and does not include any guaranteed investment for the insured or the beneficiary. As a result, the investment requirements on premiums paid to property and casualty insurance companies are usually less restrictive than on life insurance companies.

Proprietary trading (Prop trading)   A department or function within a sell-side firm that invests the firm's capital to profit based on market knowledge gained in the process of the firm's other market operations. (See also "Position trader" and "Treasury department.")

Prudent man rule   A rule established by legal precedent requiring that any manager of funds in a trust be held to the measure that he or she must manage the funds as a prudent man would manage his own affairs.

Purchases and sales (P&S)   The department in a securities firm responsible for keeping track of customer trading activities prior to settlement, including comparison activity between brokers and creation of customer confirmations.

Put option   An option contract in which the writer promises to purchase a fixed quantity of the underlying at a set strike price if the holder elects to exercise the option. (See also "Call option," "Exercise," "Option," and "Strike price.")

Quote   The price at which a firm or an individual will buy or sell a security, referred to as "bid and offer" (sometimes called "ask"). A two-sided quote consists of a bid and an offer for the security. A one-sided quote is only the bid or the ask. (See also "Bid," "Offer," and "Ask.")

Reference data   Data generally provided by vendors (and thus originating outside the purchasing firm) that is used primarily for post-trade processing. Historically, reference data was considered materially different from "market data" because the latter tended to be delivered in real time, and the former was delivered periodically and in bulk. Also, a good portion of reference data comes from the market, and thus, the distinction between market data and reference data fails to be aptly named. Perhaps the best distinction between what is commonly referred to as market data and reference data is that market data is generally input into trading decisions. Pricing and news helps in the evaluation of potential and actual trading decisions including indications of interest, instant messaging and tweets, last sale prices (dynamically updated), quotes, news, research, and commentary. In contrast most reference data—historical data, capital changes, counterparty data, issue identifiers, and data linking issues and the entities to which they belong—all support post-trade applications. Even this distinction breaks down because historical prices can, in turn, be input to future trading decisions. (See also "Market data.")

Registered market maker   A generic term for a market maker registered with a specific exchange or trading venue. (See also "Market maker.")

Registered representatives   A commonly accepted term for retail salespersons, particularly from traditional retail firms. The name suggests that the salesperson must be licensed by a regulator or self-regulator and is thus registered to perform the roles permitted by the licensing authority. (See also "Financial consultant.")

Regulations   Laws and rules passed by regulators and self-regulators governing the operation of markets and controlling the financial responsibilities and procedural requirements of market participants. (See also "Regulators" and "Self-Regulation.")

Regulators   An organization, usually created as a part of a government, that is responsible for overseeing a process or activity such as the financial markets or its participants.

Regulatory accounting   Any accounting that must be performed as a result of regulatory mandate. (See also "Statutory reporting.")

Reorganization or Reorg   A department particularly within a sell-side firm that handles the issues related to holdings that are subject to stock splits, dividends, warrants, buy-backs, mergers, and acquisitions.

Research analyst   An individual working for a buy-side firm, sell-side firm, or third-party vendor that creates investment research to help prospective investors evaluate instruments considered for investment. (See also "Research.")

Research or Investment research   The activity undertaken by buy-side firms, sell-side firms, and third-party research firms to assess the value and possibly the market price of investment assets.

Retail brokers   Firms, divisions of firms, and individuals that target individual investors providing investment advice, transactional support, and asset management. (See also "Retail sales" and "Wealth management.")

Retail investors   Individuals who are managing money for their own benefit or that of their family. (See also "Individual investor.")

Retail sales   That portion of the sales activities of both buy- and sell-side firms that is directed at individuals.

Retail services   A collective term for all services provided by a financial institution for individual customers.

Risk   A generalized term for uncertainty that can affect the profitability, and in some cases survival, of a financial organization. (See also "Risks.")

Risk management   A name given to both the process and support systems used to measure and ameliorate risk. Because there many different definitions of risk, any discussion of risk management must begin with agreement regarding what types of risk are being discussed and what management means to the participants.

Risks   The aggregate term for all the potential causes of losses for portfolios and positions controlled by entities in the markets. As many as 20 unique types of risk have been identified. (See also "Risk.")

Safekeeping   The general term for warehousing instruments and instrument positions in the trading markets.

Sales   The activities within a securities firm that are directed at generating more customers or more revenue-generating activities from existing customers.

Sales and marketing   A general term for selling instruments or portfolios, but particularly those functions employed by buy-side firms to acquire new customers for investment products.

Sales trader   An individual in a trading room of a broker/dealer that has customer responsibility. The sales trader can typically execute orders from customers that are below limits established by a position trader at the firm's established quote. May also be referred to as an "institutional salesperson." (See also "Institutional sales" and "Position trader.")

Secondary market   The term used to describe trading in a security or instrument after it is issued initially. Securities are issued in the primary market. Once issued, trading occurs in the secondary market. (See also "Primary market.")

Securities lending or Stock loan   The function of lending securities either from a firm's own securities or from customer positions (with permission) for use by firms taking short positions and/or for settling instrument sales when the principal is unable or unwilling to deliver securities as required by a transaction.

Securities movement and control   The functions required to monitor, and in some cases manage, the post-trade processes for a buy-side firm.

Securities valuation   The process of finding and verifying official prices for all the holdings in a portfolio, firm position, packaged instrument, or customer account.

Securitized financing   Any financial service offered in the form of a security or other traded instrument. (See also "Securitized.")

Securitized or Securitization   The process of converting bespoke financial services or assets into securities that can be traded easily in the financial markets. For example, converting a short-term bank loan into commercial paper or home mortgages into mortgaged-backed securities.

Security certificate   (See "Certificate.")

Segregated   Instrument holdings that are separated from other holdings for a special purpose such as collateral for a loan.

Self-regulation   The practice in financial markets of allowing the participants in the market to establish their own regulations, usually subject to oversight by a governmental regulator. Self-regulation evolved because participants in markets needed the ability to establish and enforce rules to ensure the market operated efficiently.

Sell short   An order to sell a security that the seller does not own; a sale affected by delivering a security borrowed by, or for the account of, the seller. Trading venues and regulators often have very specific conditions under which a short sale can be executed.

Sell side   Organizations such as brokers, dealers, banks, and exchanges that provide services required to trade securities and currencies. Also known as the "wholesale marketplace."

Settlement   The process of delivering securities and making payment.

Settlement date   The agreed date on which settlement takes place. For most equity transactions, the date is three business days following the transaction (T+3). For some debt securities and many derivatives, it is the next business day (T+1).

Shareholders   The individuals who own equity securities in a firm that is organized as a corporation.

Shares   The units of ownership in corporations and other instruments that use the structure of equity securities. The term has its historical roots in the Dutch East India Company, the first issuance of modern common stock in which an investor was entitled to share in the profits of a specific shipping voyage to the Orient. Although universal, the term "shares" is most prevalent in Europe. (See also "Stocks.")

Short or Short position   A term referring to a trader that has a negative (borrowed) security position. The term can also mean the firm or individual that must deliver money (buyer or the buyer's agent) in clearing. (See also "Long or Long position.")

Single capacity   The concept in the United Kingdom prior to "Big Bang."

Size   The quantity of securities in a quote or limit order.

Soft commissions (noun, U.K.) or Soft dollars (noun, U.S.) or Softing (verb, U.K.)   The notion that services are supplied to buy-side firms by their sell-side intermediaries in exchange for the promise (either implicit or explicit) that the buy-side firm will compensate the sell-side provider with commissions to offset the value of the services provided. Investment research is a widely accepted soft-dollar service. Other services that assist in the provision of investment services (e.g., the provision of market-data services) are less straightforward but are acceptable in some markets.

Specialist   Combination agent/dealer on an exchange trading floor who manages the market in the specific securities allocated to him or her. Specialist units are independent companies with corporate or partnership structures.

Speculator   Generalized term for a trader who is interested only in short-run price movements. This term can include day traders in the equity markets, and hedge funds and locals in the futures markets.

Spread   The difference between the lowest offer and highest bid. When a dealer or market maker provides the bid and offer, the spread represents the dealer's potential profit at any moment.

Stamp duties   Taxes applied by national governments to instrument transactions.

Stock loan and borrow   (See "Securities lending.")

Stock options   (See "Options.")

Stock splits   A capital change that occurs when an issuing company chooses to divide (or in some cases combine) stocks in a fixed proportion. The transaction leaves all stock holders unchanged in terms of their proportion of ownership, but often by splitting stock shares become more affordable to smaller investors. This is particularly used when an equity security experiences a strong run-up in price.

Stocks   The familiar name for equity securities that convey ownership rights in a company or other organization. In addition to common shares, there are variations such as preferred stocks that promise a dividend if there are sufficient revenues. Other variations may have different amounts of voting rights. (See also "Equity" and "Shares.")

Street name   Customer-owned securities registered in the name of the securities firm where the customer has an account. The use of a street name significantly facilitates the clearing and settlement of securities transactions.

Street-side activities   All activities related to trading and settling securities transactions.

Strike prices   The set price at which options can be purchased at exercise (a call option) or at which the underlying can be sold at exercise (a put option).

Suitability rules   Rules that specify what types of instruments and transactions are acceptable based on the perceived capacity of the investor to understand the purpose of the transaction and the risks involved. Generally applicable only for retail investors. A broker/dealer that sells a product or service to a customer that is not suited to the product or service may be subject to regulatory sanction and may be the target of a civil litigation.

Swap   A transaction usually associated with complex derivatives and financial engineering in which an income stream or payment or specific risk is exchanged for a different feature or attribute. These trades permit investors to exchange a type of income or exposure they do not want for something else they do want or are willing to accept. These transactions can be complicated and presuppose that the parties understand the implications of the exchange.

Syndicate   A group of broker/dealers that come together to share the risks of an investment banking transaction and also to sell the instruments created.

Syndication   The process in an investment banking transaction in which the firm known as the lead underwriter puts together a group of other investment banks and broker/dealers to initially purchase a new issue and then divide the shares issued among the syndicate for resale to investors.

Systems   One of the three major categories of technology supporting the financial markets.

Tax lots   For investments such as trusts where the investment itself is taxable, every different execution price for the holdings in the account must be recorded so that capital gains can be accounted for tax purposes. Also, the tax cost or basis enters into decisions about what holdings should be sold to minimize the tax effects of partial liquidations of holdings.

Term   The life of an instrument.

Term-life insurance   Life insurance that involves insurance only against death and does not include any residual investment as occurs with whole-life insurance. (See also "Whole-life insurance.")

Terms-and-conditions   The common term for an information service that provides access to details usually found in registration documents when an issue is created. This information is critical to understanding how to price instruments with unique attributes such as the ability for a bond to be called before maturity.

Ticker   Dynamically updated instrument prices. The term stems from the ticking noise made by telegraph-based pricing devices as they printed to paper tape.

Ticker symbol   The commonly used symbol for a security such as "IBM" for International Business Machines, Inc., or "T" for AT&T. The root symbol for the security is often granted by the listing exchange, but the full ticker symbol (e.g., "IBM.N" to indicate IBM traded on the NYSE) is developed by the quote vendor and is not standardized.

Time   The component of interest calculations that determines how long the interest rate assumption applies. Often it is expressed as a series of earning periods (e.g., years, quarters, months) over a total investment period.

Time-deposit accounts   Interest-bearing bank accounts from which money can be withdrawn only after a time delay and sometimes with a fee for early withdrawal.

Trade (or deal)   A completed (executed) order.

Trade allocation   (See "Allocation.")

Trade report   Official notification (by whatever means is accepted) to an exchange or clearing corporation of the successful match of a buy order and sell order.

Traded options   A term to distinguish exchange-traded options from bespoke puts and calls. (See also "Options.")

Trader-of-last-resort   A description of a market maker that is committed, usually by the rules of a market, to trade to satisfy customer demand when no other customer trades can be found. This concept usually suggests that the market maker is asked to provide liquidity and immediacy even when the market maker's best interests may not be served by the trade.

Trading (noun and verb)   The division or department within a financial markets firm that is charged with executing customer orders, proprietary trades, and market making. Also, the process of executing all orders.

Trading mechanics   A combination of rules, operating procedures (on a physical market), and computer algorithms (for an electronic market) that define how orders are handled, the sequence in which trades are executed, and how price is established.

Traditional retail broker/dealers   Retail broker/dealers that interact with their customers through branches in which registered representatives of financial consultants provide sales and customer service. Historically, these sales personnel were paid by commission, but increasingly firms use assets-under-management as a unit of pricing. (See also "Discount brokerage," "Electronic access broker/dealers," and "Assets-under-management.")

Treasury department   A department within a bank, and sometimes an investment bank, that is focused primarily on managing the firm's capital to satisfy regulatory requirements. While firms may try to profit from their employed capital, the Treasury's primary goal is to maintain adequate capital.

Trust   An account set up with an entity having trust powers (usually a bank) that requires the assets managed be handled with greater care than normal business obligations would suggest. A trust must be managed by the trustee "…with the same care with which a prudent man would manage his own affairs." Trusts originated in English Common Law and have many variations. They are often used to protect the assets of very young or incompetent beneficiaries. (See also "Beneficiary," "Corporate trust," "Fiduciary," "Personal trust,""Trust powers," and "Trustee.")

Trust powers   The capabilities of a trustee (individual or entity) that generally include most of the rights and capacities of the beneficiary of the trust including suing to protect assets and making investment decisions.

Trustee   The entity or individual vested with trust powers. The trustee has a special duty of care in managing the assets of a trust. (See also "Beneficiary," "Corporate trust," "Trust," and "Trust powers.")

Underlying   The instrument, index, or commodity on which a derivative security is based.

Underwriting   The process of raising money for a company or governmental unit through the issuance of stocks or debt instruments in the capital markets. (See also "Investment banking" and "Primary market.")

Unit trust   An investment vehicle that is very similar to a mutual fund where participation in the fund is purchased as units rather than shares.

Unit of trading   A measure of the quantity of an instrument that is most commonly traded. The unit may be the smallest indivisible quantity such as a share of a bond, but commonly it is a fixed multiple of the smallest quantity often known as a "round lot."

Units   The elements of ownership of a unit trust. The equivalent of shares.

Universes   A group of similar entities, portfolios, funds, or the like grouped for measurement purposes. Vendors publish periodic attributes for the universes the vendor monitors, and members of that universe are then able to compare their own attributes against statistics for the universe.

Vendors   Companies that supply information, technology, and services to the financial markets. In particular, firms such as Bloomberg and Reuters that provide market data.

Venture capitalists or Venture capital firms or VC   Financial intermediaries, usually partnerships, that help finance startup companies in exchange for an equity interest in the startup. When the startup becomes successful, the VC helps create an IPO and is repaid by the market appreciation of the VC's equity interest.

Voice broker   Archaic term for an interdealer broker in the currency markets. The term dates from the time when these IDBs dealt with their dealer/customers over the phone. (See also "Broker's broker" and "Interdealer broker.")

Warrants   Financial instruments issued by a company that the holder can exercise like a call option to buy company shares at a predetermined price. Although a warrant works like an option, the warrant is issued by the company often as an alternative to paying a dividend if the company wishes to retain its earnings. In contrast, an option is created in the secondary market and does not affect the company directly. (See also "Options.")

Wealth management   A term for traditional retail brokerage particularly where the customer is considered "upscale" and where the method of pricing is assets-under-management rather than commissions. (See also "Traditional retail broker/dealers" and "Electronic access broker/dealers.")

Whole-life insurance   Life insurance that includes an element of investment in addition to the insurance against death. (See also "Term-life insurance.")

Wholesaler   A dealer in the business of carrying inventory in large numbers of instruments as a service to other brokers and dealers that can satisfy customer demand for securities. The broker or dealer with a customer order can come to the wholesaler and buy or sell without having to maintain an inventory.

Wrap accounts   Accounts developed by broker/dealers in conjunction with investment management firms that pool modest portfolios from brokerage customers and provide the accounts with the benefits of professional money management.

Writer   The individual who creates an open interest by writing an option to sell (put) or buy (call) an underlying instrument at a future date. Note that the writer takes the opposite side of a contract. A purchaser of a put contract has the right to sell to the writer. The writer receives a premium when the contract is first sold.

Ascher, K. (2005). *The Works: Anatomy of a City*. New York: Penguin Books.

Bernstein, P. L. (1998). *Against the Gods: The Remarkable Story of Risk*. Hoboken, NJ: John Wiley & Sons, Inc.

Bernstein, P. L. (2005). *Capital Ideas: The Improbable Origins of Modern Wall Street*. Hoboken, NJ: John Wiley & Sons, Inc.

Bernstein, P. L. (2007). *Capital Ideas Evolving* (1st ed.). Hoboken, NJ: John Wiley & Sons, Inc.

Brooks, J. (1997). *Once in Golconda: A True Story of Wall Street 1920–1938* (2nd ed.). New York: John Wiley & Sons, Inc.

Brooks, J. (1999). *The Go-Go Years: The Drama and Crashing Finale of Wall Street's Bullish 60s* (2nd ed.). New York: John Wiley & Sons, Inc.

Bruck, C. (1989). *The Predators' Ball: The Inside Story of Drexel Burnham and the Rise of the Junk Bond Raiders* (2nd ed.). New York: Penguin Books.

Choudhry, M. (2004a). *Advanced Fixed Income Analysis*. Oxford: Butterworth-Heinemann.

Choudhry, M. (2004b). *Corporate Bonds and Structured Financial Produces*. Oxford: Butterworth-Heinemann.

Choudhry, M. (2004c). *An Introduction to Credit Derivatives*. Oxford: Butterworth-Heinemann.

Choudhry, M. (2006). *The Bond & Money Markets: Strategy, Trading, Analysis*. Oxford: Butterworth-Heinemann.

Eales, B. A., & Choudhry, M. (2003). *Derivative Instruments: A Guide to Theory and Practice*. Oxford: Butterworth-Heinemann.

Farwell, L. C., Gane, F. H., Jacobs, D. P., Jones, S. L., & Robinson, R. L. (1966). *Financial Institutions* (4th ed.). Homewood, IL: Dow Jones-Irwin.

Fink, R. E., & Feduniak, R. B. (1988). *Futures Trading: Concepts and Strategies*. New York: Institute of Finance.

Garbade, K. D. (1982). *The Securities Markets*. New York: McGraw-Hill Book Company.

Gastineau, G. L. (1975). *The Stock Options Manual*. New York: McGraw-Hill Book Company.

Giles, T. G., & Apilado, V. P. (Eds.), (1971). *Banking Markets and Financial Institutions*. Homewood, IL: Richard D. Irwin, Inc.

Goetzmann, W. N., & Rouwenhorst, K. G. (2005). *The Origins of Value: The Financial Innovations That Created Modern Capital Markets*. New York: Oxford University Press.

Hieronymus, T. A. (1977). *Economics of Futures Trading: For Commercial and Personal Profit* (2nd ed.). New York: Commodity Research Bureau, Inc.

Lee, R. (1998). *What Is an Exchange? The Automation, Management, and Regulation of Financial Markets*. Oxford: Oxford University Press.

Lewis, M. (1990). *Liar's Poker* (2nd ed.). New York: Penguin Books.

Loader, D. (2007). *Fundamentals of Fund Administration: A Guide*. Oxford: Butterworth-Heinemann.

Neftci, S. N. (2008). *Principles of Financial Engineering* (2nd ed.). Boston: Academic Press.

Parks, T. (2005). *Medici Money: Banking, Metaphysics, and Art in Fifteenth-Century Florence*. New York: W.W. Norton & Company, Inc.

The Staff of the House Committee on Interstate and Foreign Commerce (1975). *Legislative History of Securities Acts Amendments of 1975*. Washington, DC: U.S. Government Printing Office.

Note: Page numbers followed by *b* indicates boxes, *f* indicates figures.

Printed in the United States
By Bookmasters